OLAR'S

$\mathcal{S}$Book of the
PIRITS

Other books by Zolar

Zolar's Encyclopedia of Ancient and Forbidden Knowledge
Zolar's Encyclopedia and Dictionary of Dreams
Zolar's Book of Dreams, Numbers, and Lucky Days
Zolar's Compendium of Occult Theories and Practices

ZOLAR'S

Book of the SPIRITS

PRENTICE HALL PRESS   o   New York

The History of Spiritualism, by Sir Arthur Conan Doyle, on pages 34, 47, 60, 61, 62, and 63 is quoted by permission of Dame Jean Conan Doyle.

Nothing So Strange, by Arthur Ford and Margueritte Harmon Bro on pages 67, 70, 72, 74, 75, 76, 82, 84, and 232 is quoted by gracious permission of the Spiritual Frontiers Fellowship.

Quotations from the works by Carl Jung on pages 17, 18, 52, and 53 are taken from the following volumes: "Synchronicity," from *The Collected Works of C. G. Jung*, trans. R.F.C. Hull, Bollingen Series XX, Vol. 8: *The Structure and Dynamics of the Psyche*. Copyright © 1960, 1969 by Princeton University Press. "On Occultism," from *The Collected Works of C. G. Jung*, trans. R.F.C. Hull, Bollingen Series XX, Vol. 18: *The Symbolic Life*, copyright 1950, 1953, 1955, copyright © 1958, 1959, 1963, 1968, 1969, 1970, 1973, 1976 by Princeton University Press.

———— O ————

*Published by Prentice Hall Press
A Division of Simon & Schuster, Inc.
Gulf + Western Building
One Gulf + Western Plaza
New York, NY 10023*

PRENTICE HALL PRESS is a trademark of Simon & Schuster, Inc.

Library of Congress Cataloging-in-Publication Data

Zolar.
Zolar's book of the spirits.

Bibliography: p.
Includes index.
1. Spiritualism. 2. Mediums—Interviews.
I. Title. II. Title: Book of the spirits.
BF1261.2.Z65 1987   133.9   86-43178
ISBN 0-13-984048-6

Designed by Irving Perkins Associates

Manufactured in the United States of America

10 9 8 7 6 5 4 3 2 1

First Edition

This work is dedicated to
the loving memory of
Anne and Erlo Van Waveren . . .
friends, healers, Jungian analysts.
So new in spirit . . . so old in soul!
And to Rev. Dr. Clifford Bias
who, though he will be missed,
will never be absent!

ACKNOWLEDGMENTS

Zolar would like to thank Lorraine M. Walla, D.A., for her help in editing and preparing this manuscript.

CONTENTS

———o———

INTRODUCTION
———o———

A Chat with Zolar

Spirits! The very word both frightens and fascinates us!

If you grew up, as I did, in a Protestant family (Methodist, to be more exact), the idea of actually conversing with spirits was something that never crossed your mind.

As a somewhat precocious Bible student, I knew of various biblical injunctions against witchcraft, magic, and conversing with spirits. But I also knew that, throughout the Old Testament and New Testament, various angels of the Lord were said to have appeared and conversed with various Prophets. Was an angel some kind of spirit? I didn't know.

Certainly, it seemed logical to assume, in accordance with the laws of modern physics, that since nothing could not give rise to something, the mere fact that we were born suggested we must have indeed come from somewhere.

So, too, it seemed illogical to assume that when we die we just disappear. Because if we do, how could we have come from someplace to begin with.

To primitive minds and those not so primitive, the connection between soul, breath, and life was an early realization. When a baby was born, it appeared lifeless; as the first breath was taken, it cried out and was alive. An old man was dying. He heaved and stopped breathing. He was dead. Life was gone.

Anima in Latin means both *soul* and *breath*. Hence one could say that we actually breathe in our soul when we are born. But once again, where does this thing called soul come from?

It is interesting to note a little-known superstition that a stork flew around Christ while he was being crucified, in order to comfort him. This would certainly suggest a belief that the stork is some sort of divine messenger that transports the soul from one place to another.

But what is this soul, and where does it come from to begin with?

I am reminded of the story of a young boy who attended a Sunday sermon in which the minister preached from Genesis on the idea that we all come from dust and that when we die, we return to dust. Upon returning home, he called his mother to his bedroom and made her bend down and look under his bed. "Look, Mom," he said. "Someone's either coming or going!"

To the primitive mind and to primitive persons (children), the coming and going of life has always been and will always be a great mystery. In short, how can we know until we *go*?

In my own experience, it was not until adulthood that an opportunity presented itself for me to actually attend a session with a real-life medium who, I was told, could actually talk with the other world.

I do recall, though, my Aunt Laura and other family members playing with the spirit-contacting device known as the Ouija Board. If my memory serves me, this was probably sometime during World War II when, due to the great loss of lives, there was a renewed interest in spirit contact.

Many years later, while I was teaching at the New School for Social Research, a student of mine presented me with a very fine Ouija Board, which he had made. For many years, I had it hanging on my office wall.

With the advent of the Aquarian Age, the last decade has seen a great resurgence of and interest in spirit contact, whose beginnings coincided historically with the discovery in 1790 of the planet Uranus, not coincidentally the ruler of Aquarius. It is only natural that many persons should now be seeking to make contact with other worlds through various kinds of mediums.

A somewhat different twist to the old linen is found in the claims of many modern spiritualists that they are channels for various beings rather than simply a means to make contact with those who have passed over to the other side. An example is the phenomenal success and publicity given the late Jane Roberts, who claimed to channel an entity called Seth.

From a psychological standpoint, such claims represent a movement in ideology from the conception of powers that are limited to simply contacting a family member who has passed through transition, to the seemingly unlimited ability to commune with beings who apparently have access to the Akashic Records, or what Jung called the Collective Unconscious.

As I write this work in New York City, I can even turn on my television and watch a weekly cable program on which a medium, Julie Winter, channels an entity called Micciah while surrounded by a host of spellbound followers. Twenty, perhaps even ten years ago, this would not have been possible.

From yet another perspective, while mainstream Christianity has often been highly critical of the contact with spirit, calling it the working of Satan, there now exists a fast-growing charismatic movement that is attempting to investigate, explain, and even encourage such practices as spiritual healing, the casting out of spirits (devils), and speaking in tongues (xenoglossia). Who can say where this movement will take Christianity?

In picking up the threads of spiritualism and weaving them from their origins in the phenomena of hypnotism and clairvoyance down to their everyday use by hard-core financial advisers, I have sought to present in this work only enough facts to make sense without risking losing your valued interest. In short, I will give you cake crumbs and icing rather than a cookbook of recipes.

To do this, I have divided the book into two parts. The first presents a brief history of spiritualism from its origin to the present. The second is a more practical, how-to-do-it-yourself method whereby you can begin to make your own contact with the world of spirit.

In order that the second half of this work may be truly of value, I have interviewed a number of mediums and channels who tell, in their own words, how they began their work as mediums and how they developed their psychic abilities.

I especially appreciate the assistance I received from the Universal Spiritualist Association, whose national headquarters is located at Maple Grove in Anderson, Indiana, and especially the late Rev. Dr. Clifford Bias.

I am also eternally indebted (better be careful what I say here!) to the Lily Dale Assembly, Lily Dale, New York, for their inestimable assistance, and for the friendship and openness extended to me by their directors and the staff of resident mediums, whose names appear throughout this work.

I have also been enlightened by conversations with Rev. Joseph H. Merrill, President of the National Spiritualist Association of Churches.

Last, to my many friends and faithful readers around the world who have asked for this book by their continued support of my writings, I would invite you to join me in a journey through time, space, and plane . . . a journey in search of a soul . . . your soul!

—Zolar

Declaration of Principles: National Spiritualist Association of Churches

———— O ————

1. We believe in Infinite Intelligence.
2. We believe that the phenomena of Nature, both physical and spiritual, are the expression of Infinite Intelligence.
3. We affirm that a correct understanding of such expression, and living in accordance therewith, constitute true religion.
4. We affirm that the existence and personal identity of the individual continue after the change called death.
5. We affirm that communication with the so-called dead is a fact, scientifically proven by the phenomena of spiritualism.
6. We believe that the highest morality is contained in the Golden Rule: "Whatsoever ye would that others should do unto you do ye also unto them."
7. We affirm the moral responsibility of the individual, and that he makes his own happiness or unhappiness as he obeys or disobeys Nature's physical and spiritual laws.
8. We affirm that the doorway to reformation is never closed against any human soul here or hereafter.
9. We affirm that the precepts of prophecy and healing contained in the Bible are divine attributes proven through mediumship.

1

---o---

The Mesmer Connection

It is, however, comparatively rare that scientific investigators disagree regarding the demonstrable facts pertaining to a subject under investigation. Yet this is the condition in which we find the science of hypnotism after more than a century of research by some of the ablest scientists of the world. They are divided into schools today, as they were in the infancy of the science. Indeed, the science is still in its infancy.

—Thomas Jay Hudson,
THE LAW OF PSYCHIC PHENOMENA

Hypnotism, from a Greek word signifying "sleep," was in Hudson's words, "a compromise sufficiently noncommittal." Scottish surgeon James Braid chose it to describe the phenomenon of trance, which he believed could be induced independently of personal contact or suggestion. But to understand Braid's break from the traditions of the past, we must first look at the work of Anton Mesmer.

Franz Anton Mesmer was born on May 23, 1734, in Iznang, Swabia, near Lake Constance. He was the third of nine children and was born three years after his parents' marriage, when his father was thirty-one years old. Curious?

Anton's father, Antonous Mesmer, was the son of a head gamekeeper, and his mother, Maria Ursula, was the daughter of a locksmith.

As a child, Mesmer was given to wandering off by himself. He attended a local monastic school from his ninth to his fifteenth year.

1

While he excelled academically, he preferred to be out of doors, rambling along the banks of the Rhine. He was very much concerned with the cycles of nature and seasonal changes, ever seeking at first hand an explanation as to how things really came to be.

He was said to have been always able to hold the attention of those around him, a quality that later made him an able magnetist.

In 1750 he entered the University of Dillingen in Bavaria on an archbishop's scholarship, one of the few available entrances into knowledge for a person of little means. After completing four years at Dillingen and finding no inclination for the priesthood, Anton sought to further his studies at the larger Bavarian University of Ingoldstadt, where he apparently earned a doctorate in philosophy while also studying physics, mathematics, and astronomy, together with modern and ancient languages.

It was here that he found himself especially attracted to the study of astronomy, which was then attempting to break free from the ancient belief in astrology. Here, no doubt, he encountered the writings of Paracelsus, the German physician, who accepted the belief in planetary influence as reality.

Toward the end of a four-year course of study, Mesmer turned his attention to the study of law and was enrolled as a law student at the University of Vienna in 1759. In the autumn of 1760 he was admitted as a first-year medical student at Leiden in Holland and stayed there to complete the prescribed six-year course.

In the last year of his studies, he submitted the customary thesis in Latin; two copies of the printed text have survived. He had chosen as his topic the influence of the planets on the human body, no doubt because of his lifelong interest in astrology. In May 1766, he was awarded the degree of Doctor of Medicine, with highest honors. His original diploma is preserved to this day in the Kerner Museum at Weinsburg.

While various later critics of Mesmer and his work may point to the topic of his thesis as indicative of a belief in fortune-telling, placing his thesis in the historical perspective of the academic community in which he lived shows him to have been an individual of rare insight and scholarship.

Mesmer held no belief in astrology or other preternatural theories. His thesis simply examines the forces emanating from the sun as to their purely physical influence on living organisms. Central to his thesis were an examination of Newton's laws of gravity and his hypothesis of "a certain subtle spirit" pervading all material life. This energy, said Newton, also caused movements of the human body that were the result of its "vibrations along the filaments of the nerves."

It is also interesting to note that in his thesis Mesmer uses the term *animal gravitation* for the force (fluid) that animates all living bodies. Later he was to substitute the term *animal magnetism*. According to Mesmer, when the flow or ebb of this universal fluid within man became out of harmony with that of nature, nervous or mental disorders resulted.

(Please forgive me, dear reader, if I have gone to great lengths in describing Mesmer's education. I have deliberately done this to point out that he was, by all standards and for the century in which he lived, a scholar and a highly educated physician. This fact is often neglected by present-day scholars who, given our current knowledge of hypnosis, would place Mesmer's animal magnetism theories in the same category as bloodletting and leaching. To do this would clearly be to throw out the baby with the bath water.)

In 1775 Mesmer, who by then had commenced a private practice as a physician, learned of the use of various magnets for healing from his friend Maximilian Hell, court astronomer and head of the observatory of Vienna. Hell told Mesmer that he had learned about the use of magnets for healing from an Englishman traveling in Vienna, and that he had made his own experiments and had had about twenty successes in curing various illnesses. Hell had published his discoveries in a locally distributed newssheet, and Mesmer felt he should publish a reply.

Being first and foremost a scientist, Mesmer obtained some magnets of suitable shape from Hell and proceeded to test them on various patients.

In his first published report, Mesmer mentioned various cases that were cured by the application of magnets, including apoplexy, epilepsy, hysteria, melancholia, and fitful fever. It was Mesmer's contention that almost anything could be a conductor for this animal magnetism: metals, paper, silk, stone, glass, water. Steel magnets were not required.

By 1778 Mesmer was in Paris achieving great success with his animal magnetism manipulations. By this time he had abandoned the use of magnets altogether, after being introduced to the work of Father Gassner, a controversial priest who healed by touch alone.

While the medical profession had already begun to shrink away from him, his popularity with the general public and various members of the court continued.

Seeking to prove the validity of his discovery, Mesmer finally consented to a complete investigation of his methods by physicians and members of the Academy of Sciences appointed by the King of France. The investigating committee consisted of four physicians, Borie, Sallin, d'Arcet, and Guillotin, and five members of the Academy: Franklin, Leroy, Bailly, de Borie, and Lavoisier.

At no other time in French history would so extraordinary a group of minds be assembled. It included the American discoverer of electricity and the French discoverer of oxygen (Lavoisier).

After extensive investigation of Mesmer's claims, the committee concluded that there was no basis in fact to conclude the existence of magnetic fluid and that whatever claims arose did so because of the imagination of the patients, the pressure of hands and fingers, or the imitation of the behavior of other patients.

A second commission likewise judged that animal magnetism was both useless and dangerous, and that members of the Society should be prevented from practicing its methods. As a direct result of these investigations, twenty-one members of the Society were tried and ordered to give up their use of magnetism. Seventeen submitted rather than lose their membership in the prestigious Society.

While Mesmer's personal fame began to wane, causing him to be driven into exile and eventually to die on February 25, 1815, it was to the credit of his disciple, the Marquis de Puysegur, that his original theories were revised and his name kept alive.

Puysegur discovered that patients could be placed in what he wrongly called a somnambulant state by a combination of suggestion and the light rubbing of the eyes. Not only did patients placed in this state respond to the oral suggestions of the mesmerist, but they also exhibited a heightening of faculties such as the ability to diagnose illness in themselves or in others, absent or present, and the ability to clairvoyantly glimpse the present and peer into the future.

It is because of this clairvoyant faculty, which was brought into prominence through induction of the trance state, that in 1825 the Royal Academy of Medicine in France ordered a new investigation. After six years of investigation, a report was issued declaring the therapeutic value of mesmerism as well as accepting proof of the clairvoyant phenomenon.

The controversy in Britain and the United States continued into the 1830s and 1840s. In Britain, the hostility of orthodox medicine reached great proportions, causing a leading mesmerist, John Elliotson, to resign his teaching position at a London hospital.

Fortunately, a Manchester surgeon of stout Scottish descent, James Braid, chose to take an intermediate position between those who felt the phenomena were caused by some kind of fluid and those who believed the whole effect to be a grand fraud.

From 1842 on, Braid employed mesmerism in his own practice, renaming it hypnotism and proving that the success of the induction of the trance state had nothing to do with whether or not objects had been magnetized, or the magnetic ability of the operator. The essential ingredient was simply whether or not the subjects believed that they could be and would be entranced.

Hence it was Braid's conclusion that the hypnotic state is simply one in which subjects are abnormally responsive to suggestions made by the operator, either explicit or implied.

Now that we have gotten through a brief history of hypnosis, let us return to the reason for our original inquiry—clairvoyance.

While Braid admitted that he had "never been able to produce [the higher phenomenon] by my mode, though I have tried to do so," investigators in other parts of Europe often reported magnetism as the remedial agent that released the clairvoyant state. Generally speaking, those who were successful in a clairvoyant way accepted the theory of a magnetic fluid, while those who found no success rejected its existence and sided with Braid.

The intellectual belief of the operator would seemingly have no influence over the induction and limits of the trance state, if Braid's theory regarding the nature of suggestion is correct. Yet the history and growth of spiritualism would seem to point otherwise.

Jean Deleuze, a professor of natural science at the Paris botanical gardens, was one investigator who cautiously approached the clairvoyant phenomenon, opposing experimentation in any branch of magnetism other than therapeutics.

In various letters to Dr. G. Billot, published in 1836, he wrote:

> Yes, a great number of somnambulists have affirmed that they have conversed with spiritual intelligences and have been inspired and guided by them, but I will tell you why I have thought it best not to insist on such facts and proofs of spirit communication. It is because I have feared that it might excite the imagination, might trouble human reason and lead to dangerous consequences. . . . I have suppressed many things in my works because I considered it was not yet time to disclose them.

Clearly the beginnings of spiritualism were cleverly swept under the rug of materialism, at least in Europe. But in the United States, founded on the principle of freedom of thought, spiritualism was different.

To the best of our knowledge, animal magnetism came to the United States during the summer of 1829 in Fanny Wright's Hall of Science in New York, where another Frenchman, Dr. Joseph Du Commun, an instructor in French at West Point, delivered a series of three lectures. Du Commun had been a student of Puysegur while in France.

It was not Du Commun, however, but another Frenchman, Charles Puyen, who must be given the credit for creating the then soon-to-be-popular movement. While a medical student, Puyen had taken ill and consulted a medical clairvoyant in Paris. During an extended visit to the West Indies, he discovered in Martinique and Guadeloupe, where members of his family owned plantations, that a number of French planters had for many years been experimenting with animal magnetism, using their slaves as unwilling subjects. It took Puyen only a few months of study to become an expert magnetist himself.

Seeking to improve his still unstable health, he sailed to New England and landed in Portland, Maine. After living with an uncle in Haverhill, Massachusetts, he moved to Lowell. In 1836, encouraged by the mayor of Lowell, Dr. Elisha Bartlett, he began giving lectures in Boston. Slow in starting out, because of lack of funds and personal unattractiveness, he eventually succeeded in accumulating a circle of physicians and medical students, and commenced lectures, instruction, and demonstrations of his methods.

By accident, he discovered an extraordinary "magnetic" subject, Miss Cynthia Gleason, then an underpaid weaver in a textile mill. Known as the sleeping beauty, Gleason toured most of New England with Puyen, giving demonstrations in which she proved to be a gifted medical clairvoyant. While under magnetic influence, Gleason could diagnose the ailments of any patient by slowly passing her hand over the patient's body from the head downward. She claimed that the body of the patient became transparent and that she could actually see the various organs. Often her descriptions were homespun—she would describe white spots on the liver or pimples on the stomach—but they were proven unusually accurate nonetheless. She could even diagnose a person's illness from a lock of his hair and would later recognize that person should she meet him on another occasion.

After New England, magnetism spread to New York State and then moved west to Ohio. By the early 1840s demonstrations of magnetism, often accompanied by clairvoyant phenomena, were crowd drawers wherever they appeared.

It was only a small step from the ability of a magnetized subject to diagnose illness to what has been called *telesthesia*, or traveling clairvoyance. Clairvoyance is the ability, allegedly supernormal, to see persons and events distant in time and space. The word literally means "clear vision."

As has been pointed out, the experiments with animal magnetism, mesmerism, and hypnotism were found to coincidentally yield greatly heightened abilities to see, feel, and even taste. In a few instances the entranced subject was able to taste and smell foods eaten by the operator.

Still further experiments demonstrated the ability, in some instances, of the operator to cause the subject to perform certain acts or respond in certain ways by merely mentally instructing the subject to act in that manner.

Explorers among primitive tribes frequently brought back stories of the ability of medicine men, shamans, and priests in America, Africa, India, and Tibet to describe with great accuracy things going on at a distance after placing themselves in a trance state.

Frederick Meyers, in his 1903 classic *Human Personality and Its Survival of Bodily Death*, suggests that the faculty is a combination of such paranormal abilities as telepathy, retrocognition, and precognition. Simply put, traveling clairvoyance seems to deny our ordinary conceptions of time and space, which suggest that a person must be physically present in order to perceive a particular event that is taking place. Of course, methods of modern communication, such as television, have proved this to be not so, though it may be argued that the television camera is a physical extension of a given person's abilities.

Whether or not hypnotism was used to produce clairvoyance among the ancients is not known for certain. What is known, however, is that as early as 1785, one of Puysegur's associates, Baron de Berstett, reported that his niece, while entranced, accurately described events occurring at a distance. In this particular instance the Baron, unable to bring his niece out of the trance state, became alarmed and left her in trance to obtain the assistance of a physician twenty miles away.

While the Baron journeyed to Nantes and before his return the next day, his niece was able to describe an altercation that had occurred between her uncle and a stranger, her uncle's movements and his conversation with the physician, and the physician's clothing. She even knew when she was approached by the physician that her uncle was waiting in the next room.

It was almost as if she were "seeing" through the eyes of her uncle. In this case, the entranced subject was most likely reading the thoughts and perceptions of the operator, her uncle.

William Gregory, professor of chemistry at the University of Edinburgh and a practicing physician, in his *Letters on Animal Magnetism*, cites fifteen cases in which magnetized subjects were able to describe distant places.

In one instance, Dr. Gregory sent a sample of a woman's handwriting to his friend and colleague, Dr. J. W. Haddock, who for some time had been magnetizing a clairvoyant named Emma. Emma was placed in trance and given the handwriting, about which Dr. Haddock knew nothing, and which he had assumed, because of its bold script, to be that of a man.

Emma proceeded to describe in accurate detail a woman "below middle height, dark complexioned, pale," who looked ill. She then went on to describe the home of the woman, her dress, her furniture, and several pieces of Bohemian glass that were placed near her writing desk. She also mentioned that this woman had recently taken the cure in a spa in Germany.

This is an unusual case, for clearly Emma was not reading the mind of Dr. Haddock, since he knew nothing of the woman in question. Nor was Dr. Gregory present at the time. Hence one must assume that Emma, through the handwriting of the woman and the entranced state, was somehow able to "see" what she was seeing and feeling.

The ability of Emma is also most important for our present investigation since upon various occasions while entranced she described the world of spirit and conversed with deceased friends. It is here that we also find the beginnings of what would become the philosophy of spiritualism.

While speaking of the discarnate friends with whom she communicated, Emma never used the word "dead" but invariably used instead the word "shelled." When asked while entranced to explain this word she simply replied, "They have left their shell and gone away."

While the seeds of spiritualism were well planted within animal magnetism, no attempts had been made to delineate the belief system upon which it rested. In brief, spiritualism was a phenomenon and not an *ism* or religion.

For one of the first cogent attempts to theologize the spiritualist doctrine, we will now examine the work and teachings of Emanuel Swedenborg, who should rightly be given the credit for the popularization of belief in a spiritual world that is the final resting place for all mortals and that can be contacted through the trance state.

2

Swedish Massage: The Medium Way

Swedenborg is, in fact, a madman in most men's views, and this judgment has much to support it. The great bulk of his teaching—almost the whole content of Arcana Coelestia—*has undergone a singularly unfortunate downfall. A seer, a mystic, cannot often be disproved; his visions may fall out of favor, but they still record one man's subjective outlook on the universe.*

—F. W. H. Myers,
HUMAN PERSONALITY AND ITS SURVIVAL
OF BODILY DEATH

Emanuel Swedberg was born in Stockholm on January 19, 1688, the son of the Lutheran Bishop of Scara and former professor of theology at Upsala.

Emanuel completed his education at the University of Upsala in 1710 and then traveled to Britain, Holland, Germany, and France. In England he was befriended by no less than Sir Edmund Halley, of later comet fame, and John Flamsteed, the first director of the Royal Greenwich Observatory.

About 1715, he returned to Stockholm, where he began to edit a journal entitled *Daedalus Hyperboreus*, which dealt primarily with mechanical inventions. Much of his time was then devoted to the independent study of natural science and engineering.

In 1716, due to his growing reputation, he was appointed by King

Charles XII as a special assessor to the Royal College of Mines. So absorbed was he with his pursuit of science and engineering that he turned down an appointment as professor at Upsala for the practical experience he would gain from mining. During this same time he published many papers on mathematics and mechanics.

Sometime in 1718 he invented a means of transporting boats over land for fourteen miles, conceived of plans for a vessel that would travel underneath the ocean, attempted to design a flying machine, and conceived of an air gun that could fire sixty or seventy shots without reloading.

Eventually his fame reached the royal household, causing Queen Ulrica to elevate him and his family to nobility, and to change his name to Swedenborg. Now that he sat in the House of Nobles, Swedenborg's political observations began to carry great weight, though he was thought to be far too democratic by his critics.

During the years 1720 to 1747, he totally immersed himself in various private studies and published numerous works on science, anatomy, and geology. In 1744 he published *On the Infinite and Final Cause of Creation*, a book in which he attempted to discuss the relationship between soul and body.

It was about this time, at the age of fifty-five, that he was overcome by a profound change in disposition. He began inquiry into the world of spirit rather than pursue the world of politics and science.

Almost spontaneously, Swedenborg found himself entering the trance state. He received extraordinary dreams and visions daily. Suddenly he heard conversation originating from the world of spirit and felt impelled to found a new church. He began to work for spiritual ends alone and resigned his various positions, taking a pension of half pay.

Unlike other magnetic subjects, he was in conscious, direct communication with the world of spirit. In answer to his many critics and skeptics, he wrote the following:

I am well aware that many persons will insist that it is impossible for anyone to converse with spirits and with angels during his lifetime in the body; many will say that such intercourse must be mere fancy; some, that I have invented such relations in order to gain credit; whilst others will make other objections. For all these, however, I care not, since I have seen, heard and felt.

Again, it is important to note that for Swedenborg this unusual departure from the world of physics to that of metaphysics was that of a respected scientist who had rejected becoming professor of astronomy in order to explore the business of mining. In a case that is much like that of Mesmer, we have here the sudden rebirth into cosmic consciousness of a highly educated intellectual.

In the context of our discussion of spiritualism, Swedenborg's contributions are important from a great many standpoints. First, it is important to note that Swedenborg was the first person to break from the tradition of the animal magnetists who suggested that a person must first be magnetized in order to enter spiritual realms. Second, not only did Swedenborg not have to be mesmerized in order to make spirit contact, but he was able to do so by himself, without the assistance of an operator. This practice established an entirely new method of procedure for those who would become mediums. Lastly, he maintained that contact with the world of spirit was something he and others could do, each and every day, throughout their lives, and that one did not have to die in order to enter spiritual realms.

The importance of Swedenborg's teachings to the growth of spiritualism is best presented in *The Debatable Land Between This World and Next*, written by Robert Dale Owen, the renowned English socialist and humanitarian, who became a spiritualist at the ripe old age of eighty-eight, after attending a sitting with the American medium, Mrs. Hayden. According to Owen, the move from the Quakerism of George Fox to the spiritualism of Swedenborg was a great advance.

Swedenborg taught the following: First, men in this world can have communion with spirits in the next world. Second, this communion can be reliable and valuable or mischievous and misleading, according to whether men are world-minded (sensual) or spiritually inclined. Third, there are no angels, good or bad, no fallen angels, nor any Satan or Prince of Hell; self-love is the only Devil. Fourth, men carry with them to the next world the very same characteristics that distinguish them here. Fifth, Heaven is reached through a love of truth and goodness, and not by faith or baptism. Sixth, love of God and one's neighbor comprises all divine truth. Seventh, after death men very soon enter an intermediate state between Heaven and Hell, where they have free liberty to choose which way they will travel. Eighth, God does not punish one with Hell or reward one with Heaven. Rather, each spirit is attracted to one or the other according to its ruling passions, much the same way as on earth one may seek the companionship of virtuous associates or befriend evil persons. Ninth, all the sufferings ascribed to the next world are self-inflicted, and Hell is constituted by self-loving and wordly minded souls. Tenth, the occupations and duties of Heaven are not restricted to a single rite but are manifold and represent a world of activity.

Despite the extraordinary scope of his philosophy, Swedenborg the man remained throughout his life unpretentious and hardworking. He never married nor sought to found a new sect, believing instead that his followers could be of any denominational persuasion. It was his sincere belief that he was a divinely appointed instrument of God's revelation to man. He relied on the truth of his visions, believing that while God in his essence was unknowable, in his human form he can be seen and realized. "God is man," he had written.

Though he himself daily communicated with spirits, he was vehement in his belief that others should not follow in his footsteps unless they received divine sanction. Of course, this particular aspect of his theology was abandoned by later spiritualists who believed that spirit contact was available to anyone who sought it.

Spirits could be actors of rare gift, according to Swedenborg, having the ability to impersonate anyone, living or dead. His warnings were very clear against messages supposedly coming from famous personages such as Moses, Saint Paul, Francis Bacon, and even Christ. If a person receiving the message *believes* it is coming from a famous person, this in turn causes the spirit to believe that he *is* that same personage, and thus the deception becomes compounded.

After his moment of cosmic consciousness and throughout his remaining life, Swedenborg continually presented evidence of his clairvoyant ability to transcend time and space.

The best-known example was quoted by the philosopher Immanuel Kant, who said that while attending dinner in Göteborg with fifteen other guests, 280 miles from Stockholm, Swedenborg suddenly retired to the garden and returned a few minutes later to announce to all assembled that a fire had broken out in Stockholm, razing the house of a friend, and that it was fast approaching his own home. This first pronouncement happened at about six o'clock. Again, around eight o'clock, he momentarily left the table, returning to announce that the fire had been extinguished before reaching his house.

Needless to say, the astonished guests spread the story, and on the next day Swedenborg was called to the provincial governor, who questioned him at great length about the disaster. Swedenborg answered meticulously, telling how the fire started, its duration, and so on. The day following his interview with the governor, a messenger, having been dispatched to Göteborg arrived, followed by a royal courier. As did the later published reports in various Stockholm newspapers, both messengers' reports agreed in detail with what Swedenborg had clairvoyantly seen.

It is almost impossible to accurately assess the length and breadth of the influence of Swedenborg on the later development of spiritualism and philosophy. Even Carl G. Jung could not fail to make mention of this seer in his discussion of synchronicity (*Collected Writings*, Ch. 8, p. 912):

When, for instance, the vision arose in Swedenborg's mind of a fire in Stockholm, there was a real fire raging there at the same time, without there being any demonstrable or even thinkable connection between the two. I would certainly not like to undertake to prove the archetypal connection in this case. I would only point to the fact that in Swedenborg's biography there are certain things which throw a remarkable light on his psychic state. We must assume that there was a lowering of the threshold of consciousness which gave him access to "absolute knowledge." The fire in Stockholm was, in a sense, burning in him too. For the unconscious psyche, space and time seem to be relative; that is to say, knowledge finds itself in a space-time continuum in which space is no longer space, nor time, time. If, therefore, the unconscious should develop or maintain a potential in the direction of consciousness, it is then possible for parallel events to be perceived or "known."

What better way to leave our discussion of this man of most unusual talent than once again with the words of F. W. H. Myers from *Human Personality and Its Survival of Bodily Death* (p. 354): On the whole, then, with some stretching, yet no contravention, of conclusions independently reached, I may say that Swedenborg's story—one of the strangest lives yet lived by mortal man—is corroborative rather than destructive of the slowly rising fabric of knowledge of which he was the uniquely gifted, but uniquely dangerous, precursor.

Or in the words of J. H. Noyes, when asked to describe the spiritualist movement in the United States: "Swedenborgianism Americanized!"

3

John the Baptist

I confess that my impressions are adapted more to the rising generations than to those already in being; because the present notions and possessions of the earth are too fixed and unprogressive to breathe the heavenly exhalations of newly discovered and fast unfolding truths.

—Andrew Jackson Davis

In our discussion thus far, we have examined the contributions of two highly educated individuals, Anton Mesmer and Emanuel Swedenborg, to the development of modern spiritualism. In both instances we found individuals who by all standards were men of arts and letters who moved in society's highest circles. As we move ahead in our discussion, we will see that this is one of the peculiarities of spiritualism—that it has always appealed to some of those who would be considered well-to-do.

In this chapter, though, we shall examine the other side of the coin and the contributions of one seer who claimed his only education to have been five months at a rustic school and the reading of a single tale called "The Three Spaniards."

Andrew Jackson Davis, known as the Poughkeepsie Seer, was born in Blooming Grove, Orange County, New York, on August 11, 1826. He was the last-born child and only son in an existing family of five daughters, only one of whom lived to adulthood. According to his autobiography, *The Magic Staff*, he was given his impressive name by a somewhat alcoholic uncle who greatly admired the future president.

Andrew's father was a weaver and a shoemaker who barely supported himself by these trades and hired himself out as a farm
worker during the summer. Though his parents were honest and
respectable, his father was given to drinking bouts that often left the
family to care for themselves. At the age of twelve, Andrew moved
with his parents to Poughkeepsie, and by fifteen he was apprenticed
out to a shoemaker named Armstrong, with whom he worked for
about two years.

By chance, if anything so happens, in 1843 he attended a series of
lectures in magnetism given by Professor Grimes and was persuaded by a tailor named Levinston to be magnetized himself. After
a series of magnetic sessions, in March 1844, by his own account,
he wandered into the countryside and there he experienced a spontaneous trance, during which time he was instructed by no less than
the Greek physician Galen and Swedenborg about his mission to
mankind.

Later on, in describing his first magnetic session, he wrote:

> It seemed that the whole earth, with all its inhabitants, had been
> suddenly translated into an Elysium. . . . A few moments more, and
> I not only beheld the exteriors of the individuals in that room—
> clothed with light as it were—but I easily perceived their interiors,
> and then too, the hidden source of those magical emanations. I could
> see all the organs and their functions—the liver, the spleen, the
> heart, the lungs, the brain—all with the greatest possible ease. The
> whole body was transparent as a sheet of glass.

As Davis' powers developed, he reached the conclusion that his
gifts should not be demonstrated for the merely curious but ought to
be used to heal and prescribe for the sick. Hence, a clinic was
opened, and he began a practice as a medical clairvoyant. After
working in this manner for a year or so, and having delivered a
number of lectures while in the trance state, he became aware that
his future work lay in the area of lecturing and writing of his perceptions while in a trancelike state. To do this he needed to choose yet
another magnetizer and someone reliable who would write down the
lectures as he gave them. For these functions he chose Dr. Lyon, a

Bridgeport, Connecticut, physician, and Rev. William Fishbough of New Haven.

The technique he followed was very simple. Dr. Lyon would place him in the magnetic trance. Davis would begin to dictate his discourse. Dr. Lyon would repeat each utterance as he heard it, and Fishbough would record it.

Commencing in November 1845, and extending over fifteen months, nearly eight hundred closely printed pages were produced and published under the title *Principles of Nature, Her Divine Revelations, and a Voice to Mankind.*

While it is obvious that this method of dictation meant filtering the discourse through the minds of two very literate individuals, the writings were attested to by three permanent witnesses as they were dictated. Before he delivered the lectures, Davis announced, while entranced, that he was to be excluded from any personal financial gain.

When finally privately published by Lyon and Fishbough, the book began selling at once, and, according to Dr. George Bush, Professor of Hebrew Language and Literature at New York University, sold nine hundred copies in one week alone. In fact, the initial sales of the book were almost solely the result of the reviews of the work, which were written in the *New York Tribune* by Bush, a Presbyterian who had converted to Swedenborgianism a few years earlier.

Joining Bush in the initial enthusiastic reviews of the book were George Ripley, who had founded the experimental commune Brook Farm, and Parke Goodwin, a disciple of the French social theorist Charles Fourier. Both reviewed the work in their publication *Harbinger*, with Ripley writing seven pages and describing *Principles of Nature* as "the most surpassing prodigy of literary history." Goodwin in another issue called it "extraordinary in every light in which we may regard it."

Although reviews from other members of the literati were forthcoming, the work did go through at least fourteen editions and was by all standards a spiritualist best-seller. But was Davis really a spiritualist?

While Davis believed in spiritualism and taught it, his own works did not come through any particular spiritualistic channels nor any regular form of mediumship. His initial work was not dictated to him by spirits but was rather produced by his own unconscious powers, somehow heightened by the magnetic trance. While his works may be said to have been clairvoyantly prompted, they were not, in a strict sense, given or dictated to him by spirit.

In fact, in his later career he abandoned the need for the magnetic trance altogether and rather employed a self-induced trancelike state that did not require any outside assistance. He described this state as one of abstraction; he would withdraw from the outer world and center his attention on the inner, spiritual world. This to him was the normal and natural evolution of spiritual growth, to which anyone might attain. Of this independent clairvoyant state, Davis wrote as follows, calling it "The Superior Condition":

> The Superior Condition is a development of every spiritual power, the subjection of every animal propensity, and the bringing of the *real* man into immediate conjunction with spirits, causes and principles. . . . Individuals who enter The Superior Condition, whether through the agency of human magnetism, or by constitutional and spiritual development, are subject to that universal law whereby the human spirit is *educated* by experience. That is to say, the mind improves and learns by familiarizing itself with influences and phenomena, whether in the body or out of the body, whether in this world or in the higher spheres of existence.

As to exactly what took place when he was entranced, Davis took pains to be exceedingly clear on page 38 of *Principles of Nature*, realizing how difficult it would be for others to comprehend how and where his ideas actually came from:

> The mind becomes free from the organism, except as connected by the medium before mentioned [by a slender thread of magnetism, by which the spirit can be drawn back to the organism]: and then it is capable of receiving impressions of foreign or proximate objects according to the medium with which it particularly becomes associ-

ated. The medium existing between thought and thought, between mind and mind, and between time and eternity, is the only active pervading medium which I am dependant on for the conception of thought, and for the perception of all things of a refined, ethereal or spiritual constitution. . . . I am not impulsed or impressed by the thoughts or feelings of a foreign person, though I am cognizant of them through the medium above termed ethereal.

When I pass from the body, it is not the distance—the indefinite space through which the mind proceeds, that is necessary to enable it to obtain its information, but it is the transition or metamorphosis of the principle of mind to its second sphere of existence.

Attempting to clarify this point yet further, on pages 43 and 44, he wrote:

It is impossible by *words* to convey a full and adequate conception of the manner in which I arrive at truth. I can only employ such words as convey all the idea that words can convey, of this process. My information is not derived from any *persons* that exist in the sphere into which my mind enters, but is the result of a *Law* of truth, emanating from the Great Positive Mind, and pervading all spheres of existence. By this truth is attracted to and is received by, the mind.

To Davis, all things that existed in the material world possessed a spiritual or immaterial or inner side. All movement, all life, all growth emanated from the spiritual. While all things, then, could be said to be dual in nature, this was so only in respect to their mode of existence and not their essential nature, which was always spiritual.

In support of his contentions is the fact that Davis, while formally uneducated, nonetheless appears in his various writings to be perfectly at home in all branches of science and philosophy. Even speculation as to the number of planets may be found in his writings, which postulated eighth and ninth planets long before their actual discoveries.

It is not until the very last section of *Principles of Nature* that we find the seeds for the development of spiritualism and the reason why mention of Davis must take place in a work of this nature.

Briefly stated, Davis conceived of seven distinct spiritual spheres, with various subdivisions in each. Starting with the earthly life, spirits progress through the seven spheres, taking an eternity of time to travel them all. According to Davis, the Third Sphere is one so beautiful that human words cannot be found to describe it. No one on earth has yet attained this or any sphere beyond this.

After completing his first book, *Principles of Nature*, Davis authored *The Great Harmonia*, a work in five volumes. It is here that one can find the clearest exposition of this seer. Volume 1, entitled *The Physician*, contains an account of the threefold nature of man in body, soul, and spirit, and includes a description of the nature and phenomenon of death from the clairvoyant viewpoint. In addition to *The Great Harmonia*, Davis later published a total of twenty-four other volumes, including his autobiography, *The Magic Staff*, in 1857.

From his first work until his death in 1910, Davis was generally considered as the unofficial leader or director of the spiritualistic movement. Much of his time was spent lecturing and writing.

In 1880 he threatened to leave the ranks of spiritualism, claiming that too much emphasis was being placed on phenomena and not enough on philosophy. It is the philosophy behind the manifestation that he wished people to understand and study: not the icing of seances and circles, nor the cake of rappings and apports (time transports) but rather the law that makes the recipe work in the first place.

How may Davis be judged then? This is a difficult question indeed. Certainly he provided a literate vehicle for a growing interest in spiritual alternatives to a highly material world. In the area of religion, he dared attack the dogmas of the church by insisting that Christ and all men were divine, as the spirit in each is an integral part of the infinite spirit. While Christ was more spiritually developed than most men, he was in principle no more God than all men are God. Certainly, Unitarian ministers gained great strength from such ideas as these.

Perhaps the best summary of Davis' influence may be found in *Modern American Spiritualism*, by Emma Hardinge:

A. J. Davis and his friends, ridiculed, despised, condemned and slandered as they were, on the one hand startled the age from the worship of atoms, in which material science pretended to discover the sources of mind; and on the other, embodied the vague transcendentalisms of credal faiths in the distinct and tangible form of an electric, living, silver cord, uniting the shadowy phantasmagoria of matter with the deathless and changeless principle of spirit. . . . The irresistible influence which he has exercised upon the opinions of the age, unquestionably formed the John Baptist [name given Davis by early spiritualists] which inaugurated that sunlit day when faith became knowledge, hope of immortality a glorious realization, and the dark, spectral shade of death became transfigured into the radiant form of a ministering spirit, in the bright illuminating beams of modern Spiritualism.

And so, another chapter was written. It was not an uneducated cobbler, though, who was destined to formally launch the spiritualist rocket but rather two young girls living in the small hamlet of Hydesville, New York, in the township of Arcadia.

4

---○---

The Fox Sisters:
Telegraph to Eternity

The reality of rappings does not depend on the Fox sisters. In 1888 it was too late for denial and their recantation proves nothing. It is deplorable that from 1849 onward the Fox family should have given theatrical performances for payment, but this no more invalidates the facts than the patents taken out by Wells and Morton for the use of ether contradict the facts of anesthesia.

—Dr. Charles Richet,
THIRTY YEARS OF PSYCHICAL RESEARCH

The history of spiritualism is fraught with oddities and contradictions. The difficulty seems to arise from the fact that there is something within each and every one of us that would have us believe in the reality of life after death and our ability to maintain contact with those who have passed over the veil.

In our current discussion we are faced with a great many questions as to whether the phenomenon that shall be soon described is indeed genuine.

The Amazing Randi, a contemporary magician of renown, has many times duplicated the phenomena of psychics and spoon benders alike. That this can be done so easily does not prove that all that happens or has happened in the annals of spiritualism is fraudulent. It simply means that one must be wary as well as prepared to admit that fraud may indeed be at hand with profit and not prophecy the motivation.

Eileen J. Garrett, one of the world's most respected psychics, relates the following story on page 121 of her classic work *The Sense and Nonsense of Prophecy:*

> The peasant mind of the Italian medium, Eusapia Palladino, did not take the simulation of fraud as a serious crime. She frankly answered when confronted with fraud, "The poor things. What would you do. This public demands it and must have a show," and that, of course, has been only too true. Some people have excused fraud on the grounds that the medium is usually surrounded by a group of eager enthusiasts who want their money's worth, and that he is therefore compelled to give the proceedings a little help in the right direction, that direction being a demonstration of the unseen "friends" interested in our earthly welfare.

Fortunately for the world of spiritualism, its humble beginnings were captured in print by an alert literati, E. E. Lewis, who just "happened" to arrive in Hydesville on April 4, 1848, four days after the rappings first appeared in the Fox family home. Motivated by what appears to have been curiosity and a sense of journalistic significance, Lewis began to interview the Foxes as well as their neighbors and friends, and he obtained no less than twenty-two signed statements. These he deftly combined with other materials, including a hastily drawn woodcut of the house, and he published a forty-page treatise entitled "A Report of the Mysterious Noises Heard in the House of Mr. John D. Fox."

As to the number of copies of this publication that were printed and distributed, little is known. The pamphlet remains as the undisputed first publication in the history of spiritualism, and according to Slater Brown, only four copies are known to exist.

Sir Arthur Conan Doyle, best known for his creation of the Sherlock Holmes stories, in his classic work *The History of Spiritualism* also mentions this pamphlet and his inability to obtain nothing more than a copy.

Briefly, the facts of the Hydesville incident are as follows: John D. Fox, his wife, Margaret, and their two daughters, Margaretta, age fifteen and a half, and Kate, just shy of twelve years old, had been living in a rented, ramshackle frame house in Hydesville, New York, since March 1848.

The house itself, about forty years old, was one and a half stories high and consisted on the ground floor of two small rooms, a kitchen and a buttery. Upstairs there was a low-ceilinged attic and downstairs a dirt-floored cellar.

John Fox was a blacksmith by trade and was said to have been a recovered alcoholic. Both he and his wife were Methodists. During his less sober days, he and Margaret had lived apart for about twelve years. The couple reunited after the birth of Maggie and Kate. While separated from her husband, Margaret had experienced a difficult time trying to support her four older children, who in 1848 were grown and married. Mrs. Fox has been described as simple, kind, and possessing a strong sense of family loyalty.

The two younger girls were simple country folk, with very little formal education or aptitude for schooling. As can be seen from various portraits, neither of the girls could be called beautiful; of the two, Kate's features were the more delicate.

According to Mrs. Fox, mysterious noises began to be heard in the house around March 20, 1848. Sometimes it sounded as if furniture was being moved. On other occasions it was as if someone was pounding on the walls or floor. So loud was this rapping that actual vibrations could be felt. Although the family began to search the house, up and down, inside and out, for the source of these disturbances, nothing could be found.

Having been kept awake until midnight on March 30, the entire family retired at about seven on Friday, March 31. For protection, the two girls had moved their trundle bed into their parents' room.

Once more, the rapping sounds began. Somewhat playfully, Kate snapped her fingers and asked the raps to answer. Much to the amazement of the family, that is exactly what happened. When Maggie followed by clapping her hands and asking the raps to reply, they mimicked her clapping. Mrs. Fox next asked the raps to indicate the ages of her six children, which facts she knew would be unknown to a stranger. Not only did the raps indicate the age of each correctly, but after the six were given, there was a pause and three more raps took place, indicating the age of a seventh child who had died three years previously.

According to her sworn statement, Mrs. Fox next inquired as to whether it was a human being who was making the noise. No raps were heard. She then inquired if it was a spirit; if so, it was to manifest with two raps. Two raps were heard. She continued by asking if it had been injured in the house, if the person was living that injured it, and if its remains were buried under the dwelling. Raps to the affirmative were heard in all instances.

Mrs. Fox immediately dispatched her husband to the home of a neighbor, Mary Redfield, who in her deposition attested to finding the two girls pale and frightened. After hearing her correct age sounded out as well as receiving responses to other personal questions, she hurried off to her husband and returned with two other neighbors, Mr. and Mrs. Duesler.

Mr. Duesler, at first doubting what he had been told, began to question the spirit, hoping to learn more of the alleged murder. When he asked if a former resident of the house, John C. Bell, had injured it, the entire bedstead upon which Duesler sat was shaken harder than ever before.

After a period of questioning, it was determined that the source of the rappings was the spirit of a dead peddler who had been murdered for his money some five years before and whose body was buried in the cellar, to which Mrs. Redfield's husband was sent.

In order to further prove the validity of the intelligence, Mr. Duesler, after learning the details of the supposed murder, began to question the entity on various personal matters, including his age, his wife's age, the ages of family members, the number of children in different families in the neighborhood, and the number of deaths that had taken place in these families. In each instance, the correct number of raps was received.

Other neighbors were also called in: Mr. and Mrs. Jewell; Mr. Hyde, who was the son of the owner of the house; and his wife; and two fishermen who were spearing suckers in Mud Creek.

Seeking to discover the name of the peddler, Mr. Duesler ingeniously conceived of the idea of reciting the alphabet, letter by letter, after requesting the spirit to designate (rap) when the correct letter had been stated. From this he determined that the peddler's initials were C.B. As it was now close to midnight, Mrs. Fox took her two daughters to the home of a neighbor, leaving her husband and Mr. Redfield to occupy the house alone.

The following day, several hundred persons gathered to hear and question the knockings. Various ad hoc committees were formed to investigate the matter. Attempts to dig up the cellar floor in search of the *corpus delicti* were thwarted by water that filled the hole as fast as they dug.

On Sunday, the third day of the knockings, Duesler ordered everyone out of the house except two neighbors, Stephen Smith and Benjamin Clark, with whom he went down to the cellar. Upon entering the basement a single dull blow was heard. Immediately, Smith went upstairs but found nothing.

On April 12, Duesler issued the following signed report attesting to his inability to explain the rappings:

> It is a mystery to me, which I am wholly unable to solve. I am willing to testify under oath that I did not make the noises or rappings which I and others heard, that I do not know of any person who did or could have made them, that I have spent considerable time since then in order to satisfy myself as to the cause of it, but cannot account for it on any other ground than that it is supernatural. . . . I never believed in haunted houses, or heard or saw anything but what I could account for before, but this I cannot account for as yet.

John C. Bell, the former resident of the house who had been accused of the murder of the peddler, was at the time of the incident blacksmithing in Lyons, a town about twelve miles from Hydesville. Upon hearing of the charges made against him, he came forward to confront his accuser. Of course, in any court of law, such would have been impossible, for the accuser was not of this world!

Since Bell had been well known in town before relocating, a great many neighbors came to his defense and signed a statement attesting to his good character and the falsity of the charges against him. This statement, also included in Lewis' pamphlet, bore the signature of no less than forty-five persons.

Had a murder actually taken place? A young former servant of the Bells, Lucretia Pulver, presented a circumstantial story: During her employment five years earlier, a peddler had come to the house who was never seen again, and she had been dismissed the very afternoon he had appeared. Mrs. Bell proceeded to leave town for three days to visit friends and upon returning sent for Lucretia. According to Lucretia's statement, she found Mrs. Bell in possession of two new thimbles and two old overcoats, which she now believed to have been in the possession of the murdered peddler. She also stated that a little while later, she herself heard knockings in the house and footsteps in the buttery. She further claimed to have stumbled over some loose earth in the cellar that Mrs. Bell claimed was the work of rats.

What is to be made of her story? First, at the time of the incident, Miss Pulver was fourteen and certainly not of an age to be left alone in the house with Mr. Bell while his wife went off to visit friends. Were her impressions simply those of an impressionable teenager? Another statement from Lucretia's mother was to the effect that soon after the alleged murder had taken place, she had called upon Mrs. Bell, who had complained of hearing strange noises in the house. Yet another deposition from other neighbors claimed that during the summer of 1844, Bell's well water had been "very offensive and bad."

Hannah and Michael Weekman had occupied the house in 1846 and 1847. According to their depositions, they too had heard rappings on the outside door; when they went to investigate, they found no cause for the sound. They further testified that their daughter, who occupied the room in which the rappings were heard by the Fox sisters, had awakened crying violently, that she had felt something cold moving over her face and head. Michael also claimed that on one occasion he heard his name called but could find no source for the sound. This had happened when his wife was not at home.

Here again, one must question why the Weekmans took so long to come forward with their report. Perhaps they had just brushed their experiences off as many of us would do. On the other hand, the thought of having their experiences immortalized by Lewis might have provided enough fuel to rekindle their imagination. We will never know for sure.

The Foxes' son David, only after considerable digging in the basement, which had to be continually pumped free of water, later in the summer claimed to have discovered a few bones, hair, and some teeth. In 1904, the owner of the house announced that he had uncovered a human skeleton in the foundation wall of the cellar when it had collapsed. In neither case, though, were these remains submitted to medical examiners for valid identification. It was rumored that the owner of the house had actually planted these artifacts, since by then the house had become a spiritualist shrine; it was in fact moved to Lily Dale Assembly Grounds in 1927, where it stood for veneration until it was destroyed by fire in 1937.

It is unfortunate that Sir Arthur Conan Doyle, who depicted Sherlock Holmes as a master of logic, did not go back and reread his own stories before penning his *History of Spiritualism*. Seeking to prove the existence of the peddler's spirit as the source of the rappings, Doyle wrote as follows:

> There was discovered a peddler's tin box as well as the bones, and this box is now preserved at Lilydale [sic], the central country headquarters of the American Spiritualists, to which also the old Hydesville house has been transported. These discoveries settle the question and prove conclusively that there *was* a crime committed in the house, and that this crime was indicated by psychic means.

The question is, of course, what would Holmes have said?

Charles B. Rosma, as the peddler was, supposedly named, was never found, nor did any of his relatives come forth to claim that he had disappeared. This, too, was explained away by Doyle, who claimed that perhaps the name as given by the spirit had been misinterpreted: that it was really Ross or Rosmer and that this error had prevented accurate identification.

In any event, neither Bell nor anyone else was ever tried for the crime, if there was one, and no medical examination of the remains was ever conducted.

What became of the Fox sisters? After the Fox family decided to leave their Hydesville home, they temporarily settled at the home of their son David. Unfortunately, they were soon to discover that the rappings had followed them to David's home. What had never been realized was that the rappings occurred *only* in the presence of the girls. No one who had witnessed the phenomenon had realized that it was not due to the presence of the supposed spirit but rather was somehow connected to the sisters themselves. (Duesler had come close to making this realization when he had noted that the raps responded only when questions were asked.)

If, indeed, the girls had produced the rappings without detection, how had they done it? According to various observers, the rappings sometimes continued for four or more hours, certainly an exhausting task.

The other unanswered issue lies in the unusual manner in which the raps provided accurate answers to questions posed by various persons, answers that were not known to the sisters. Even if one were to dismiss the raps themselves, certainly the accuracy of the answers suggested some kind of paranormal or clairvoyant ability.

In yet another attempt to quiet the scene, in case the manifestations required the two sisters to remain together, it was decided that Kate would return to her sister Leah's house, when she appeared for a visit at David's. Leah at the time was thirty-four and had a daughter of her own, age twelve. She had been living with a young man, ten years her junior, Calvin Brown, since her husband had left her.

The rappings continued at David's and began at Leah's in Rochester as well. In fact, Kate's presence in Leah's house released a host of what was later described as poltergeist activity. Objects were mysteriously thrown through the air, dishes and seashells were tossed about, blankets were removed from beds, beds were shaken at night, and a variety of sounds of every description were heard, at least according to Leah. These disturbances continued for about a month.

Isaac Post, a friend of the Fox family and a Quaker, on learning of Duesler's repeating the alphabet in order to obtain the peddler's name, suggested that this technique, if followed on a regular basis, might quiet the spirit activity. This was done, and the first message was received, "We are all your dear friends and relatives." A method for turning the rappings into language had been devised, and the first spirit telegraph was invented.

Under the able guidance of E. W. Capron, who lived in Auburn, New York, some seventy miles from Rochester, Kate and Maggie began to travel and conduct public seances. Kate especially had been well prepared for the stage since she had lived in the Capron's boardinghouse and in the homes of many of his friends where she had conducted numerous demonstrations.

As reported by Capron,

> We heard the sounds on the wall, bureau, table, floor and other places, as loud as the striking with a hammer. The table was moved about the room, and turned over and turned back. Two men in the company undertook to hold a chair down, while at their request, a spirit moved it, and notwithstanding they exerted all their strength, the chair could not be held still by them.

In time, under the direction of Leah, working as their manager, the Fox sisters began giving seances in hotels in various cities of New York, charging the unheard-of sum of one dollar for public seances and five dollars for private ones. Public seances were held until noon, from three to five o'clock in the afternoon, and from eight to ten o'clock at night. Private seances were scheduled in between. Up to thirty persons were normally accommodated in the public seances, and private readings, duly chaperoned, were held in the small anterooms of hotels.

As to exactly how the rappings, the mainstay of the reported phenomena, were produced became the subject of a great deal of controversy. Many investigators concluded that the raps were in some manner produced by a mechanical device concealed under the sisters' skirts.

The most famous of the Fox sisters' ever-stalwart supporters was Horace Greeley, who wrote the following in the *New York Tribune*:

> The rooms which they have occupied at the hotel have been repeatedly searched and scrutinized; they have been taken without an

hour's notice into houses they had never before entered. They have been all unconsciously placed on a glass surface concealed under the carpet, in order to interrupt electric vibrations; they have been disrobed by a Committee of Ladies appointed without notice and insisting neither of them should leave the room until the investigation had been made, etc. etc., yet we believe no one to this moment pretends that he has detected either of them in producing or causing the rappings, nor do we think any of their condemners has invented a plausible theory to account for the production of these sounds, nor the singular intelligence which (certainly at times) has seemed to be manifested through them.

In 1851 Leah (who was assumed to have powers too) and Maggie were invited to perform before three professors at the School of Medicine in Buffalo. A statement was later published by this group in the *Buffalo Commercial Advertiser* to the effect that they had heard the raps in various rooms and in different parts of the same room, and that in their opinion the sounds were not produced by any mechanical device either attached to the sisters or to any of the furniture.

It was their final opinion that indeed the sounds were produced by "one or more of the movable articulations of the skeleton." Thus it was concluded that Maggie had produced these rappings by a voluntary dislocation of her knee joints, which was done with sufficient force to vibrate doors and tables. Leah, who no doubt felt that if these opinions persisted Maggie's career would be finished, immediately challenged the professors to prove their theory.

After many hours of grueling examination, during which time there were raps and also a long period of silence, Maggie appeared to break down; she cried, though she finally managed to produce a number of raps. Since she seemed unable to produce any sounds while her knees were being held, however, the professors concluded they had proved their claim. While they admitted they were "unable to explain fully the precise mechanism by which the displacement is effected" and exactly how Maggie could throw her knee in and out of joint for extended periods of time without causing permanent, painful injury, they were convinced that both knees were "endowed with sonorous powers."

Despite the scientific air of the report, skeptics and critics alike found little fuel in the content. The findings failed to explain rappings heard in other parts of the room, the movement of physical objects, and the ability of the rappings to answer correctly questions to which the girls could have had no prior knowledge. Unfortunately for the sisters, the controversy did not end here.

On April 17, 1851, Mrs. Norman Culver, David Fox's sister-in-law, who had recently quarreled with the Fox family, issued a statement to the press in which she claimed unequivocally that Kate had shown her how the raps were produced by snapping all ten of her toes, as well as her ankles when louder sounds were required. Mr. Capron, in quick refutation of this statement, issued his own, which showed that on the day and time when this supposed confession took place, Kate was actually residing at his house, some seventy miles away! Dirty pool? Perhaps!

In retrospect, a great many questions concerning the nature of the Foxes' mediumship were raised that unfortunately were never adequately answered, in much the same manner as the question of the alleged body in the cellar! No one will ever really know whether or not the phenomenon caused by the presence of the sisters was indeed caused by spirit or simply by some sort of psychokinetic force emanating from the girls . . . perhaps from their knees.

Certainly it is possible to argue that even if the rappings were caused by the girls themselves, this in no way disproves the presence of disembodied spirits as the causal agent.

Neither of the girls claimed to have been guided by a particular spirit control, a deceased family member, or friend or other being.

To conclude this chapter, the words of Eileen Garrett perhaps make the most sense:

The Fox family quarreled bitterly and, forty years later, Margaret Fox stated that all her revelations had been frauds. The other sister, Kate, far gone in drink, supported Margaret's confession. But in 1892—a little late, I think—both Margaret and Kate retracted their confessions. These unfortunate facts prove nothing, for it is not enough merely to say there was fraud; it must also be shown how the fraud was perpetrated—and this the Fox sisters were never able to do. Most mediums who work for money use tricks at one time or another—the audience demands it—and although their shameful admissions seem to damn the whole group, actually it does not prove that there is nothing to mediumship. A curious chapter might be written on the pseudo-confessions of pseudo-mediums. In 1847 the Fox sisters were mere children. Is it logical that two little girls organized a hoax that was tested many times during their lifetime?

5

The Amazing D. D. Home

But, although I attribute much value to what evidence
exists in the case of Home, it cannot but be deplored that
the inestimable chance for experiment and record which
this man afforded was almost entirely thrown away by
the scientific world. Unfortunately the record is
especially inadequate in reference to Home's trances
and the evidence for the personal identity of the commu-
nicating spirits.

—F. W. H. Myers,
HUMAN PERSONALITY AND ITS SURVIVAL
OF BODILY DEATH

If the world of spirit is the essence behind the world of matter, then
certainly it must be unlimited in its scope. One name above all else
stands out as a beacon to prove the supremacy of spirit: D. D.
Home.

Daniel Dunglas Home (pronounced "Hoom") was born in Cur-
rie, near Edinburgh, Scotland, on March 20, 1833. Daniel's father,
who called himself Humes, was apparently an illegitimate son of
Alexander, the tenth Earl of Home. Daniel, himself, since he never
mentioned his father in any of his autobiographical writings and
since he was adopted at an early age by his mother's sister, is also
assumed to have been illegitimate.

Of Daniel's mother, little is known except that she was a High-
lander of the McNeal clan and was supposedly gifted with "second
sight."

Of his early years, little is known. At the age of nine, he was brought by his foster parents, Mr. and Mrs. Cook, to Norwich, Connecticut, where he lived until 1850. Although his father had emigrated to Greenville, Connecticut, several years earlier, Daniel appears by all record to have had little contact with him. In fact, upon returning to England in 1855, he changed his name from Humes to Hume to Home. As for his absent mother, Daniel seemed to miss her greatly.

At the age of thirteen, Daniel began to reveal various psychic abilities. (It is interesting that, as in the case of the Fox sisters, this should occur at puberty.) Daniel and a friend, Edwin, pledged that whoever died first would come and present himself to the other.

About a month after Home had moved a few hundred miles away from Edwin, he announced to his aunt that he had seen a vision of Edwin, and that he had died. Two days later, the death was confirmed.

In 1850, he had a vision of his mother in his bedroom and heard her say, "Dan, twelve o'clock." At the time he was ill in bed. He called loudly for his aunt, to whom he described this vision. The next day news was received that confirmed his mother's death at the hour described. At the time, Daniel was seventeen and his mother forty-two.

A few days after the death of Daniel's mother, various rappings began to appear in the house as the Cooks sat down for breakfast. This was accompanied by the movement of furniture. Mrs. Cook, a staunch Presbyterian who had heard rumors of the rappings at the Fox house, suggested that Daniel was the cause and that he had brought the devil into her quiet household.

When he objected that the raps were not his doing, she lost her temper and even threw a chair at him. Despite her objections, the phenomena continued, and Daniel found the rappings and other manifestations becoming more insistent. Even in the homes of friendly neighbors, Daniel found that the rappings were tapping out messages.

When Daniel was eighteen years of age, he was either thrown out of the house by his aunt or left on his own accord. For the next five years he lived with various friends and families. During this time his mediumship began to develop very rapidly, and he gave as many as six or seven seances a day; since he did not realize the drain they were placing on his already frail health, he was frequently ill.

He lived in Boonton, New Jersey, and Brooklyn, New York, for a while. He arrived in Springfield, Massachusetts, in 1852, where he lived with Rufus Elmer, a prosperous businessman and ardent spiritualist. It was while living there that Home began to gather around him a number of well-to-do believers; people of this type were his followers throughout his life.

Among those who sought to investigate his strange powers were William Cullen Bryant, the poet; Professor Wells of Harvard University; Judge Edmonds of the New York Supreme Court; Professor Bush; Bishop Clark of Rhode Island; and David A. Wells, who had authored a number of textbooks on geology and physics.

During Home's first seance of note, conducted in a well-lighted room (Home throughout his career preferred to work in the light rather than in the dark, as is the practice of many modern spiritualists), the table was described to have moved "in every possible direction and with great force." Despite the efforts of two of the party to restrain the movement of the table, it was seen to rise up from the floor and seemingly float for several seconds! When Wells attempted to seat himself on the table, much like a horse it reared up on two legs. When all three, Wells and the two local businessmen, sat together on the table, it yet moved in various directions.

On another occasion, an attempt was made to measure the force the spirits exerted, which experiment Sir William Crookes attempted to duplicate at a later date in Home's career. In this instance, a scale was attached to one end of the table, which indicated that it took nineteen pounds to lift it free from the floor. Spirits were then requested to increase the weight, and the scale showed an increase of from six to twelve pounds. According to a signed statement by nine witnesses, Home was not even in the room when the experiment was performed.

Besides possessing the ability to somehow alter the physical weight of material objects, Home on other occasions demonstrated an ability to tilt a table as much as forty-five degrees by simply touching it with the tip of his fingers—and the objects placed on the table did not slide off!

Following is Dr. R. T. Hallock's account of a seance that occurred in June 1852. Seven persons were present:

> On the table around which we were seated were loose papers, a lead pencil, two candles, and a glass of water. The table was used by the spirits in responding to our questions, and the first peculiarity we observed was that, however violently the table was moved, every-thing on it retained its position. When we had duly observed this, the table, which was mahogany and perfectly smooth, was elevated to an angle of thirty degrees and held there, with everything remaining on it as before. It was interesting to see a lead pencil retaining a position of perfect rest on a polished surface inclined at such an angle. It remained as if glued to the table and so of everything else on it.

During this same seance, the spirits were asked if they could move the table with a man on top of it. When they replied that they could do so even with two men, Hallock and Charles Partridge, editor of the *Spiritual Telegraph*, climbed onto the table. Even though their combined weight was 350 pounds, the table was rocked back and forth until both men were thrown off.

In another demonstration of Home's ability, an accordion played any song requested when he held the side opposite the keys. Again, this was done in a brightly lit room. Of this particular phenomenon, demonstrated while Home was still a guest at Rufus Elmer's home, Elmer writes:

> Then an accordion, held under the table in one of Mr. Home's hands [the other being on the table] with the keys downward, was played in strong tones, three parts being maintained and any tune performed that was called for—even foreign music. The instrument was also played upon while held in the same manner by each person present— all hands except the one holding the accordion being upon the table in sight.

This particular ability of Home's was the subject of a detailed investigation by Sir William Crookes when Home relocated in England.

So great was the affection of the childless Mr. and Mrs. Elmer for Home and his unusual abilities that they offered to adopt him and make him their heir if he agreed to change his name to Elmer.

Since Home had also exhibited remarkable healing powers, a number of friends persuaded him to study for the medical profession. Due to the stress of his seance work, however, and the general state of his poor health, especially his lungs, he was advised instead to leave for England as a sort of missionary of spiritualism. This he did in 1855, with his trip financed by Professor Bush and two sympathetic friends.

On April 9, 1855, Home arrived in England and stayed at Cox's Hotel in Jermyn Street in London. In the autumn of the same year, he went to Italy and held seances for many royal personages, including the Czar of Russia.

It should be pointed out that, unlike the Fox sisters, Home, during the thirty years of his career, never charged a single shilling for his gifts. He did, however, accept room and board and various gifts of jewelry. In 1857 he was offered two thousand pounds for a seance by the Union Club in Paris. He refused it with these words: "I have been sent on a mission. That mission is to demonstrate immortality. I have never taken money for it and I never will!"

Though courted by kings and royalty throughout his lifetime (Napoleon the Third provided for his only sister, and the Czar of Russia sponsored his marriage), Home never lost his humility. Of his philosophy of life, he wrote:

> I have these powers. I shall be happy, up to the limit of my strength to demonstrate them to you, if you approach me as one gentleman should approach another. I shall be glad if you can throw any further light upon them. I will lend myself to any reasonable experiment. I have no control over them. They use me, but I do not use them. They desert me for months and then come back in redoubled force. I am a passive instrument—no more.

On yet another occasion, a lecture given in London on February 15, 1866, he said:

I believe in my heart that this power is being spread more and more every day to draw us nearer to God. You ask if it makes us purer? My only answer is that we are but mortals, and as such liable to err; but it does teach that the pure in heart shall see God. It teaches us that He is love, and that there is no death. To the aged it comes as a solace, when the storms of life are nearly over and rest cometh. To the young it speaks of the duty we owe to each other, and that as we sow so shall we reap. To all it teaches resignation. It comes to roll away the clouds of error, and bring the bright morning of a never-ending day.

Though Home's career as a medium was totally without fraud, he nearly lost his prestigious following through what became known as the Home-Lyon affair.

After many years of struggling, a band of his followers in 1866 organized a new society to promote spiritualism and to provide Home with a fixed position as secretary. This society was called the Spiritual Athenaeum.

It was during this time that Home made the acquaintance of Mrs. Jane Lyon (then seventy-five), a wealthy and childless widow. Like the Elmers, it was her desire to adopt Home, with the provision that he would take the name of Lyon. This Home did and was presented with a sum of money amounting to either twenty-four or sixty thousand pounds (two accounts are given of the amount), supposedly presented "as a free gift."

According to Sir Arthur Conan Doyle, Home had never sought this money to begin with and had in fact argued with Mrs. Lyon to the effect that this rightfully belonged to her heirs, to which she had countered that it was hers to do with as she wished. In any event, after only a few months, Mrs. Lyon sought to revoke her gift and, in April 1868, sued to recover the money in the Court of Chancery, alleging fraud.

Although Home had not removed the money from England or placed it where it could not be recovered, and although he presented numerous affidavits from persons of distinction attesting to his powers, character, and honor, after what has been described as "ten days of hilarious proceedings" the Court ruled in Mrs. Lyon's favor, not being satisfied that her gifts were "acts of pure volition uninfluenced."

Again, according to Doyle, the incident occurred in the first place because Mrs. Lyon had imposed upon Home so that she would be introduced to all his wealthy and influential friends and supporters, which he refused to be blackmailed into doing. Doyle also maintains that had Mrs. Lyon simply asked for the return of the money, it would have been immediately forthcoming. Instead, she proceeded at once to bring a cause of action against Home. Of the final decision, Doyle writes:

> Of all the men of honour who called him friend, it is not recorded that he lost one through the successful machinations of Mrs. Lyon. Her own motives were perfectly obvious. As all the documents were in order, her only possible way of getting the money back was to charge Home with having extorted it from her by misrepresentation, and she was cunning enough to know what chance a medium—even an amateur unpaid medium—would have in the ignorant and material atmosphere of a mid-Victorian court of law. Alas! We can omit the "mid-Victorian" and the statement still holds good.

Before we proceed to discuss other aspects of Home's unusual mediumship, further mention must be made of the social circles in which he moved. In 1858, he had married the seventeen-year-old daughter of Count de Kroll, a Russian general. Alexis Tolstoy attended as a representative of the Czar, and Alexander Dumas, famed author of *The Three Musketeers*, stood in as Home's godfather. (Home's wife died before the Home-Lyon affair, and her modest fortune did not pass to Home.)

In England he was welcomed at many homes of the nobility. He crossed paths with many of the authors of the time; those who attended his seances include the Robert Brownings, Edward Bulwer-Lytton, Frances Trollope, Dante Gabriel Rossetti, Ivan Turgenyev, Sir Edwin Arnold, John Ruskin, and William Makepeace Thackeray. Charles Dickens, however, refused repeated invitations to attend the seances and sought instead to attack Home in the press whenever possible, alleging he was a ruffian and scoundrel.

Robert Browning, too, was convinced that Home was simply an imposter and a cheat, his opinion most likely stemming from a seance he and his wife had attended at the home of John Snaith Rymer, a retired solicitor. At the incident in question, Home had caused a garland of clematis flowers to rise from a table and land on the head of Elizabeth Barrett Browning, much to her delight. In a letter penned to her sister, Henrietta, Elizabeth described what happened as follows:

> At the request of the medium, the spiritual hand took from the table a garland which lay there and placed it upon my head. The particular hand that did this was of the largest human size, as white as snow and very beautiful. It was as near to me as this hand I write with, and I saw it distinctly. . . . I was not troubled in any way and felt convinced in my own mind that no spirit belonging to me was present on the occasion.

While Elizabeth may have not been troubled, Robert certainly was. It may have been that he was offended at the apparent interest spirit and Mr. Home had taken in his wife. Or, as Home suggested in one of his recollections, since Browning rose from his chair as soon as the garland moved in his direction, perhaps he was disturbed at the thought that it had been intended for himself.

In any event, a few days later, when Rymer and Home called at Browning's house, he pointed to Home and yelled out in rage, "If you are not out of that door in half a minute, I'll fling you down the stairs." Before Home could leave, Elizabeth (again, according to Home), grasped both his hands in hers and said emotionally, "Oh dear Mr. Home, do not, do not blame me. I am sorry but I am not to blame."

To get even with Home in the only way he could, Robert immediately composed a long satiric poem, "Mr. Sludge, The Medium" (see appendix 2), making sure his circle of friends knew exactly upon whom he had patterned Mr. Sludge.

Of this incident, Doyle later wrote, without mentioning the incident in detail, "Truly Mrs. Browning was a better judge of character than her spouse, and Sir Galahad a better name than Sludge."

While many physical mediums, both before and after Home, had demonstrated the ability to move objects, and to cause rappings and the materialization of spirit hands and faces, Home must be given credit for being one of the few mediums—if not the only one—to possess the ability to elongate his body, or parts of it, and to demonstrate an immunity to heat and flame.

Through a means unknown to his investigators, Home was able to increase his height by as much as eleven inches. According to one witness, this elongation took place from the waist upward. Another witness claimed to have seen Home elongate his legs as much as six inches and yet remain able to walk on them while they were in this paranormal state. On another occasion he was seen by Lord Adare and H. D. Jencken, the London solicitor who later married Kate Fox, to shrink himself down to five feet so that his shoes disappeared into his trousers.

He was able to handle hot, live coals without being affected in any way. Lord Lindsay claimed that he had seen Home do this at least eight times and that once, wishing to prove to himself that the coals were indeed hot, he had touched one with his finger and had received a "blister as large as a sixpence." At other times, Home would take hot coals and hand them to other sitters who like himself showed no trace of being burned.

On one occasion, Lord Adare related that Home had "placed his face right among the burning coals, moving it about as though bathing it in water." H. D. Jencken further elaborated that Home, after stirring the coals with his hands, "to our horror and amazement placed his face and head in the flames, which appeared to form a bed, upon which his face rested. I narrowly watched the phenomenon and could see the flames touch his hair. On withdrawing his face from the flames, I at once examined his hair; not a fibre was burnt or scorched."

After all is said and done, though, it was Home's ability to levitate that made him more famous than perhaps any other medium in the world.

While there were perhaps one hundred observers of this phenomenon, there were only some thirty published accounts, of which seven were cited by Lord Adare. The most famous seance in which Home demonstrated this ability took place on December 16, 1868, at Adare's rooms at 5 Buckingham Gate, London.

Unlike most of Home's seances, this particular one had been conducted in the dark. According to Lord Adare's account, there was no light in the room except for that coming through the windows (there had been a new moon two days earlier).

Present at the time were Lord Adare, who had followed Home's career for a number of years; the Master of Lindsay, who would later become Lord Crawford; and Captain Charles Wynne, who was Lord Adare's cousin. Adare had been a correspondent for the *Daily Telegraph* during the Abyssinian War and had twice served as Under-Secretary of State for the Colonies. He was twenty-six at the time of the incident. The Master of Lindsay, who was in his early twenties, would later become a Fellow of the Royal Society and serve as President of the Royal Astronomical Society as well as a Trustee of the British Museum. Of Captain Wynne, little is known.

The most complete account is that written by the Master of Lindsay on July 14, 1871. Why it was not written until some two and a half years after the incident is not known, nor has this fact been commented upon by either contemporary or later scholars. In any event, this is Lindsay's account:

I was sitting with Mr. Home, and Lord Adare and a cousin of his. During the sitting Mr. Home went into a trance, and in that state was carried out of the window in the room next to where we were, and was brought in at our window. The distance between the windows was about seven feet six inches, and there was not the slightest foothold between them, nor was there more than a twelve inch projection to each window, which served as a ledge to put flowers on. We heard the window in the next room lifted up, and almost immediately after we saw Home floating in the air outside our window. The moon was shining full into the room; my back was to the light, and I saw the shadow on the wall of the windowsill, and Home's feet about six inches above it. He remained in this position for a few seconds, then raised the window and glided into the room feet fore-most and sat down.

In July 1869, Lindsay offered another account of the incident for the Committee of the Dialectical Society:

> I saw the levitations in Victoria Street when Home floated out of the window. He first went into a trance and walked about uneasily; he then went into the hall. While he was away I heard a voice whisper in my ear, "He will go out of one window and in at another." I was alarmed and shocked at the idea of so dangerous an experiment. I told the company what I had heard and we then waited for Home's return. Shortly after he entered the room. I heard the window go up, but I could not see it, for I sat with my back to it. I, however, saw his shadow on the opposite wall; he went out of the window in a hori-zontal position, and I saw him outside the other window [i.e., the next room], floating in the air. It was eighty-five feet from the ground.

Lord Adare's account is as follows: "We heard Home go into the next room, heard the window thrown up and presently Home appeared standing upright outside our window; he opened the win-dow and walked in quite coolly."

After the levitation had occurred, Lord Adare had gone to shut the window out of which Home had gone, which was in the next room. When he returned to the seance room, he remarked to Home that he could not understand how he had gone out through so small a space, as the window had barely been opened:

> I remarked that the window was not raised a foot, and that I could not think how he [Home] had managed to squeeze through. He arose and said, "Come and see." I went with him; he told me to open the window as it was before; I did so; he told me to stand a little distance off; he then went through the open space, head first, quite rapidly, his body being nearly horizontal and apparently rigid. He came in again feet foremost, and we returned to the other room. It was so dark I could not see clearly how he was supported outside. He did not appear to grasp, or rest upon the balustrade, but rather to be

swung out and in. Outside each window is a small balcony or ledge nineteen inches deep, bounded by stone balustrades eighteen inches high.

According to Doyle, once the reports of Adare and Lindsay had been published, a Dr. Carpenter who had been a continual critic of the incident was quick to comment that there had been a third witness present who had not written his account, assuming that "Captain Wynne's evidence would be contradictory."

Captain Wynne wrote to Home on February 2, 1877, "The fact of your having gone out of one window and in at the other I can not answer to." To this he added, "If you [Home] are not to believe the corroborative evidence of *three* unimpeached witnesses, there would be an end to all justice and courts of law."

What is to be made of this particular incident? Certainly it is possible to argue that Home in some way had succeeded in hypnotizing or mesmerizing his three witnesses and while they were under trance, presenting them with a vision that they later swore had been reality. That their statements were written years after the fact would further serve to blur from their memory the truth of the happening.

On the other hand, continued examination of Home by Sir William Crookes, one of England's foremost scientists and the discoverer of thallium, convinced him that all the paranormal phenomena, including the levitations, were indeed genuine.

Carl G. Jung, in *On Occultism*, cites verbatim the following passage written by Crookes and published in the *Quarterly Journal of Science*. His remarks were based on his investigations during 1870–73.

The most striking cases of levitation which I have witnessed have been with Mr. Home. On three separate occasions have I seen him raised completely from the floor of the room. Once sitting in an easy chair, once kneeling on his chair, and once standing up. On each occasion I had full opportunity of watching the occurrence as it was taking place. There are at least a hundred recorded instances of Mr. Home's rising from the ground, in the presence of as many separate persons, and I have heard from the lips of three witnesses to the most striking occurrence of this kind—the Earl of Dunraven, Lord Lindsay, and Captain C. Wynne—their own most minute accounts of what took place. To reject the recorded evidence on this subject is to reject all human testimony whatever; for no fact in sacred or profane history is supported by a stronger array of proofs. The accumulated testimony establishing Mr. Home's levitations is overwhelming. It is greatly to be desired that some person, whose evidence would be accepted as conclusive by the scientific world—if indeed there lives a person whose testimony *in favour* of such phenomena would be taken—would seriously and patiently examine these alleged facts. Most of the eye-witnesses to these levitations are now living, and would doubtless be willing to give their evidence. But, in a few years, such *direct* evidence will be difficult, if not impossible, to be obtained.

As to whether or not Home's phenomenon was caused by contact with spirit can never be proved at this juncture in time and space. It must remain one of the unanswerable mysteries of psychic phenomena.

At the age of fifty-three, Home's overall frail health and exceptionally poor lungs caught up with him. He died and was buried with the rites of the Greek Orthodox church in a Russian cemetery at St. Germain-en-Laye in 1886. On his gravestone was placed a brief inscription taken from the writings of Paul (1 Cor 12:10): "To another discerning of Spirits."

6

---o---

Allan Kardec:
Spiritist Burr in the
Spiritualist Saddle

The doctrine of our freedom in the choice of our successive existences and of the trials which we have to undergo ceases to appear strange when we consider that spirits, being freed from matter, judge of things differently from men. They perceive the ends which these trials are intended to work out—ends far more important to them than the fugitive enjoyments of earth.

—Allan Kardec

Just as Andrew Jackson Davis may be said to have been the primary spokesman for the American spiritualist movement, Leon Denizarth Hippolyte Rivail, known to the world as Allan Kardec, to this day stands without equal in Latin America, though he was French by birth.

For the most part, Kardec's research into what he called spiritism, rather than spiritualism, fell on somewhat deaf ears in France and was expounded in England by a sole disciple, Miss Anna Blackwell, who translated his works into English. His influence in South America, especially Brazil, is no less than staggering.

For facts regarding Kardec's life we are indebted to Anna Blackwell, who translated his book *Livre des Esprits* from French into English in 1875.

———O———

Leon Denizarth Hippolyte Rivail was born in Lyons, France, on October 4, 1804, to a genteel family of Bourg-en-Bresse, which had for many generations distinguished itself in the magistracy and at the bar. Both his grandfather and his father were barristers of high character. His mother was considered beautiful, accomplished, elegant, and amiable.

He was educated at the Institution of Pestalozzi at Yverdum, where he demonstrated an interest in scientific investigation that was coupled with a love of free thought, traits that persisted throughout his life. As he had been born in a Catholic country but had been educated in a Protestant one, as a youth he meditated on how he might bring about a unity of belief among the various Christian sects.

In 1824 he returned to Lyons, having finished his studies and intending to devote himself to the law, as his father and grandfather had done. When he witnessed a number of acts of religious intolerance, he felt disillusioned and abandoned his plans, going instead to Paris where he supported himself by translating standard French books for young persons, such as *Telemachus*, into German.

When he decided to enter the educational profession, he purchased a flourishing boys' school in 1828 and devoted himself to teaching, for which he felt a natural predilection.

In 1830 he began the practice of hiring, out of his own pocket, a large hall in the Rue de Sevres, in which he presented lectures on chemistry, physics, comparative anatomy, and astronomy, without charge to those attending. He continued this practice for more than ten years, sometimes drawing as many as five hundred persons from all ranks of society.

He invented a somewhat ingenious method of computation, constructed a mnemonic table of French history, which enabled students to remember the events and discoveries of each period, and authored and published a number of educational works. Among these are *A Plan for the Improvement of Public Education* (1828), *A Course of Practical and Theoretic Arithmetic on the Pestalozzian System* (1829), *A Classical Grammar of the French Tongue* (1831), *A Manual for the Use of Candidates for Examination in the Public*

Schools (1848), and *Normal Dictations for the Examinations of the Hotel de Ville and the Sorbonne* (1849). Many of these works were still in use in many French schools at the time of Rivail's death.

He was a member of a number of learned societies, including the Royal Society of Arras, by which he was awarded the Prize of Honor for authoring an essay on the question "What is the System of Study most in Harmony with the Needs of the Epoch?" He was also the secretary of the Phrenological Society of Paris, and belonged to the Society of Magnetism, in which he was first exposed to the phenomena of trance and clairvoyance.

About 1850 he witnessed for the first time the phenomenon of table-turning that had by then overtaken Europe. He attended a rather exclusive Paris salon in which the hostess, much to his surprise, made the guests play table-rapping. Sitting and placing his hands on a heavy round table, Rivail was astonished when the table began to rap out messages. It not only told where Mme. X had misplaced her jewels but that Mlle. Y would soon marry and with whom. When the spirit identified itself as that of a famous and long dead poet, all the guests save Rivail laughed. For Rivail, the fact that these messages might indeed come from the deceased was reason to take them seriously. If there really were spirits, surely their existence would have an effect on science.

Continuing his investigation, Rivail was led to a friend of his who had two daughters who had become mediums. While the girls were generally gay, lively, worldly, and somewhat frivolous, Rivail's presence always transformed their communications to that of a grave and serious nature. Finally, according to Blackwell, in one sitting he was told that "spirits of a much higher order than those who habitually communicated through the two young mediums came expressly for him, and would continue to do so, in order to enable him to fulfill an important religious mission."

To test the truthfulness of this announcement, he began to draw up a number of questions. These he submitted to spirit through the two young mediums, who devoted a couple of evenings each week to this purpose. The answers he received served as the basis for his later books.

After the passage of two years' time, during which he continued to receive various answers to his questions, he shared with his wife his idea of publishing what he had received:

> It is a most curious thing! My conversations with the invisible intelligences have completely revolutionized my ideas and convictions. The instructions thus transmitted constitute an entirely new theory of human life, duty and destiny, that appears to me to be perfectly rational and coherent, admirably lucid and consoling, and intensely interesting. I have a great mind to publish these conversations in a book; for it seems to me that what interests me so deeply might very likely prove interesting to others.

When Rivail submitted his idea to his unseen friends through his usual mediums, they responded that it had been they who had caused this idea to enter into his mind in the first place. He was told that the time had come for him to publish such a work and that he should call it *Le Livre des Esprits* (The Spirits' Book). It should not be published under the name Rivail, which he should keep for his own books already published, but under the pseudonym Allan Kardec, which was an old Breton name in his mother's family.

So popular was this work that it rendered Allan Kardec a household name. He was called by this name throughout the remainder of his life, except by his old personal friends and family members.

Soon after the publication of *The Spirits' Book* in 1856, he founded the Parisian Society of Psychologic Studies, for which he served as president until his death in 1869. Every Friday evening this group met at his home for the purpose of obtaining instructions from spirits. He also went on to found and edit a monthly magazine, *La Revue Spirite*, dedicated to the advocacy of the views set forth in *The Spirits' Book*.

Various spiritist associations were established in many different countries. They contributed to his research and resulted in the publication of a revised edition of his original treatise in 1857. In addition, he went on to publish four subsequent works, using essentially the same material as a basis: *The Book of Mediums* (1861), *The Gospel as Explained by Spirits* (1864), *Heaven and Hell*

(1865), and *Genesis* (1867). He also published two short treatises entitled *What Is Spiritism?* and *Spiritism Reduced to Its Simplest Expression*.

Physically, Kardec has been described by Anna Blackwell as somewhat under middle height, strongly built, with a large, round, massive head, well-marked features, and clear gray eyes. According to her, he looked more German than French. He is said to have been energetic and persevering, grave, slow of speech, and unassuming in manner.

As a result of the success of his publications, he lived modestly but well, spending his winters in Paris and his summers at the Villa Segur, a semirural retreat. He continually received numerous visitors from various stations of life and was himself received by the Emperor Napoleon II at the Tuileries a number of times, in order to discourse upon his work.

Having suffered from heart disease for many years, in 1869 Allan Kardec drew up a new plan for a spiritist organization that he hoped would continue after his passing. To do this he established a legal entity called the Joint Stock Company for the Continuation of the Works of Allan Kardec, which was empowered to buy and sell, to issue stock, and to receive donations and bequests. To this he intended to bequeath the copyrights to all of his writings and *La Revue Spirite*.

Before his plans could be finalized, however, the aneurysm from which he suffered ruptured, and on March 31, 1869, he passed on to that world about which he had spent much of his life learning. No doubt he was welcomed with open arms. It was left to his widow to carry out his plans, which she is said to have done with great exactitude.

His remains were interred in the cemetery of Montmarte with a gathering of a great many friends. To this day, on the anniversary of his passing hundreds of persons congregate at his graveside, where commemorative words are spoken, and flowers and wreaths are laid.

While it is difficult to accurately assess the extent of his influence, Sir Arthur Conan Doyle thought enough of it to include significant reference to Kardec in his *History of Spiritualism*.

For the most part, Kardec's beliefs in two areas separate him and his followers from the rest of the spiritualist movement. According to Harry Boddington, in his *University of Spiritualism*, the essential difference between Kardec and other spiritualists centered around two beliefs: first, his belief in the doctrine of evocation, which held that if you call upon individual spirits with a sincere motive, they will respond; second, Kardec and his followers taught the belief in reincarnation, which for most spiritualists represented a denial of the doctrine of evolution. It is the latter belief that caused his doctrines to be generally unacceptable by both English and American spiritualists.

Doyle summarizes Kardec's beliefs as follows:

This Spiritist philosophy is distinguished by its belief that our spiritual progression is effected through a series of incarnations.

1. Spirits have to pass through many incarnations; it follows that we all have had many existences, and that we shall have others, more or less perfect, either upon this earth or in other worlds.
2. The incarnation of spirits always takes place in the human race; it would be an error to suppose that the soul or spirit could be incarnated in the body of an animal.
3. A spirit's successive corporeal existences are always progressive, and never retrograde; but the rapidity of our progress depends on the efforts we make to arrive at perfection.
4. The qualities of the soul are those of the spirit incarnated in us; thus, a good man is the incarnation of a good spirit, and a bad man is that of an unpurified spirit.
5. The soul possessed its own individuality before its incarnation; it preserves that individuality after its separation from the body.
6. On its re-entrance into the spirit world, the soul again finds there all those whom it has known upon the earth, and all its former existences eventually come back to its memory, with the remembrance of all the good and of all the evil which it has done in them.
7. The incarnated spirit is under the influence of matter; the man who surmounts this influence, through the elevation and purification of his soul, raises himself nearer to the superior spirits, among whom he will one day be classed.
8. Incarnated spirits inhabit the different globes of the universe.

Again, according to Doyle, when Kardec posed to his contacts the question "What is the aim of the incarnation of spirits?" he received the following answer: "It is a necessity imposed on them by God, as the means of obtaining perfection. For some of them it is an expiation; for others, a mission. In order to obtain perfection, *it is necessary for them to undergo all the vicissitudes of corporeal existence*. It is the experience acquired by expiation that constitutes its usefulness."

Writing in 1924, Doyle says of the controversy promulgated by Kardec's work:

Spiritualists in England have come to no decision with regard to reincarnation. Some believe in it, many do not, and the general attitude may be taken to be that, as the doctrine cannot be proved, it had better be omitted from the active politics of Spiritualism. Miss Anna Blackwell, in explanation of this attitude, suggests that the Continental mind being more receptive of theories, has accepted Allan Kardec, while the English mind "usually declines to consider any theory until it has assured itself of the facts assumed by such theory."

Doyle then goes on to quote Mr. Thomas Brevoir (Shorter), an editor of *The Spiritual Magazine*, writing in 1876:

When Reincarnation assumes a more scientific aspect, when it can offer a body of demonstrable facts admitting to verification like those of Modern Spiritualism, it will merit ample and careful discussion. Meanwhile, let the architects of speculation amuse themselves if they will by building castles in the air; life is too short, and there is too much to do in this busy world to leave either leisure or inclination to occupy ourselves in demolishing these airy structures, or in show-ing on what slight foundations they are reared. It is far better to work out those points in which we are agreed than to wrangle over those upon which we appear so hopelessly to differ.

Perhaps of greatest interest are the comments of the notable D. D. Home, written in response to an article on Kardec's beliefs by Alexandre Aksakof. Home writes with rare wit:

I meet many who are reincarnationists, and I have had the pleasure of meeting at least twelve who were Marie Antoinette, six or seven Mary, Queen of Scots, a whole host of Louises and other kings, about twenty Alexanders the Great, but it remains for me yet to meet a plain John Smith, and I beg of you, if you meet one, to cage him as a curiosity.

Of the apparent split in France between Kardec's beliefs in reincarnation and those of M. Pierart, publisher of the opposition journal, *Le Revue Spiritualiste*, the *London Spiritual Magazine* sought to comment in 1865:

To this doctrine—which has nothing to do with Spiritualism, even if it had a leg of reason or fact to stand on—all the strength, and almost all the space of these journals is devoted.

These are the things which give the enemies of spiritualism a real handle against it, and bring it into contempt with sober minds. Reincarnation is a doctrine which cuts up by the roots all individual identity in the future existence. It desolates utterly that dearest yearning of the human heart for reunion with its loved ones in a permanent world. If some are to go back into fresh physical bodies, and bear new names, and new natures, if they are to become respectively Tom Styles, Ned Snooks, and a score of other people, who shall ever hope to meet again with his friends, wife, children, brothers and sisters? When he enters the spirit world and enquires for them, he will have to learn that they are already gone back to earth, and are somebody else, the sons and daughters of other people, and will have to become over and over the kindred of a dozen other families in succession! Surely, no such most cheerless crochet could bewitch the intellects of any people, except the most especial bedevilment of the most sarcastic and mischievous of devils.

Strange as it may appear, though, after presenting a number of quotations decidedly *against* the doctrine of reincarnation, Doyle blatantly says the following:

On the whole, it seems to the author that the balance of evidence shows that *reincarnation is a fact*, but not necessarily a universal one. As to the ignorance of our spirit friends upon the point, it concerns their own future, and if we are not clear as to our future, it is possible that they have the same limitations. When the question is asked, ''Where were we before we were born?'' we have a definite answer in the system of slow development by incarnation, with long intervals of spirit rest between, while otherwise we have no answer, though we must admit that it is inconceivable that we have been born in time for eternity. Existence afterwards seems to postulate existence before.

As to the natural question, ''Why then, do we not remember such existences?'' we may point out that such remembrance would enormously complicate our present life, and that such existences may well form a cycle which is all clear to us when we have come to the end of it, when perhaps we may see a whole rosary of lives threaded upon the one personality. [Italics added]

The controversy generated by Kardec's work still has repercussions today. To learn whether modern spiritualists accept the doctrine of reincarnation about which I have an open mind, I sought out and spoke with Rev. Joseph H. Merrill, president since 1973 of the National Association of Spiritualist Churches (N.A.S.C.).

According to Merrill, the N.A.S.C. holds the position that reincarnation is *not* part of spiritualist teachings since it is not a *proven* theory. He says, ''We are not opposed to individuals believing whatever they want to believe. We do *not* believe that they should be *teaching* something that is a *theory* only . . . that is not a proven fact . . . in relation to spiritualism.

''Our definition of spiritualism is that it is a science, philosophy, and religion. Science, because we classify, analyze, and we *prove* our phenomenon. Whereas reincarnation has never been proved. It's a theory only!''

While Merrill says the N.A.S.C. has the power to censure churches that teach reincarnation, ''It has not happened up to the present time.'' He added, ''It is a very sticky subject. I have not accepted it in all my years of spiritualism, because in my early days in spiritualism, I studied Rosicrucianism in Boston.

''There was a period while I was studying that I thought I could go to a certain house in Paris, to an art colony, and that I could go right in and say 'I'm home.' I began to believe that maybe this was true. And so I asked my spirit helpers, 'Give me something. Is it true or isn't it? Help me to believe.' And the answer I got from spirit has satisfied me all through these years. In the spirit world, it's as much a theory as it is here in the earth world!

"There are those who have come into spirit who believed in it while on the earth. There are those who did *not* believe in it on the earth, and they come into spirit *not* believing it." He continued, "We have not yet seen anyone reincarnated. So until that is proven, it's all theory. So with that . . . all of a sudden, it [i.e., his belief in reincarnation] left!"

Merrill then applied his common sense to analyze why this belief had come to him in the first place. He discovered that the origin of his family name, de Merle, was in the Alsace-Lorraine region of Europe. Artistic talent had been inherited in his family (Merrill's father and he were both photographers and artists). Hence Merrill concluded that one of his ancestors, who had been an artist, had overshadowed his mind and might have lived in a certain house in Paris. Thus Merrill felt that if he had physically gone there, he could have said he "was home."

When I asked Merrill to clarify this point still further, he responded by saying, "Spiritualism believes in progression, continual progression. In the aeons of time, you go back to the godhead. You came from the fountainhead and you're going back there eventually. But through that you are going to go through progressive channels of understanding, growing, and learning, until that point is reached. Then you go back to where you came from, God. Since we believe in contact with the spirit people, and we prove it, at some point if they reincarnate, how can we contact them?"

Merrill is fond of telling the story of being in a church where a medium friend of his was attempting to bring a message from a departed grandmother. The parishioner said "No" repeatedly. Trying to press it to her, the medium finally asked, "Don't you have a grandmother on your mother's side who is in spirit?"

"No," the parishioner replied. "She reincarnated fifty years ago!"

"Where's spiritualism?" Merrill asks.

Merrill related having met the well-known author Jess Stearn, who was visiting the spiritualist community of Lily Dale one year. He had been writing about Taylor Caldwell and later published a book about her previous lives. "We had a two-hour conversation about reincarnation," Merrill said. "I asked him to show me *why* he believed it. He himself was not sure that it was true. And Taylor Caldwell did not beleive it. She later made a statement. So anyway, it's a theory and not part of spiritualism."

Merrill continued by saying, "We do have spiritualist mediums in our organization, who in their private interviews go and give past-life readings, which is very wrong and should be stopped!" The problem, according to Merrill, is that "the organization [N.A.S.C.] has not made an official statement or put a stop to this practice."

While Merrill could not say why his organization has not taken a definite position on this issue, he feels that "at some point we will have to take a stand because it is spreading so, it is diluting what we spiritualists believe in as far as our mediumship is concerned."

One thing is certain, as will be seen later on in this work: The issue of reincarnation is undisputedly the burr in the saddle of modern spiritualism.

Striving to further clarify this point, Harry Boddington offers the following suggestions in *The University of Spiritualism*:

> The majority of Spiritualists oppose the doctrine of reincarnation because they believe the next phase of life contains all the elements essential to progress. The idea of a "good time" on earth usually relates to physical adjustments rather than spiritual development. The doctrine is often attributable to vanity . Conceit desires glory; so we conjure up dreams of past splendors and quite forget that if we are worse off now than we were, we must have retrogressed and not gone forward. "Overshadowing" by a discarnate spirit, or semi-control, produces sensations attributed by many to memory of prior existence. Traveling "in the spirit" induces similar ideas owing to

the inability of the physical brain to express psychic experience correctly. Telepathy, prophetic vision and psychometric contact with the past often produce similar ideas.

The issue of reincarnation ultimately diluted Kardec's long-term influence in France (as well as in England and the United States), but his influence in Latin America is staggering. It is estimated that in present-day Brazil there are no fewer than 3,000 Kardek (as it's spelled there) temples in which physical illnesses are allegedly cured by mediums who believe they possess the ability to project healing energy into the aura of those who are ill—a technique that has come down in a number of forms from ancient times.

Kardec's teachings were brought to Rio de Janeiro by a nobleman of the Brazilian court when he returned from Europe carrying a copy of Kardec's research, first published in 1856 with the title *The Spirits' Book*. No doubt this work was what the upper-class Brazilians were looking for. First, it had been written by a Frenchman of obvious culture. Second, the author was a scientist. Third, he was white. And last, he told them what they all wanted to hear; namely, "There is no death."

His writings were immediately translated into Portuguese, and Kardekian centers rose up all over the country. For the most part, it was initially the better educated and those of the upper class who attended these meetings, in which they learned the laws of the spirit world and received messages. Surely, the Brazilians were seeking answers to questions concerning the perpetuity of life that neither European Catholicism nor pagan African candomblé could provide. This they easily found in Kardec's teachings.

What better way to end the discussion of Allan Kardec than to recall the opinion of Anna Blackwell, his lone English supporter: "These works are regarded by the majority of Continental Spiritualists as constituting the basis of the religious *philosophy of the future*—a philosophy in harmony with the advance of scientific discovery in the various other realms of human knowledge; promulgated by the host of enlightened Spirits acting under the direction of Christ himself. [Italics added]"

Is Anna correct? Only the passage of time will tell.

7

Arthur Ford: The Man Who Summoned the Dead

Old Church men think I'm mouthing the words of the devil, but the young ones know the spirit never dies and never leaves.

—Arthur Ford

On Monday morning, January 4, 1971, at 12:45, as reported in the *Miami Herald*, the world's most-renowned medium, Arthur Ford, uttered three words, "God help me," and passed over the threshold "to be with his good friend Fletcher," (with whom for over forty-three years he had been in constant contact—but whom he had never met!).

To adequately describe the worldwide influence of this man born in Titusville, Florida, with its grand population of only three hundred, one must certainly have a great many more pages than we have at our disposal.

What D. D. Home had been to nineteenth-century Europe, Arthur Ford was without question to twentieth-century American spiritualists. But his transition, like his life itself, was shrouded with mystery and left many of his followers doubting his abilities to make genuine spirit contact.

The reason for this sudden doubt was simple. While researching a biography of Ford, which was later published as *Arthur Ford: The Man Who Talked with the Dead*, authors Allen Spraggett and

William V. Rauscher came upon various newspaper articles and obituaries that contained information corresponding with what Arthur had presented while in trance at the famous televised Ford/Pike seance. Even though one particular obituary of the Rt. Rev. Karl Morgan Block had been clipped some *nine years before* the infamous seance took place, its presence among Ford's personal papers caused doubt in Spraggett's and Rauscher's minds as to his integrity and ethics. Additional handwritten notes, similar to crib sheets used in academic examinations, had also been found that contained references that had been represented as coming from spirit. Whether these were taken down by someone attending the seance or had been used by the late Ford himself could never be determined.

A former secretary with whom Ford had parted on unfriendly terms, and who he had called "a goddamned queer," also maintained that Ford never held an important seance without first researching the lives of those who would be in attendance. He would start with school records and then just follow the trail up to the current moment. Allegedly, he had done this *before* attending the Pike seance.

This same informant charged Ford with carrying about a suitcase of notes that he had code-named his "poems." Before a sitting, he would read a little "poetry," which he supposedly kept up-to-date by constantly reading newspapers and cutting out obituaries from all over the United States. This would enable him to pretend to have insights received in a trance state.

Most damaging of all was the statement by the secretary that Ford had told him "that anybody who could perform 100 percent of the time was a fraud."

Was this the truth about Arthur Ford? Who can say in retrospect, after all these years? Certainly the obituaries that were found could have been clipped and sent to Ford as proofs or confirmations of things that he had told those who attended his many seances.

The truth of the matter would seem to lie somewhere between Ford and his Maker. But we are getting well ahead of our story.

Arthur Augustus Ford was born January 8, 1897, at 10:30 A.M.

The exactness of the report of his birth time was no doubt due to his later interest in astrology.

According to Ford's autobiography, *Nothing So Strange*, his father was a steamboat captain, whose name he later found out had been Albert Fordeaux. He and his stepsister had been raised by Ford's grandmother when her husband was reported to have drowned while sailing to New York.

In later years, Ford enjoyed telling friends that he had been "born in jail," which was half true, as his grandfather was a deputy sheriff who lived in the county building that also housed the jail. It was here at home that Ford was born. Ford's mother, Henrietta Brown Ford, had come back home to her family in Titusville specifically for his birth.

When Arthur was three weeks old, she returned to Fort Pierce to join her husband, at which time, according to his father's wishes, Arthur was christened in the Episcopalian church. Describing his father, Ford would say, "He was an ardent, non-church-attending Episcopalian, of which the world still has a few."

It was not without a certain amount of familial discord that Arthur was baptized in that faith, however, as his mother and her family were "staunch, indoctrinated, unequivocal, vociferous Baptists"— which I assume is Ford's way of saying that they took their religion more than a bit seriously!

It was due to the influence of his uncle, Arthur Brown, editor of the Fort Pierce newspaper, and his father that he developed a life-long addiction to reading everything he could lay his hands on, including numerous periodicals, from which he daily clipped and saved interesting articles.

Unlike some mediums, Ford had no recollection of any particular psychic experience as a child. Of this he writes:

> If I had psychic experience in my childhood I was unaware of the fact. Anything unorthodox would have been frowned out of me while a religious vision or an allergic prophecy would have been bragged into my consciousness, but looking back I realize that I was often aware what people were going to say before they spoke and aware what they were thinking when they did not speak.

Arthur's social life as a young man centered around church and Sunday school, beginning early in the day and continuing on late into the evening.

But boyhood friends of Arthur's, who were Catholic, first exposed him to the idea of contacting the spirit of someone who had passed on; being Catholic, they called these spirits saints. It was in this family that Arthur met and was befriended by a "stocky agile chap," whom he never saw after he was nine years old but who later reappeared to guide him into the world of spirit. This boyhood friend became the most famous spirit guide in the world. His name was Fletcher.

At about the age of fifteen, Ford discovered two booklets that had been left in a room his mother rented out to the northern tourists they called "damnyankees," who had begun to discover Florida as a winter resort. Both booklets gave addresses, together with the promise that one could obtain future publications, free, by simply writing. They were *The Metropolitan Opera News* and *Evolution and Religion*, published by the King's Chapel, a Unitarian church in Boston. Both were read by Ford and his father, while his mother confiscated them whenever she could. The latter booklet led Arthur to attend a local Unitarian church started by a retired clergyman named Simpson, who had moved to town from the North.

As a result of these associations, when Ford was sixteen, he found himself called before the deacons and elders of his church and questioned about his beliefs—Unitarians did not accept the divinity of Christ. By the end of his interrogation, he had knowingly hanged himself and was "churched," which was Southern Baptist for excommunicated.

It was through Simpson that Ford was told about the Johnson Academy in Kimberlin Heights, Tennessee, where he could work and finish school at the same time. Since his local school had only a two-year course and since things had gotten "hot" after he had been churched, Ford hastily left for Tennessee with only $40 in his pocket.

According to Ford, the Academy was run solely by faith, with both the students and faculty praying daily over the names of prospective donors. Of this he writes:

Each of us boys had a list of donors for whom we prayed. I became known as one of the most effective prayers in the school. . . . I worked in the office and one of my tasks was making up the list of names to be prayed for. I am afraid I placed on my own list some of the likeliest prospects. Nevertheless, I did pray earnestly and some of my more unlikely prospects came through with gifts.

One of his prayers was for the opportunity to go to college. In the fall of 1917, he entered Transylvania College in Lexington, Kentucky, on a scholarship. At the same time, he entered the R.O.T.C., even though as a ministerial student he was exempt from the draft.

In 1918, Ford gave in to his conscience and enlisted to do his duty. He was sent to an army officers' camp in Sheridan, Illinois, and attained the exalted rank of second lieutenant in ninety days. He was then reassigned to Camp Grant, Illinois.

It was while Ford was in the military service that the world of spirit began to appear to him. Ford wrote of this later in his life: "During the months I saw military service I was often puzzled by 'voices' and 'visions.' I knew nothing of spiritualism. It was something in which respectable people did not engage. Because of my ignorance I was frightened at my experiences. I felt that I must be cracking up."

The strange form in which Ford's ability began to manifest itself was that he would hear a name spoken by one of his voices and find it on the casualty list a few days later. According to Ford's autobiography, this unusual psychic ability took a strange turn during the Spanish flu epidemic in 1918.

Each morning Ford would awaken with a list of names of those who had died of flu during the night. This continued for a week, bringing him to the brink of insanity. The pattern then changed, and he began to dream casualty lists of company members who had gone overseas.

On Armistice Day, November 11, 1918, Ford's visions touched him personally for the first time. He dreamed he saw his brother George, who had been stationed at a camp in the South. While George was smiling in the dream, Ford nonetheless felt a sense of sadness. A few days afterward, he received word that his brother had died of the flu, having taken ill on the day of his dream.

Returning to Transylvania College in 1919, Ford was fortunate to encounter a psychology professor, Dr. Elmer Snoddy, who encouraged him to accept and seek to develop his strange abilities. In the words of Allen Spraggett, one of Ford's biographers, he convinced Arthur that he was "psychic and not psychotic."

While Ford's academic career was for the most part undistinguished, he did excel at preaching. In his junior year he served as the interim pastor of St. Matthew's Church near Louisville, which brought him a call from the Christian Church in Barbourville, Kentucky.

Since the demands of this pastorate were great, Ford would have to quit college if he assumed the post. This he did. Though he had not yet graduated, he was ordained by Dr. Alonzo Fortune at the Chestnut Street Christian Church in Lexington, Kentucky.

This event seems to have marked an end to Arthur's formal education, though over the years various biographical accounts have mentioned him as having a master's degree from the University of Kentucky. (The *New York Times* even referred to him as the Rev. Dr. Ford in a 1967 description of his family television seance with Bishop Pike.)

Ford was twenty-five when he assumed his first pastorate in 1922. In the same year, he married Sallie Stewart. The marriage ended in divorce five years later.

After a year and a half in the pastorate, he was congratulated by the local press, as he had succeeded in doubling the already sizable church membership and tripling the Sunday School attendance.

During this time, Arthur consciously continued to expand his psychic abilities by holding experimental seances and even allowing himself to be hypnotized. In 1921, Arthur had traveled to New York City, where he affiliated himself with the American Society for Psychical Research (ASPR). He became the confidante and close friend of Gertrude Tubby, the Society's secretary.

In his second year at Barbourville, Arthur met Dr. Paul Pearson, founder and president of the Swarthmore Chatauqua Association, which managed lecture circuits in New England. Pearson persuaded Ford to resign from the ministry and join his staff as an expert in psychic phenomena. So great was the love of his congregation that they asked him to name his successor, and in 1924, he hit the lecture trail.

Once again receiving rave reviews for his public speaking ability, Ford found himself immersed in a new career, which allowed him to base himself in New York City, near the ASPR. While in New York he met his lifelong friend and patron, Francis Fast, a wealthy businessman and dedicated spiritualist who was convinced of Ford's potential as a medium.

In the chapter of his autobiography entitled "The Training of a Psychic," Ford recalls the ancient mystical injunction "When the disciple is ready, the teacher will appear." In his own case, the teacher took the form of the famous yogi Paramahansa Yogananda, who had first come to America in 1920.

Swami Yogananda, later the author of the best seller *Autobiography of a Yogi*, had founded the Self-Realization Fellowship in order to disseminate to Westerners the ancient teachings of yoga.

According to Ford, it was Swami Yogananda who first instructed him in how to meditate and how to enter a trance state by himself, which allowed him to make contact with the world of spirit. Of his special relationship with Yogananda, Ford wrote:

> Swami Yogananda accepted me, not so much as student in any formal sense of the word, but as friend. Such powers as mine were nothing new to him, nor did he rate them as significant except as they might be used to deepen awareness.
>
> I often traveled a considerable distance to hear him lecture, for he never failed to challenge the commonplace. From him I learned that truth belongs to neither East nor West, but is a universal thing, which only seems different when one does not look beneath its varying cultural expressions.

While Ford was able to see and discern spirit to a limited degree, it was not until 1924 that his mediumship reached new heights. It was then that his guide Fletcher announced himself and said that he was now Arthur's partner on the unseen plane. This event happened indirectly when a friend of Arthur's who was having a sitting was told, "Tell Ford that I am to be his control and that I go by the name of Fletcher."

When asked at a later sitting exactly who he was, Fletcher said he was one of the French Canadian boys whom Arthur had played with as a young boy in Fort Pierce and that he was using his middle name, Fletcher, so as not to embarrass his Roman Catholic family. He added that his family, after leaving Fort Pierce, had gone to Canada and that he had been killed in action during World War II. He went on to present details as to the name of his company, when and where he had been killed, and the current address of his family.

Ford wrote to the family asking about various members, including Fletcher, without disclosing his reasons for writing. One of Fletcher's brothers wrote back confirming that Fletcher had been killed at the time and place that he had conveyed to Arthur.

So like many other mediums, Ford now had a control . . . a control named Fletcher. As to exactly how he and Fletcher worked together, Ford wrote the following:

> When I wish to go into a trance I lie down on a couch or lean back in a comfortable chair and breathe slowly and rhythmically until I feel an indrawing or energy at the solar plexus. Then I focus my attention on Fletcher's face as I have come to know it, until gradually I feel as if his face presses into my own, at which instant there is a sense of shock somewhat as if I were passing out. Then I lose consciousness, appearing to be asleep. My body is in a state of sleep and when I waken at the end of a session I feel as if I had had a good nap.

Once Ford was in trance, Fletcher would announce his arrival to those sitting by simply saying "Hello" in a slight French Canadian accent.

From the very moment Fletcher appeared, Arthur's mediumship took on a different dimension. By the late 1920s, his gifts were so well established that a number of devoted followers organized The First Spiritualist Church of New York, which met at Carnegie Hall Studios and appointed Arthur Ford its pastor, a position he held for two years.

In the spring of 1927, he traveled to England for the first time, where he met and became friends with Sir Arthur Conan Doyle, Sir Oliver Lodge, and Mrs. St. Clair Stobart. His introduction to the British spiritualist world came unexpectedly when Sir Arthur, upon concluding his lecture on spiritualism at Grotrian Hall in London's Mayfair district and after quieting the applause for his own lecture, introduced Ford as follows: "We have on the platform tonight a well-known American medium, Arthur Ford. I am going to ask him to give a public demonstration of his clairvoyant gift!"

Totally unexpectedly Ford found himself pushed to the center of the platform, from which he began to call out names and details, one by one. Of this night he later wrote, "I felt as if the reputation of American mediumship was at stake. Back home, I always considered my public work an experimental sort of thing, as the audiences in Carnegie Hall well knew. I never claimed to be a professional medium."

The next day the *London Express* carried a story written by Doyle that began, "One of the most amazing things I have ever seen in forty-one years of psychic experience was the demonstration of Arthur Ford."

After relating but a few of the specifics that Ford had presented to his audience, Doyle concluded his article: "So he went on, without pause or mistake, for twenty minutes, as a thousand can testify. And yet this young man had only landed in England forty-eight hours before, and there was not, outside the platform, one person in that audience whom he knew." Ford's reputation was clearly established. Mrs. St. Clair Stobart described the evening in a single word, "Magical." Ford was never again to experience so serene and straightforward a triumph in his career.

Of all of Ford's new friends in England, it was perhaps the influence of Doyle that meant the most to him. In the chapter of his autobiography that describes this part of his life, he writes:

> Before I left England, Conan Doyle laid upon my conscience the matter of becoming a professional medium. He felt that both ministers and mediums were called of God, but that since there were more ministers than mediums, I should choose mediumship. Finally I agreed with him and made the decision, but it was a good many years before I understood my calling.

Back in the United States, in October 1927 Ford crossed swords with the renowned American magician Howard Thurston, who claimed, as quoted in the *New York Herald* (October 3, 1927), to have personally exposed more than three hundred mediums. He said that he had a gadget that could create an ectoplasmic phantom that would duplicate all the events of a seance.

So outraged by Thurston's comments was Ford that he openly challenged him to meet in public debate at Carnegie Hall, offering him $10,000 if he could prove his claims. (The money for the challenge had been provided by one of Ford's affluent friends, John Bowman, president of the Bowman Biltmore Hotel Corporation.)

When the evening of the meeting arrived, amid a packed hall of magicians and press, Ford openly challenged Thurston to simply produce the names, addresses, times, and places of exposure of only twenty-five mediums, together with the proof that they were so exposed. Thurston could name only three, all of whom were dead. Arthur went on to ask him for the names of twenty-five families that had broken up due to the influence of spiritualism—another of Thurston's claims. Thurston responded with none.

When Ford asked him to produce his "rubber spook" in front of the audience and to let it walk over to him and tell him the real name of his father (i.e., Fordeaux), Thurston said he had forgotten to bring it along.

Needless to say, the whole encounter was more than a great personal success for Ford. The next day's *New York Telegram* headlines declared, "Spiritualist Hurls Defiance At Ghost Deriding Magician."

It was not Howard Thurston but another magician of even greater fame, Harry Houdini, with whose name Ford's would be eternally linked.

Houdini had spent most of his life debunking fraudulent mediums. On his deathbed on October 31, 1926, he had given his wife a code with emphasis on one word, known only to her; if conveyed to her by a medium, it would serve as proof that he lived on. Originally, Beatrice had offered a $10,000 reward to anyone who could communicate the message she and her late husband had agreed upon. Later on, she withdrew the reward, having been advised by spiritualists that they could more easily reach Houdini if the reward was not an issue.

The beginning of the breaking of the Houdini code came on February 8, 1928, when Fletcher announced through Ford at a seance in Ford's apartment that the mother of Harry Weiss, known to the world as Harry Houdini, had come forward with a message her son had waited all his life to hear. The word was "Forgive" and was to be given to his wife who was the only person in the world who knew the word. It seemed that before his mother's passing, a rift had occurred in the family when Sadie, Harry's sister-in-law, had left Harry's brother Nathan for another of Harry's brothers, Leopold. Harry had broken off all contact with Leopold and vowed never to forgive his brother unless ordered to do so by his mother. Unfortunately, his mother had passed away before he could discuss the matter with her.

Francis Fast, who had been in attendance at this sitting, had taken down Fletcher's message and shared it with Ford after he came out of the trance state.

The next day this message was taken to Mrs. Houdini, who made a public statement that this was "the sole communication received among thousands up to this time that contained the one secret key word known only to Houdini, his mother, and myself."

During this first seance, Fletcher had ended his communication with the words, "She is going now, and she says that since this message has come through it will open the channel for the other."

"The other" was the famous message based on a ten-word code that was part of the pact Houdini had made with his wife prior to his death. At the time of his passing, considerable press coverage had been given to this secret message, and while many messages had been presented to Mrs. Houdini, none had been acknowledged by her as valid.

It was not until November 1928 that Fletcher brought forth the first word of Houdini's own message. Why this should have taken so long is not known. The spelling-out of the entire message took eight sittings, which stretched over a period of two and a half months.

At the final sitting, Fletcher asked to dictate the exact message. The message was, "Rosabelle . . . Answer . . . Tell . . . Pray . . .

Answer . . . Look . . . Tell . . . Answer . . . Answer . . . Tell.''

Fletcher then went on to say that the message must be signed by those present and then be delivered to Mrs. Houdini, who must make it public; that she would be accused of complicity; and that Harry Houdini was there (in spirit) and had brought this message to her. He then asked that upon receipt of this message she be brought for a sitting of her own, at which time, she would return to her husband a code that would be understood only by the two of them. The two together would spell a word that would be the message he wished to convey to her.

The next day, Fast and John W. Stafford, associate editor of *Scientific American*, delivered the message to Mrs. Houdini, who agreed to let Ford, three members of his group, and a member of the press come to her house.

Upon arriving, Ford went into trance and through Fletcher continued to explain the code that eventually yielded the final word, ''Believe.'' The exact code was that used by the couple in a mind-reading act at the start of his career. Mrs. Houdini commented that the code was such a secret that ''even though the stage hands knew the words, no one except Houdini and myself knew the cipher, or the key, and its application.''

Despite charges of fraud, Mrs. Houdini stood her ground as the national press declared that the legendary Houdini code had been broken.

While it may be argued that since Mrs. Houdini did herself know the code, it is certainly possible that Ford with Fletcher's help may simply have telepathically extracted the message. However, since Mrs. Houdini was not present at any of the sittings during which, word by word, the message came out, even if this was an example of telepathy, it was certainly one of no ordinary dimensions. If the telepathy explanation is accepted, it would not serve to prove Houdini's continued existence in spirit, but it would not disprove Ford's or Fletcher's extraordinary abilities.

From Beatrice's statement, which was signed and witnessed by H. R. Zander of the United Press, Mrs. Minnie Chester, who was a lifelong friend of Mrs. Houdini, and John W. Stafford, one must conclude that there was no doubt in her mind that she had received a message from her late husband that proved his continued existence. And isn't this what spiritualism is all about?

Besides the Houdini code breaking, Ford is best known for the Bishop Pike seance that was to cast such doubt on his ability after his death. The seance made history by being televised. During the seance, televised in September 1967, Ford made contact with the son of Bishop James Pike, also known as James.

Allen Spraggett arranged the event. He apparently contacted Ford well in advance, using Bishop Pike as bait to attract Ford, who was then seventy-one years of age. The seance proved as controversial as the earlier Houdini affair.

The suicide of James Pike at age twenty in February 1966 was followed by a rash of unexplainable phenomena. In Cambridge, in the apartment the father had shared with his son, clocks had stopped at exactly 8:19, the alleged time of his death. Postcards with James' handwriting mysteriously appeared in unusual places, a shaving mirror once belonging to the youth supposedly moved under its own power, and milk placed in the refrigerator soured immediately.

While the Bishop had originally thought that his grief was the cause of these phenomena, he had sought the advice of his English friend, Rev. Canon John Pearce-Higgins, a leader in the Churches Fellowship for Psychical and Spiritual Studies. Pearce-Higgins had sent Pike to Enna Twigg, the famous British medium, who had brought him some evidential messages that he thought came from his late son.

Because of what had already transpired, and no doubt due to Ford's reputation, Pike was quick to assent to Spraggett's idea for the seance. During the actual seance, Ford showed all indications of having gone into trance during which time he presented material alleged to come from Pike's deceased son.

After the seance took place, the prestigious *New York Times* carried a page-one story with the headline "Pike Asserts He Got Messages From Dead Son at TV Seance." In the article Ford was identified as "the prominent American medium whose powers have been pronounced authentic by several American psychiatrists."

Once again, newspapers around the world made page-one news of a seance held by the same medium who had made headlines during the Houdini affair.

Did Arthur Ford fake the Pike seance? One will never know.

It is interesting to recall that in Spraggett and Rauscher's book itself, mention is made in an early chapter of the youthful Ford's propensity to read everything he could lay his hands on and to regularly *clip and save articles of interest*, a habit once endorsed by Will Durant.

This being the case, why was it that Spraggett and Rauscher were shocked to find clippings, notes, and obituaries in Arthur's apartment? Hadn't they already known about this particular habit?

Then there is the reference by the former secretary to what Ford called his "poems." Again, earlier in the biography, Spraggett writes, "In his spare time, America's most famous medium wrote song lyrics. They were mostly romantic ballads and were mawkishly sentimental, judging by an example that has survived entitled 'Henrietta.' " Could these not be the poems to which Ford made reference?

It would seem that the evidence pointing to Ford's faking his seances is by Spraggett's own admission, scanty and circumstantial. The question remains, then, as to why Spraggett and Rauscher would seek to discredit their friend, who was no longer present on the earth plane to defend himself. Had a rift occurred between Ford and his biographers, perhaps over the alcoholism that had plagued him in his early days? We will never know the answer to these questions.

Like other lights along the spiritualist path, it is impossible to assess Ford's influence. Certainly, the cofounding of the Spiritual Frontiers Fellowship (S.F.F.) has done much to place the realm of spirit back in the mainstream churches, where it first originated. Who can say how many persons first learned of spiritual gifts because of S.F.F.? Later on in this work mention will be made by a number of mediums of this very question.

Speaking of his work with various churches, Ford wrote near the end of his biography:

I wonder if the interest of these new-old frontiers may not bring back into the churches some of the thousands of members who have been lost to the cults and esoteric movements which for the past half century have taken over the psychic aspects of religion. . . . Survival is not the only tenet of the gospel but it is the one without which the others lose much of their significance. One has only to see the transformation in the lives of some who suddenly realize that personality is not lost in death to know how basic this assurance is. Likewise one has only to experience the cooperation of unseen presences still animated by love and dedicated to service to know that the company of the righteous is invincible.

One thing that can be said of Arthur Ford is that, throughout his life, he remained independent and unaffected by what others might want him to think. For example, although he had served as the president of the National Association of Spiritualists (founded in 1899), one of the largest spiritualist bodies in the United States, he had his own belief in reincarnation:

Reincarnation alone makes God's justice comprehensible. It is the dominant idea in the lives of two-thirds of the world's population. It was clearly taught by the early church. It is true to nature since modern science has proven that everything is constantly passing from one form of existence to another.

Reincarnation is not a law, it is a method. Karma is the law, the law of compensation. It is the law of cause and effect applied to the personality. Reincarnation utilizes physical birth so that a spirit, an ego, may solve a karmic problem, that is, one deriving from wrong thoughts or deeds in a previous earthly lifetime.

Arthur Ford died as he had lived. He was a man of extraordinary power who before transition had taken two hundred shots with a defibrillator in an attempt to normalize his heartbeat. He wanted to pass on to the world he alone knew so well, yet modern medical science bade him to tarry a little. In the end, Ford, not medical science, won out. According to Patricia Hayes, his personal secretary at the time of his death, ''he left behind few material possessions except a large trunk filled with letters from over the years, from loyal and dedicated people who had written him about their inner feelings of the spirit.''

Ford was spiritualism's Caesar, venerated and then probably betrayed by his associates. We will never really know him, and perhaps the most that can be said are the words of another Caesar: *"Veni. Vidi. Vici."*

8

Lily Dale:
The Town Free Spirits Built

*Probably the best-known camp [for spiritualists] is Lily
Dale, situated on an island in Lake Cassadaga, Chautauqua County, New York. Like some of the others it has
hotels, motels, and cottages for the accommodation of
visitors. At Lily Dale some two hundred members own
their own homes, and families have come for four or five
generations. There is an auditorium which seats twenty-
five-hundred people and has a splendid pipe organ. Skidmore Memorial Library is housed in a handsome brick
building and has thousands of volumes which any psychic investigator is free to use—almost everything in
print or out. Recently a healing temple has been built on
the grounds and I watched some remarkable work in
spiritual healing. Interests are many-sided at Lily Dale,
even including sports.*

—Arthur Ford,
NOTHING SO STRANGE

Today, where can you get a room in a quaint nineteenth-century
hotel for less than twenty dollars a night? Answer: Lily Dale.

Where can you find gathered together under one magnificent sky,
and surrounded by tall, imposing trees, some of the best mediums in
the United States and Canada? Answer: Lily Dale.

Where can you find every summer, from the end of June through

the end of August, a host of affordable courses in such areas as psychic development, spirit healing, spiritualist home circle, and color and healing, along with aura and dream workshops? Answer: Lily Dale.

Where can you find a beautiful beach, a picnic pavilion, fishing, boating, and two prize swans named Lily and Dale, for a grounds fee of less than five dollars a day? Answer: Lily Dale.

Where can you find a research library containing one of the finest and most complete collections of rare spiritualist and metaphysical books? Answer: Lily Dale.

Where can you find a museum containing genuine artifacts illustrating the history of American spiritualism, including the famed peddler's trunk from the Fox family cottage? Answer: Lily Dale.

Where can you find a memorial to the Fox family cottage at the site where the actual cottage existed until it was destroyed by fire? Answer: Lily Dale.

Where can you find hanging some of the finest examples of spiritualist painting by the Campbell brothers? Answer: Lily Dale.

Where can you walk around, meditate, or just hang out with persons of like mind who have been exploring spiritualism and its allied phenomena for many years? Answer: Lily Dale.

Truly, there is no way to describe a visit to Lily Dale, except to say that it's unlike any other place I've ever visited. Perhaps it's the stillness and quiet. Perhaps it's the departed spirits of the Indians who named Cassadaga Lake. Or possibly it's that this particular Garden of Eden has always been a place in which the shackles and bondage of rational thinking have been broken by those who dared dream dreams and think thoughts that are considered unique and liberal, and who definitely march to the beat of a different drummer.

While Lily Dale has been synonymous with spiritualism since 1879, its beginnings lie in what has been called simply the Free Thinker Movement.

As early as 1855, the Religious Society of Free Thinkers was meeting in nearby Laona, New York. During the winter of 1846–47, a Dr. Moran from Vermont had come to the area and presented a course of lectures on animal magnetism and mesmerism, practices that were all the rage and were sweeping across the nation. Jeremiah F. Carter of Laona, having attended Dr. Moran's lecture, had called on the latter with the hope that magnetic treatment might benefit his own feeble health. Unfortunately, before an appointment could be arranged, the doctor was called away.

A friend, William Johnson of Laona, who had also attended Dr. Moran's lectures, suggested to Carter that he might be able to induce the same kind of trance, if Carter was willing to experiment. The experiment was a complete success, and Carter found himself the possessor of parasentient abilities. His health began to improve rapidly as a result of the control of a spirit who gave his name as Dr. Hedges, a physician who had formerly lived in Chautauqua County. In time, Carter found he could induce the trance state without Johnson's assistance. And so it was that, because of Jeremiah F. Carter, spiritualism eventually came to Lily Dale.

In 1873 spiritualists began holding picnics in a grove on the farm of Willard Alden. Alden had set aside Sunday, June 15, with the purpose of dedicating the grove for the use of spiritualism. This one-day meeting was called the June Picnic and Sunday Assembly, and was continued until 1877, after which time it was changed to a three-day meeting.

How these meetings actually came about is another story. Carter was reading a newspaper one day in the summer of 1877 when he heard a voice telling him over and over again to "Go to Alden's and arrange for a camp meeting." The next morning he walked six miles to the Alden farm and suggested to Willard that a spiritualist camp meeting be held in his grove. Alden agreed to the proposal, with the provision that all expenses for the lecture be met by the spiritualists.

So it was that the first camp meeting actually took place in Willow Lake Hall, Alden's Grove, from September 11 to 16, 1877. The average attendance was one hundred persons daily and four hundred on Sunday. Carter collected a fee of ten cents from each visitor. So successful was this humble beginning that a ten-day meeting for the following year was planned. The next year, 1878, again saw good attendance. As a result a few cottages were built in the grove.

After Alden passed on (February 25, 1878), arrangements were made with his heirs to continue the use of the grove. However, as a result of continuing disputes over the management of the gate receipts, it was decided that a different location should be found for a more permanent camp.

On August 23, 1879, a society was organized under the laws of the state of New York and named the Cassadaga Lake Free Association. After a survey of various locations, the newly organized Board of Trustees purchased lands along the east side of the upper lake that were named the Cassadaga Lake Camp Meeting Grounds. Approximately 20⅝ acres were purchased from two brothers, John and Marion Fisher, for the large sum of $1,845.12.

In December 1879, the Association decided to rent cottage lots for the annual sum of three dollars per lot. No lots were to be sold outright. Progress was also reported in the surveying of the grounds and the construction of various buildings for the Association as well as a hotel for visitors.

On Tuesday, June 15, 1880, the new campgrounds were dedicated. It was decided that the annual season would be between July 31 and August 22. It was during this first season that the first cottage was built on the grounds. By 1893 there were 215 cottages, and about forty families lived on the grounds year-round.

By 1900 a hotel, an auditorium, and an assembly hall, which housed the library founded by Marion H. Skidmore that had formerly been operated out of a tent, were functioning to capacity.

On June 27, 1888, the Post Office was opened. However, the name was erroneously spelled Lilly Dale, rather than Lily Dale, which was the name given to this tract of land by the Aldens. As is often the case with government bureaucracy, this error was not corrected until 1927.

On December 28, 1900, a fire caused the loss of five cottages in less than two hours. On February 1, 1901, a fire department was organized to prevent such occurrences in the future.

In 1903 the name was again changed from the Cassadaga Lake

Free Association to the City of Light Assembly. In this same year the name of the hotel was changed from the Grand Hotel to the Maplewood Hotel. Finally, on December 1, 1906, the name was again changed to the Lily Dale Assembly, the current appellation.

According to Lily Dale historian Joyce LaJudice, who together with Paula M. Vogt authored a pamphlet entitled *Lily Dale: Proud Beginnings*, the Dale, as it is affectionately called by many who live there, has always been a haven for free thoughts and free thinkers.

It is no wonder that in 1891, Susan B. Anthony and Elizabeth Cady Stanton came and spoke at Lily Dale. Recalling this first, Anthony wrote:

> People came from far and near. Finally three thousand were assembled in that beautiful amphitheater, decorated with yellow, the suffrage color, and the red, white and blue. There hanging by itself was our national flag ten by fourteen feet, with its red and white stripes, and in the center of the blue corner just one golden star, Wyoming, blazing out alone. [Wyoming was the first state to recognize woman's suffrage.] Every cottage in the camp was festooned with yellow, and when at night the Chinese lanterns were lighted on the plazas, it was as gorgeous as any Fourth of July celebration, and all in honor of Woman's Day and her coming freedom.

While the Lily Dale of the past welcomed speakers of note and controversy, it mainly provided a platform for spiritualists of world renown, such as Arthur Ford.

Although it may be said that the Lily Dale of the past was but a grand experiment in free thinking, the Lily Dale of today is well established. Each summer brings about twenty thousand persons along the same roads and through the same gates that not too long ago cost but ten cents to enter.

Many of the programs conducted each day at varying times, artfully announced by the sounding of a bell, are the very same ones, in the very same places, that were held more than one hundred years ago.

For instance, each day from 1:00 to 2:00 P.M. and from 6:30 to 7:30 P.M. visitors to the Dale walk through the Leolyn Woods to a place called Inspiration Stump. Here they sit in quiet meditation or hear inspirational words from the speaker in attendance.

From noon to 1:00 P.M. each day, visitors may visit the Healing Temple, where as many as five healers are in attendance. Before serving in the Temple, each healer must present his or her ministerial credentials to the Assembly. During winter months, when the Dale is closed, the Healing Temple serves as meeting place for the Lily Dale Spiritualist Church, which holds Sunday services for healing at 10:30 A.M. and for worship at 11:00 A.M.

At 2:30 each afternoon, the bells are rung, and those on the grounds scurry to the auditorium. Here an inspiring address is presented by a guest speaker or teacher, and a message service is given by one of the many mediums in residence.

At 4:30 P.M. daily, following the auditorium service, a number of residents make their way through woodland paths to the Forest Temple. Here message services are presented by seasoned mediums and others who may be developing their newly found gifts.

At 6:30 P.M., a service at Inspiration Stump is held again, and at 8:00 P.M., the bells are sounded for a general assembly in the auditorium. Message services are again presented by various mediums, or other activities of general interest are held. These can include mixers, discussion groups, presentations of films, such as Noel Coward's *Blythe Spirit* (what else would you expect at Lily Dale?), games nights, and occasional dinners and dances.

For the most part, the various daily activities are offered without charge. Those that do require donations are generally priced at only a few dollars, much less than the cost of a movie theater ticket.

Lily Dale is very particular about its demonstration of the gifts of spirit. Next to the auditorium is found a large bulletin board on which are placed the names of those mediums who have been registered by the Assembly. These persons have presented their credentials to the Assembly office and have obtained permission to do professional work on the grounds.

In many cases, these mediums have also been certified by various spiritualist organizations as well, such as the National Association of Spiritualist Churches. Fees charged by these mediums range from as low as twenty dollars for a half hour to more than one hundred dollars. These fees are not established by the Assembly but are set by the individual mediums.

To schedule a sitting with a medium one can either telephone the number shown on the bulletin board or in some instances go directly to the medium's home. It is fun to walk around the Dale and see signs on the front porch of various cottages that say, "Medium in Residence" or "Closed. No Readings Today!".

Besides the various daily activities that have been a tradition at the Dale since its earliest days, speakers of renown offer five-day, two-day, and mini workshops, and Saturday intensives in almost every area of spiritualism and psychic development. Hypnosis, dreams, auras, meditation, psychic art, holistic healing, stress management, ancient earth energies, visualization, color healing, and crystals were just some of the courses offered in the 1986 season.

Once again—and this is why Lily Dale is definitely a "Spiritualist Best Buy"—tuition costs for various workshops are unusually fair. For instance, a five-day workshop in 1986 was under one hundred dollars, which is virtually unheard-of in today's educational marketplace.

Lily Dale is the summer home of the famous Morris Pratt Institute of Milwaukee, Wisconsin (from which one can obtain correspondence studies in the spiritualism). The Institute offers special summer courses in various aspects of modern spiritualism, under the able directorship of Rev. Joseph Sax. It is here that one can capture the essence and philosophy of pure, traditional spiritualism. A copy of the Institute's program may be obtained by writing the Assembly.

If by now you are thinking that Zolar is definitely recommmending Lily Dale, you are more than right. But you must do one thing, and that's to plan well in advance.

Programs for each season can be obtained in May of each year by sending $2.00 to cover postage and requesting same from the Lily Dale Assembly, 5 Melrose Park, Lily Dale, NY 14752. (You might want to mention that Zolar recommended you.) As housing at the Maplewood Hotel and the various rooming houses on the grounds is limited, early registrations must be made and deposits sent.

———— O ————

Before closing this chapter on the Town Free Spirits Built, I must utter a warning to those who decide to visit the Dale. In Florida there is a saying that once you get the Florida sand in your shoes, you will always return. The same thing is true for Lily Dale! There is a rare quality about the place that comes from the special combination of natural beauty and unseen energy that can only be expressed by the words of Matthew 18:20, "For where two or three are gathered together in my name, there am I in the midst of them."

ON MEDIUMS

Keep your will about you
    for what psychic readers say
        need not be.
For what the psychic says
    can enslave your will
        and your will
           is meant to be free.

It is with that will
    that you choose your destiny
        whether the choice
           be right or wrong.
Your will is not a puppet
    that must dance
        to another's song.

This does not mean
    that you should not search
        in a spiritual way.
It is good
    to seek out prophets
        and listen
           to what they have to say.

Then meditate
    upon what is said
        in your inner room.

Separate what is positive
   from that which is negative
      and speaks of doom.

Cast out that which speaks
   of doom and darkness
      for that is what causes
         emotional
            and physical ill.
This message is meant
   to guide you
      we pray that you use
         your own will.

—Robert W. Johnson,
MYSTICAL THOUGHTS FOR MEDITATION:
HE SENDS YOU KNOWLEDGE

9

Mother Macauley

Margaret Macauley makes her home in upstate New York but often comes to New York City to visit her close friend Janet Kasper, who directs the New York Chapter of Spiritual Frontiers Fellowship, and it was at her home that I talked with Margaret.

Upon first meeting Margaret, I was reminded of my own grandmother, Laura Johnston, who was surely the unofficial spiritual head of my family and who was herself psychic. Margaret could be anyone's grandmother, at home serving tea or making a cherry pie, the kinds of thing for which grandmothers all over the world are best known.

Yet Margaret is different. For the past three years, under the able encouragement of Janet Kasper, she has worked as a trance medium whose spirit guide is Tote, or Toth.

Margaret was born an only child in Hartford, Connecticut, on August 31, 1917. Her mother, born in 1900, was herself psychic, though she never used the word. Margaret's mother's parents had died within three months of each other when she was but a year old. Although both parents had come from Ireland, she had a clear memory of having lived on a plantation in the American South and described a black slave who had cared for her. At the age of forty-five, Margaret's mother passed into spirit.

Margaret was born into the Roman Catholic faith, and was married and raised her sons in the same faith.

Of her first psychic experience, she remembers little. "It has always been there," she told me. "I believe we are all born with this ability. Many things we can do we are conditioned to believe we can't do. We are conditioned to believe that there is nothing

between us but air, but we know that there is much more between us than just air. We are also conditioned that we can only see certain things.''

Upon reflection, Margaret believes she was about three years old when she had her first experience, which consisted of a feeling that someone was in the room with her. She was terrified and began crying until an adult came into her room and picked her up.

Not unusual, though, is the fact that many of Margaret's early experiences occurred around times of illness—her own or that of someone close to her. Many psychic investigators, such as Hereward Carrington, suggest that, in these moments of great physical stress, the astral or psychic self finds itself loosened or projected out beyond the physical in order to make spirit contact.

At the age of forty, Margaret suffered the first of many heart attacks. It greatly frightened her: What might become of her family if something were to happen to her? Although she eventually recovered, she had a premonition that things would not be the same after this illness for her and her husband. About a year later, he took ill and was taken to the same hospital and the same ward, at which time he passed into spirit.

During moments of her critical illnesses, Margaret realized that she was not in her physical body but rather in the astral form, able to perceive and ''seemingly look through'' the bodies of her nurses and attendants. In her own words, ''All walls were down. There was no separation.''

After the death of her husband, Margaret found herself without any insurance and greatly worried about her children. Upon perusing a local newspaper, she discovered that a local church would be holding a healing service under the auspices of the Spiritual Frontiers Fellowship. Although she had worked as a nurse, she had never attended such a healing service.

After attending a service in which she felt herself being healed, she described at great length to her mother-in-law and the minister in attendance the beautiful dark-haired woman who had assisted in the service. To her amazement, she was told that there ''had been no such woman there'' and that the person that both she and her son Kenny saw and described must have been ''in spirit.''

Rev. Joseph Sefl, who had conducted the healing service, invited Margaret to become part of his meditation group, which met weekly to read scriptures, meditate, and share with other members of the group. It was here that Margaret first became aware of her gifts.

This was the extent of Margaret's formal training in psychic matters. Like many others before her, her gift came from spirit, and it is spirit that has taught her all that she knows. Of these things she says, "It was there before. It was like coming home."

Throughout her life, Margaret has tried to reconcile her ability to see spirit with the reality perceived by others. On one occasion, she asked a nun if she believed in ghosts. The nun replied by repeating the response of *her* teacher when she had asked the same question: "There are no such things as ghosts. But if you see one, say, 'Depart in the name of God the Father, the Son, and the Holy Ghost!' "

Although Margaret may be said to have spiritual beliefs, she is not religious. She does not go to mass on a daily basis, nor does she pray daily. "For a time years back, I used to meditate daily," she said, "because I knew it would have a calming effect on my heart. It is not that I didn't want to meditate; it is simply that I have a very active homelife with my son, my grandson, cats, and dogs. It is very active and happy."

During my interview with Margaret, she began to feel the presence of Toth, her spirit guide, and suggested that he might best answer my questions. Before contacting him, however, Margaret repeated the following prayer, which she has used for many years, in preparation for the appearance of Toth, who speaks through her.

We are here in the name of our father, Jehovah; in the name of his divine and beloved son, Jesus; and in the name of the most holy Spirit that manifests itself to us at this time, we pray. We pray for the grace necessary to do thy most holy work according to thy most definite will and we offer. We offer our hands, our beings into yours, now Almighty God, for consecration. And we ask, dear Father in Heaven, we ask if there are any messages or guidance to come through thy angelic realm, thy saints, thy guides, the faithful spirits; and also the physical realm of earth, the Wisdom advisers, the Master teachers, the Master healers, and deep within the essence, the consciousness and the name and the person that is here; and ask that this may be given at this hour or in the many hours to be, again according to thy Will. And we give thanks and we give praise and we give thanks to the Almighty ever-living God who always was and always will be, world without end, Amen.

After her prayer of invocation was completed, Margaret began to channel Toth, who brought me the following message:

Greetings, my son. I am Toth that speaketh unto thee. I am Toth. We do welcome you, dear son, and we do welcome our good and beloved friend. We do say it is a nice time to be with you in these few moments in perfect communion together. You see, dear son, you have asked many questions. Many questions we would answer thee, but let us tell you, we have known thee from before. Many, many times we have walked by your side as we are now talking to thee. And know you ascend to our plane and rise up to our consciousness, as we come down to be with you.

You have asked questions about the training and where it comes from. It comes from us. For there are those on earth that have a mission and have undertaken this mission before they have come into the flesh. In this case, this was the mission of the channel you are using. However, this mission was to begin when she was not yet out of her teens. But she did ask permission to have a life of her own and then she stated she would give the rest of her time in service of God, which she is doing. The training has come from us, yes, it has come gradually as a refresher course to bring back knowledge that was gained many times before. Not as you return or the label you would give to what your channel is doing, but in another time in the ancient land of Egypt. And, of course, as an American Indian. Yes, many, many incarnations.

So you see, drawing on all that from spirit, and with us working in spirit, that is how the readings have come to be.

We do say to you that we are pleased with the work that you are doing. Much more is coming into your consciousness and much good in the following months. We will not tell you that all is going to be made easy, but it will bare much fruit and it is a work that will be well done!

Many are gathering around you in spirit, as you know, and waiting on the earth plane as well, for those in the flesh are spirits also. That is why many of us work because they *are* in the flesh.

My dear son, how training takes place is when the time is right to take a spirit aside, take them into the halls of learning, teaching; into the halls of healing to show them all planes. Yes, and then to let them pass back through the center of the diamond, which you visualize into their own consciousness.

Your channel now has stepped aside and is in a place where there is rest and no pain. So lived in this way, the work can continue.

Now, dear son, in the future any questions you ask, we would only be too happy to explain to you. For there is not any, when writing your books, you cannot reach on all planes or on the earth plane by meditation through which the answers will be given. And now may we bless you in our blessing which is the first language of the ancients.

At this point in our interview, Toth, through Margaret, his channel, gave me a special blessing, which I cannot unfortunately share with my readers.

After the blessing was completed, Margaret began to come out of trance and was noticeably disoriented. I later asked her about this and was told that always, for a few minutes afterward, she finds it difficult to get her bearings. This would seem to make a great deal of sense since unlike some mediums, Margaret has absolutely no conscious memory of what she has said once Toth takes over. Should she later hear the tapes played back, her listening is always accompanied by "a feeling of detachment."

I asked her whether she actually stepped aside so that Toth could take over. She said she would like to think that she "steps aside to a place of perfect peace."

Margaret, like many other mediums, eats little red meat. This is, by her own admission, because her body does not tolerate it, rather than for any particular spiritual reasons. In fact, "I eat very little food at all," she told me.

When I commented once again on what she told her own students when they asked for a specific method to make spirit contact, she repeated that in the end it is spirit and Toth that do the teaching. "I share with them honestly as I can. I am not really a teacher."

Margaret has over the years seen various physical phenomena occur around her on many different occasions. This has not happened because of her, but rather as the natural result of the working of spirit.

In one instance, spirit was directly responsible in obtaining a new home for her and her boys after her husband had passed through transition. On this particular occasion, her son had been playing with the Ouija Board when this message came through: "Say happy mother's day to your mother . . . even though she hasn't remembered me."

Much to Margaret's amazement, this message came from her own mother, who had passed away many years ago. The message was followed by instructions that Margaret should contact a certain real estate broker who would have a home for her, including exactly how and where this woman could be contacted, and that when she was shown the house, she should take it.

Much to Margaret's amazement, things happened exactly as her mother in spirit had told her. She was taken to a house that had been foreclosed. When she thought she would not get this house since she was not working at the time, it was suggested that her oldest son, Walter, could countersign for the house since he was employed. Although he was not yet twenty-one, it was agreed that she could rent the house for a few months until he turned twenty-one. Most amazing of all was the fact that the Federal Housing Administration made an error that, according to the brokers, they had never seen before. Somehow the customarily required down payment on all FHA homes had been disregarded and, despite efforts by the broker, was never required to close the deal. Certainly this story alone is enough to make one believe in the wisdom of spirit. It did so for Margaret!

After this, Margaret no longer could make contact with the spirit of her mother. She assumed that since she had gotten the house she was promised, the matter must have been closed, at least from spirit's viewpoint!

After living in her new house for about three years, Margaret was invited to the house of a friend, who requested that she bring along her Ouija Board. The friend was aware of how Margaret had obtained her home and wanted to see if she too could get some information.

When Margaret told her she would come to dinner but would not bring the board, the friend obtained one herself and surprised Margaret with it after dinner. Margaret demonstrated some surprising scruples at this point.

"I told you not to. I didn't know years ago that everything would turn out all right, but, here, now that the children are grown, I read some place that children shouldn't be involved in that," Margaret said.

"Oh, don't be like that. Sit down, and try this, for God's sake," the neighbor said.

Margaret, Kenny (her youngest son), and the neighbor put their hands on the planchette, which refused to budge. Finally the neighbor spoke up, "See, I told you, damn it. No one loves me here and no one loves me there either. Try it again."

Finally the planchette began to move and spelled out the following message, "Mom, go home right now. Take Kenny home. I come to protect. I am Eddy. Go home. I come to protect. I come to protect. Go home right now."

"That's it," Margaret said.

"Who is that?" the neighbor asked.

"That's my brother-in-law's spirit," Margaret said, knowing that her husband had lost his brother named Eddy when he was eighteen.

"You see," said the neighbor. "Somebody came through for you."

When Kenny went outside to wait for his mother, Margaret asked the neighbor what question she had asked the board. The neighbor confessed that she and her husband had been having marital problems and that he had placed some of their money in a separate account in his own name. She wanted to find out what to do about this. For some reason, the answer to her question would have been harmful to Kenny, so spirit intervened to keep him from harm.

People come to Mother Macauley from all walks of life, from all religious dispositions. She is indeed a very special kind of grandmother who finds a very special kind of grandchildren wherever she and Toth share their light. She says to those who come to her, "Ask anything. I think we should always feel free to ask. Whether or not we always get the answers we want, we should always ask."

Up to now, Mother Macauley has limited her readings to only a few each day. She has not written down any of Toth's teaching, as the late Jane Roberts did, but she may begin teaching at some point in the future. That is, if this is Toth's and spirit's wish.

When I inquired as to her belief in reincarnation, I was told that she felt she did not have all the answers, especially about how it was possible to make spirit contact if the particular entity had already been reborn. Her reply was both humble and profound.

"I don't believe that souls have to reincarnate. I believe the choice is theirs. It is much more involved than what we know. Also, sometimes you can tune into a person who has come back in again, who is living now, and also at the same time who they were before in a previous life. There are many, many things I don't understand. It's much more complex than we realize. There are many aspects to it. There is much that we don't know. But now I believe that we don't *have to know*. It's all right. It's all right!

"One of the things I don't understand which Toth has told people is that 'time is all one.' "

While Mother Macauley may be the able spokeswoman for Toth, in the conscious state she maintains a totally independent existence. About this she said, "One woman said to me, 'What do you think about this . . .?' I told her my advice! 'Oh,' she said, 'I asked your guide and he told me something different!' I said, 'Well, this is *my* opinion!' 'But,' she said, 'I always thought you would give the same opinion; you said something completely opposite!' 'It should be that way,' I said, 'I'm the channel and not the guide.' "

When I asked Margaret whether she could obtain readings for herself by using a friend to ask the questions while she was in trance, she answered, "Yes, but I don't always listen. Spirit always kept saying you have to go away, it's beneficial. But I just couldn't make it. So they said afterward, if you don't listen to spirit you will end up in the hospital! But I tried to work things out *my* way. I *knew* spirit was right. So, I did, I ended up in the hospital! I tried to do it my way.''

My time with Mother Macauley had now come to an end. Her grandson, Eddy, came into the room to announce that his father was downstairs in the car, waiting to drive her back upstate to her home.

Before leaving Janet Kasper's apartment, I presented Margaret with a copy of my book, *Zolar's Encyclopedia of Ancient and Forbidden Knowledge*. After looking at the cover (which had won a design award) for a short while, she looked up at me. Instantly, I knew what she was going to say.

"Could you . . . could you autograph it for me?" she asked.

"Of course," I said. "I knew you were thinking that!"

10

———o———

Pamela White and Cheryl Williams: The Return of the Fox Sisters

Truth is very simple. We think a lot of damage is done to growing people when simple truth is complicated by a lot of verbiage, metaphysical jargon, and hocus pocus by people who feel there is an easy buck to be made.

—Pamela and Cheryl

Throughout the history of spiritualism there have been a number of brothers and sisters, or people with close, siblinglike relationships, who have teamed up to produce unusual phenomena. As has already been discussed, spiritualism began with the Fox sisters. Following in their footsteps were the Davenport brothers, who were world-renowned for their physical mediumship, and the Campbell brothers (not really brothers), who succeeded in producing the most extraordinary spirit art ever manifested. One can examine the works of the latter in the lobby of the Maplewood Hotel in Lily Dale, New York.

While visiting Lily Dale, I had the pleasure of meeting and talking briefly with two other "sisters" whose abilities when working together are extraordinary by any measure and who prefer to bill themselves simply as "psychic consultants" so as not to scare away those who think spirits appear only on the dark side of the moon.

Although some critics of spiritualism like to think of mediums as

Roy Newman

little old ladies often found sipping tea, Pamela and Cheryl quickly explode this myth.

Pamela White was for many years a New York fashion model before she began a collaboration with a renowned medium, the late Dr. Pierrette S. Austin.

Contrast this with Cheryl Williams, a former professional swimmer and the first woman chosen to coach an Olympic swim team. She holds a master's degree in archaeology from David Ben Gurion University and bachelor's degrees in philosophy and physical education from Concordia College. Clearly these two women are not "typical" mediums by the world's standards.

According to Pamela, she and Cheryl connected by accident, simply as two people having a number of interests in common, especially travel and counseling.

Cheryl originally set out to become a public school teacher until she realized, as many do, that "these kids don't want to be here." So she investigated other opportunities and was offered the opportunity to go to graduate school in Israel. There she completed a degree in Middle Eastern archaeology, which she describes as "a very interesting profession but not lucrative."

Since there was a great deal of artillery fire in Israel in 1974, she planned to return to the United States. Not wishing to return to the cold weather and snow of northern Minnesota, she took out a map and let her finger do the walking. It landed on Phoenix, Arizona, and it was there that she and Pamela met for the first time.

Cheryl arrived in Phoenix about a year ahead of Pamela, during which time she tried, once more, to find a career and entered nursing school. When, once again, she realized that nurses were both underpaid and also had to work all hours of the day and night in order to advance, she took a job with the marketing company for which Pamela was working.

Pamela says that when you are called "to this work everything you have done in your life previously comes to be a part of your education." So it was that she and Cheryl each brought to their mediumship gifts of spirit that in combination have produced what has been called "the dynamic duo."

While Cheryl's background was all scientific and technical Pamela's background was more artistic and communicative, and included singing, modeling, and marketing. Together they formed a perfect partnership.

Cheryl has been a "natural psychic" all her life, while Pamela describes herself as, until the age of twenty, a "ghastly skeptic." It was at this time that Pamela met Dr. Pierrette S. Austin at the suggestion of her uncle and aunt, Rabbi and Mrs. Nathan Pearlman. She had gone to her aunt for advice after reading a book on Edgar Cayce. Especially adept in the ability to diagnose illness while in the trance state, this clairvoyant was popularly known as the Sleeping Prophet.

According to Pamela, she "had to train like a lunatic for eight years" before she was allowed to demonstrate her abilities; while for Cheryl her paranormal abilities were always "there."

In Cheryl's own words: "I thought that everybody used this. I thought they saw the same things I saw. I honestly did. And heard and felt the same things. I had no idea until later in life that people weren't plugged in. I thought everybody had it and did it."

Pamela has to raise her vibrations before she can "see and feel" psychically, while Cheryl is always "plugged in" and can "read" almost any time, all the time!

Cheryl's abilities were with her as long as she can remember and very possibly came from her father, who could dowse water, couldn't wear a wristwatch because of his own energy, and had an unusual green thumb. By trade, he was an engineer in the steel industry.

And so it was that the two met at a time when they were both seeking to do something with the somewhat unusual talents each had accumulated.

Pamela and Cheryl feel their mission is to travel around the country and stimulate people to reach their own spiritual sides. Of this Pamela says, "I don't believe that anybody ever really teaches. I think that people *instinctively* know what truth is. The best we can do is to stimulate people to stretch, to look further, and hopefully, become better, more understanding, and less judgmental."

This is a remarkable statement of purpose coming from "sisters" who were raised respectively in the Episcopalian and Russian Orthodox faiths. (Pamela's father had changed his name and disposition along the way.)

Like many others in the field, Pamela and Cheryl have struggled with the distinction that is made between the terms *spiritualist*, *psychic*, and *medium*. As neither is an ordained minister or member of any of the spiritualist organizations, they cannot rightly be called spiritualists, especially since they do not share the spiritualist belief that reincarnation has not been proven. Rather, it is their belief that each individual soul has the choice as to whether or not it will reincarnate.

According to Pamela, "Psychic is a word that really is a *descriptive* word as opposed to being a label, an adjective as opposed to being a noun. A psychic is one who receives from the dimension people call spirit. A medium is one who receives and *tells*."

To demonstrate the confusion in people's minds about the various terms, Cheryl relates the story of a woman who was walking by the cottage where she and Pamela live. The woman pointed to the sign "Pamela White, Medium" and said to Cheryl (not knowing who she was), "This woman over here. Well, I don't want to see anyone who's a medium. I just want to see a clairvoyant!"

To resolve this problem of nomenclature, Pamela and Cheryl have chosen to refer to themselves simply as *psychic consultants*. "While *psychic* is a word which is often misunderstood, the word *consultant* most people can understand," Pamela explains.

One of Pamela's and Cheryl's pet peeves is the way the media have chosen to depict the world of the psychic and paranormal as something "apart from life" and in extremely negative, frightening terms. Pamela and Cheryl have had to overcome this negative image of the occult and psychic world, despite the fact that almost everyone, at some time, has had some kind of psychic experience.

Certainly, people have always feared that which they do not understand. To the ancient Greeks a "barbarian" was simply anyone who did not speak Greek. People fear darkness only until the light is turned on. Once the world was known to be round, fear of falling off the earth ceased!

Of their many psychic experiences, perhaps none is more interesting than Cheryl's when she "died" for forty-five minutes on the operating table in April 1975. During a routine knee operation, for an unknown reason, her heart stopped. It was not due to the anesthesia used, and in retrospect, her attending physicians had no explanation as to what transpired.

Speaking of this unusual experience, Cheryl says, "I went into the tunnel; however, I never got past the tunnel. I saw this light, heard this music. I can't tell you I was hearing with these physical ears. It was like I was hearing with my whole body, like a dolphin. I heard this music. It wasn't singing, it wasn't an instrument. It is very difficult to describe. I was looking at this white, iridescent, vibrant light. It was my choice. I said, 'Should I go?' And someone said, 'It's up to you.' There were people standing in white robes with hoods, tied around their middle with white cords. I said, 'I don't think I want to make the rest of the journey. I'm real tired now.' I was actually able to see the physicians working on my body to resuscitate it. I hovered over my body and was able to recount for the physicians the instruments they dropped and all kinds of things."

In their lectures, demonstrations, and seminars, Pamela and Cheryl spend a great deal of time "helping people realize that what they are going through, such as people appearing to them and astral flight, is perfectly natural."

Not surprising is the fact that neither Pamela's nor Cheryl's family has really accepted their unusual occupations. "They are not very teachable. A prophet in his own country comes to mind," says Pamela, referring to the well-known axiom.

"They are not wearing garlic," Cheryl was quick to add, "but they are not real pleased!"

Of their general philosophy of life, Pamela says, "We don't really try to convert anybody. It's useless to try to convert. There are people who are interested, people who are ready to learn. If people are interested in these things, then hopefully we are there to spur them on."

Another point of view upon which Pamela and Cheryl agree is the need for each of their clients to develop self-reliance. Dependency upon a psychic or medium is, in their own words, "a terrible trap to fall into."

In answer to the question "How has psychic work changed your lives?" both Pamela and Cheryl are more than quick to reply.

"Our lives are constantly changing because every day new things are happening," says Pamela.

"It's exciting. I don't feel that I have any kind of magical or mystical power. For me there is no drudgery of going to work every day. I never know what it's going to be. Every day is different," Cheryl adds.

Do mediums such as Pamela and Cheryl ever consult other mediums? "If it's a real, real pressing concern we have . . . something we have been chomping at for a while, we may go to someone else," Cheryl is honest to admit.

How do you find another medium as talented as yourselves? "I think in time you watch somebody work. I can check another person's work to see if they are accurate. It's a gut reaction. I can check an audience to see if the medium is getting it," Pamela responded.

Can you read for each other? "Cheryl reads for me a lot. We can get impressions for each other, especially if we are relaxed." During public demonstrations (called "working the platform"), when only one is reading, the other will often sit in the audience and "tune in" to monitor the accuracy of the reading.

In retrospect, calling Pamela and Cheryl the Fox sisters is more than just an appellation. Just as the Fox sisters gave birth to spiritualism, so are Pamela and Cheryl attempting to give a new meaning to mediumship and the paranormal. Conducting workshops, seminars, and classes in such intriguing topics as the psychic anatomy, how to develop special psychic gifts, the power of color, life after life, and mental and spiritual laws, they bring to the unknown a quality of honesty and clarity that is far too often lacking among their peers.

Unlike many professional partnerships, there is absolutely no competition and definitely no attempts to upstage one another. Watching Pamela and Cheryl weave their psychic carpet is a truly extraordinary experience. Very often, one will start a sentence only

———————— ○ ————————

to have the other finish it with exactly the right words. In listening to them talk back and forth, one cannot but be reminded of Aristotle's definition of friendship as "one soul in two bodies."

To bring our meeting to a head, I asked Pamela and Cheryl to each describe herself in just a few words.

Cheryl answered first. "I would like to be referred to as thought-provoking and humble," was her reply.

Pamela's reply, though different, also made a lot of sense. "I suppose if I really had to stretch, which is hard for me, I would like to be thought of as a caring person and somewhat of a teacher. It's not important to *be* loved, by the way. I think *loving* is more important than being loved."

Pamela and Cheryl have been doing what comes naturally for only two years, which by any standard is but a drop of rain in the ocean. One thing is certain, however; we will be hearing of these "Fox sisters" for a great many years to come.

11

The Amazing Dr. D.

Either frags, spirits of the mind, or negative spirits which effect people's minds, cause people to be the "employees" of their thought instead of the "employer."

—Frances, Spirit Guide to Dr. D.

As we have already seen, mediumship takes many different shapes and sizes. Every once in a while a personality comes along whose entire life seems to march to the beat of a different drummer. Such a personality is the woman I have chosen to call the amazing Dr. D.

Dr. Estyne Del Rio, unlike many of the mediums I have interviewed and investigated, is highly educated (she holds a Ph.D. in psychology from Jackson State University) and is a spokeswoman for what might best be described as a brand-new breed of psychology that literally combines any elements that work in order to get a patient well.

Even Carl G. Jung resorted to the use of the horoscope in order to determine the psychodynamics of a patient he could not comprehend, but Dr. D.'s techniques have gone far beyond any that Jung himself might have imagined.

Estyne Del Rio was born on July 30 in Chicago, Illinois. Her father, who had been born in Cape Town, South Africa, had settled in Chicago. At the time of her birth, he operated a highly successful carpet and linoleum installation business. Estyne's father was,

according to what she had heard, originally from Spain, and her grandfather, a rabbi, was preoccupied with the material aspect of religion, acquiring real estate. Her mother was born in California.

Her father and his sister had been placed in an orphanage at the age of five by Estyne's grandfather, who had remarried and sought to start a new life without the burden of his children. Estyne's family name was Bernhardt. At the age of fifteen, her father ran away and joined the merchant marines and eventually returned to Chicago as an adult.

When asked whether her father was "psychic," Estyne said, "No, but my mother was!" According to Dr. D., her mother's favorite expression was, "I don't know why I am saying this . . .," after which she would present various words of wisdom for which she had no conscious source. Often she would predict something that would happen later.

At the age of seven, Estyne's parents were divorced, and she and her sister were sent off to the Leota School for Girls, a private boarding school in Evansville, Wisconsin. According to Dr. D., "Each girl had her own horse to curry and groom. They raised palominos there. I used to show ride. I love horses."

Her father remarried two weeks after the divorce, and her mother a month after the divorce. Although Estyne and her sister had tried to live with her father and their stepmother, interference from their real mother had caused her father to reach the decision that placed the two girls in the Leota School.

Estyne and her sister were at Leota from the time Estyne was seven until she was fifteen. Since Estyne's sister was younger than she, it was Estyne who always came to her sister's aid when she got into trouble.

Like many psychics, Dr. D. had her first psychic experience at a young age—when she was three. She describes it as follows: "I remember waking up in my bed in my room. I had my own room at the time, and was woken by a very lovely lady with black hair who was stroking my head. I had very curly locks. I remember looking up and saying, 'Who are you?' She said, 'I am your Guardian Angel.' I said, 'How nice!' She said, 'I have been watching you grow since you were born.' She was a very lovely lady, very pretty. I went and told my mother about the lady and the friends that she had brought with her. My mother came to the room a couple of times and said, 'Estyne, there is nobody here. There must be something wrong with your eyes.' So she started taking me to eye doctors, who put drops in my eyes that were very uncomfortable.''

Since her mother had not believed what Estyne had seen, she stopped telling her mother about her experiences with the ''lady,'' who gave her name as Frances, and the other spirit friends she talked and played with. It is Frances who guides Dr. D. today.

Once Estyne had been placed in the Leota School, she found that her spirit friends visited her less frequently, except when she was outside alone or riding her horse. Estyne was also introduced to another spirit guide, an Indian who would often ride alongside her.

She was told by these guides to tell no one else of their existence, since no one would believe her and since she alone had been given the privilege of communicating with them.

When I commented on the unusualness of Estyne's early psychic experiences, she said that even her name is unusual and that she had been told by passport office employees that no one to their knowledge had the name Estyne.

According to Dr. D., her mother had told her that ''she had had a dream in which a lady appeared to her who had long black hair and told her to call her daughter Estyne. When my mother said to the lady [who Estyne believes was Frances] that she had to name the child after someone, according to the Jewish tradition, Frances told her that my father's mother's name had been Esther, so she was naming me in the tradition but with a different name.''

After graduating from the Leota School as class valedictorian, Estyne decided to become a professional dancer. (She had started dancing as a child.) It was not until she was older that she decided that psychology would be her life's work. She completed her Ph.D. at Jackson State in Galleton, Tennessee, in 1974. (In the meantime she had married and divorced her husband, whose name, Del Rio, she has kept.)

She had met the daughter of an African minister of finance, who had advised her to complete her education at Jackson State and then to go to Ghana, where she could work and become the leading psychologist in the country.

After graduation, Estyne went to Ghana, where she worked for a year as principal psychologist, not realizing at the time she had been brought to Ghana because it was near Nigeria, the home of the Yoruba people, who practiced Santeria (the worship of saints or, more precisely, a combination of Catholic saints and native gods and goddesses).

Upon returning to the United States, Dr. D. "tried to get a job as a psychologist" without success. As a result of the frustration of unemployment, she had gained a considerable amount of weight and sought the services of a well-known holistic physician who specialized in nutrition and vitamin therapy.

After an initial interview, she was offered a job by this physician as his office manager, since he was anxious to have a Ph.D. on his staff. As a result of working both as office manager and behavior modification therapist in this office, Dr. D. eventually built up a following, which led to the beginning of her own private practice in New York City, where she now resides. She has been in private practice for twelve years.

According to Dr. D., "Frances told me when I was twenty-eight that my work was to be as a teacher, and that my work was service, but I was not accepting of it at that time. I was then thinking of business."

While Estyne went on to serve as president of a public company, to host a television show, and to do many other things, she did not receive "soul satisfaction" until she started working as a psychologist and parapsychologist.

Throughout her life, Estyne has extensively traveled and studied psychic things wherever and whenever she could. "The only continent I have not been to is Australia. I studied in Brazil at two Macumba centers and met the now-deceased healer Arigo."

In 1957 and 1958, while in Cuba, she was introduced to Santeria. Prior to this time, she had never "sat in a circle," as Frances, her guide, had told her she should not do this or she would lose her clarity. She had simply to listen to the words of Frances, which she could hear ''clairaudiently.''

Besides ''hearing'' the words of her spirit guide, Estyne can psychically read a person from their photograph, see auras, and discern various spirits.

According to Dr. D., when she asked Frances where her knowledge came from, she was told that she has been here (on earth) many times before. Frances hoped that she would learn what she had to learn this time, so that she would not have to come here again, thus suggesting a reincarnation aspect to at least this spirit guide.

In 1975, Estyne met a man who was both a spiritualist and a santero (male initiate of Santeria). It was he who introduced her to the need to perform ritual exorcisms to remove spirits that can cause numerous problems. To date, Estyne has performed more than 1,700 such exorcisms.

Initially, although Estyne had been familiar with the workings of Santeria, she had been advised by Frances not to ''make the saint,'' i.e., become initiated until she (Frances) advised.

Santeria itself began when African slaves who had been taken to Latin American countries were not permitted to worship their original African gods. To please their captives, they ''worshipped'' the Catholic saints in public but equated each with an old god whom they continued to worship in private. For instance, Saint Barbara, who is depicted with a gold cup in one hand, a sword in the other, a crown on her head, and a castle at her feet, was equated with the Yoruba god (called an orisha) Chango, the god of fire, thunder, and lightning. Hence, the tribal workings of Chango were placed under the statue of St. Barbara.

According to Dr. D., Santeria is very active, though underground, in many of the major cities of the United States. It has essentially been kept hidden due to the ritualistic sacrifice and use of animals for cleaning and feeding purposes; i.e., the santero believes that the saint must be fed by the use of offerings and that spirits may be driven out through the special use of various parts of animals.

Frances told Estyne that in order for spirit to work on the material plane, it must be energized, i.e., given a meal, since the material plane is lower than that of the spirits. Spirit takes this energy (nutrients) from the blood of animals used by humans for meat (no dogs or cats).

It must be pointed out that Santeria practices are not those commonly called voodoo, which represent the use of spiritual powers for evil or selfish ends.

Spirits and santos also eat fruit, from which they extract the essence when it is placed before them as directed by Santeria teachings. On one occasion, Estyne had bought some fruit, which she had divided up between the offering bowl for Frances and the refrigerator. Her mother, who was visiting at the time, inadvertently took a piece of fruit from Frances' bowl. After biting into it, she quickly spit it out, remarking how tasteless it was, like a raw potato.

Estyne, at once realizing what had happened, told her mother to take from the refrigerator an apple that had been bought at the same time. When her mother tasted that apple, she found that it was fine.

According to Estyne, Frances had already drawn the essence out of the fruit that had been offered to her.

When I inquired as to how long the fruit was left for the santos or Frances, I was told that it depended on the reason for the offering. Sometimes it was seven days; sometimes it was three days.

According to Dr. D., until she takes the time and writes her own book on the Santeria work, the best beginner's book on the subject is *The Santeria Experience*, by Migene Gonzalez-Wippler, an anthropologist.

The highest level in the practice of Santeria is what is called making santos, or making the saint. To do this, the candidate goes through a ritualistic initiation ceremony in which the head is shaved.

Dr. D. had followed Santeria teachings as what is considered a goddaughter for twenty-five years before she made santos. She had held off this initiation, first, because Frances had told her to do so, and second, because her spiritual practices had gone in other directions.

Describing herself, she says, "I primarily work spirit. I am a spiritual psychologist first and a santera second. In actuality, I am a behavioral psychologist 25 percent of the time, a spiritualist 25 percent of the time, and a santera 25 percent of the time. And then I ask for equal time to be a woman . . . to be Estyne, the woman.''

When I commented that most people would be unwilling to let their personal lives have only 25 percent, Dr. D. commented that she would like it otherwise too, but the demands of her practice and her dedication to serve had to be placed before her personal life, if she was to have one!

Very often, the santera's work requires various herbs for ritualistic bathing, some of which have to be flown in from as far away as Africa.

Some time in the future, Estyne the psychologist is planning to author a book on what she calls fragmentation, or multiple personalities. Using spirit, Santeria, and her gifts from God, she claims to have helped heal a great many clients who have had this problem.

Unlike most psychologists, Dr. D. seldom keeps her clients in therapy for long periods of time. She says that she is able to get them well quickly because she is told by spirit what their problems really are.

When I inquired as to how much antisocial behavior she would ascribe to the negative influence of spirit intervention, her answer was simply, "Most."

"There are a lot of earthbound spirits and they affect the mind. If you are clairaudient or have any form of mediumship, the doors are apt to swing both ways. If you have any weakness, a negative spirit will stand next to you in your energy field and put thoughts in your mind. And if you start feeling what you are thinking, you can become depressed in an instant."

Once Dr. D. performs an exorcism, she follows up for at least three months or more. According to Dr. D., "The results have been phenomenal. That's why I have more than five hundred people who have given me permission to use their case histories if I would do a book."

Certainly, the most extraordinary aspect of Dr. D.'s work is that she wears many hats, continually using whatever is needed to restore a client to complete mental health.

"If I am required to be a psychologist, I end up speaking to people about their frags or other personalities [a person creates a "frag" to deal with that which has traumatized him, usually through pain]; first you get hurt, then you get angry." Hurt is "the feeling, anger is the emotional reaction to the feeling of being hurt," Estyne told me.

When working as a psychologist, Dr. D. does not enter trance but is guided throughout each session by Frances' words, which she clairaudiently hears. Frances does not enter into her, as is normally the case when mediums go into a trance. Rather, Frances' presence is evoked by Estyne's performance of a small ritual in which, over a glass of fresh water, she says out loud the words, "To God, the Divine Master." She then takes three sips of water from the glass and places it in front of her on her desk.

Immediately after Dr. D. completes this ritual, which Frances taught her, Frances stands behind her chair and says, "Oh, this one," and begins giving her clairaudiently the qualities of the patient before her. As Dr. D. hears Frances' words, she simply repeats to her client what she is told to say.

According to Dr. D., "With spirit, water is the most important element. I can do more things with a glass of water than most people can with books and ingredients. Also, guardian spirits [such as Frances] are a higher vibration than santos spirits, which are material working spirits. The guardian spirits or angels work on two planes and usually have the assistance of the secondary or protective spirits, which santos are."

Dr. D. says that Frances has passed through her (i.e., taken possession of her) only twice and that in both cases her body ached for a week. "I am very happy that she works next to me instead of 'in' me," Estyne was quick to add.

Dr. D. offers her services on three levels—as a spiritista, a santera, and a psychologist.

Sometimes, while working as a psychologist, she will be told by Frances of the presence of spirit entities around her client. In this case, she will tell her client that the problem is not really mental but that he or she has "an intelligent, intangible, negative energy in [his or her] energy field,'' which is her way of describing what others have called an obsession.

Dr. D. clearly distinguishes between cases of obsession and those of possession, which she considers the most difficult to deal with. In both cases exorcism is the solution. Again, it is Frances who will tell Dr. D. whether someone is possessed and by how many spirits.

According to Dr. D., "Spirits are either light or dark. As depicted with halos, the light ones all have light around them. If a spirit came down and said he was Jesus Christ and I should go kill someone, I would have to question him and say, 'But you are not exhibiting any of the love energy Jesus was so famous for. Do you come in the name of God?' There are certain unwritten rules. One of them is that if you ask a spirit if he comes in the name of God, he cannot answer you falsely. So in this case, the spirit would have to leave.''

Dr. D.'s understanding of the world of spirits has come from her fifteen years of dealing with them. Her major source of information, other than her personal experience, has been the writings of Allan Kardec. Of Kardec, Estyne simply says, "Very valid. Very knowledgeable. My spiritualist prayer book is written by Allan Kardec.''

One thing that Dr. D. has insisted upon is that she is a psychologist first and that in her psychology she simply uses her mediumship as a tool. In her own words, "It makes it easy to be able to know what a person's problems really are and where they stem from without spending a lot of time keeping that patient in therapy.''

Each patient first coming to Dr. D. is requested to bring with them a recent photograph, not more than three months old. The person must not wear black nor can the background be black. After the person has left, Dr. D. uses that photograph to determine whether their problem is psychological or parapsychological. Once the cause of the problem has been determined, the solution becomes simple—either psychology, spirit, santos, or a combination of the three.

While the various spirits below God can enable changes to take place on the material plane, this is done only with God's prior approval. Estyne likes to think of herself as an instrument. God provides the power. Estyne prefers to call her power simply "gifts."

Throughout her career, Estyne has never worked with the dark side. She believes one can work only white or black, and never both. In her own words, "I have been a member of the God Squad for many years. That's the side I chose and that's where I stand!" There have been many times in which she has been offered large sums of money if she would work on the black side and cause someone injury. These kinds of assignments she has always turned down.

Like many enlightened mediums, Dr. D. looks down on the popularization of magic that allows persons to go to a bookstore and buy a book on magic, enabling them to make contact with the spirit world. While such books teach how to make contact, in her opinion most fail to explain the dangers of these practices, nor do they provide a means to break a contact once it has been made.

People seek spiritual contact today more than ever because of what Dr. D. calls "a hole in their life." While we have everything material needed to make us happy, we can still be unhappy, unfulfilled, and unsatisfied. As to why this is so, Dr. D. would say it's because we are not giving anything back. We simply take, take, take, while giving and not taking is the real nature of the universe.

As to the connection between drugs and spirituality, while Estyne acknowledges that the ancients, such as the Incas, used such drugs as cocaine in their rituals, they were digested rather than ingested and used only under spiritually controlled circumstances.

Every inner conflict of the me, myself, and I (physical, mental, and spiritual) results in a physical manifestation of some kind of illness. For instance, while working for the holistic physician, Dr. D. noticed that persons who failed to express themselves were either constipated, short of breath, or tight of chest.

When I asked Dr. D. if her spirit guide Frances would always be with her, she replied, "She will be with me until the time comes when it is my time to leave. I hope that I leave this body in better shape than when I entered it, and that I am not sent back down here again!

"Every person on earth comes down with at least one guardian spirit. We could not exist in this domain without it. And this is the spirit that tries to reach you by thought, impressions, the feeling of to do or not to do. They have nothing else to do but to take care of you. That is their whole purpose and mission in life—to help you get through life and to elevate your consciousness." She believed it happened to her because her purpose in life is to help people.

It is Estyne's belief that spirits, depending on their evolution and consciousness, have a choice as to whether or not they will be reborn. Nine days after a person has passed away, according to Estyne's practices, a mass for that soul is performed both in church and in the house, to determine where it is. She says, "It would be unintelligent of man to think that prayers for a friend who has passed go unnoticed or unheard."

When I asked Dr. D for her recommendations as to how one could make spirit contact, her answer was simply, "Seek and ye shall find. Knock and the door shall be opened to you. If your purpose in seeking spirit is to help, you cannot fall into bad hands, and you are going to attract a high level of vibration."

The actual instruments of communication are a glass of water, some flowers, and a white candle. Every day, too, one should first talk to God, and then to the spirits with whom one wishes to make contact.

Even the use of a psychic device, such as a Ouija Board, is not considered bad per se by Dr. D. Again, it is the intent of the person using the board that ultimately determines what takes place. It is true that a person can become obsessed with its use, but if the desire is positive, the result must follow along the same lines.

It has not been easy for Dr. D. to follow the Santeria path. To begin with, Santeria is primarily a Latin and black undertaking. Since she was born neither Spanish nor black, some santeras are prejudiced against her. It has taken her more than seven years to overcome this initial hostility. Dr. D. believes that she "lived before" in Cuba and also in Africa, where she was black.

In her work she has met persons from all races and religious dispositions. She has made it a practice, though, to stay away from those santeros who practice both black and white, and prefers to work "clean," as she describes it.

Unlike many mediums who follow special diets, Dr. D. simply watches what she eats as to quality and quantity. She does accept the belief that it is possible for mediums to become overweight since they are dealing with etheric energy and taking into themselves "cellular imprints of people they work with."

In order to rid herself of the influences she picks up from other persons, Estyne takes special herbal spiritual baths every day. On her stove one can always find a pot of boiling herbs, which she changes every three days.

Always, Dr. D. turns to her guide Frances, whom she considers a majordomo, in charge of 167 other spirits whom she will direct to Estyne as the need demands. Frances herself was a Jamaican black in her last life and speaks English.

When the need arises, Dr. D. will "send" or "lend" Frances to one of her spiritual godchildren, many of whom have glasses of water to Frances in their homes.

Yet another way in which Dr. D. helps others is through the use of divination by the *caracoles*, or cowrie shells, which are believed to "speak" to the santero who has been initiated into their use. Although one can become a godchild of a santero without oneself making santos, the time often comes when one feels the need for greater wisdom.

Dr. D. continues to work long hours serving her God, spirits, santos, and her patients. Her day begins at seven in the morning and ends at two o'clock the following morning. She maintains this routine five days a week and rightfully claims the weekends for herself.

So convinced is she of the rightness of Frances' guidance that Estyne assured me that if she was told to sell everything, leave her New York City apartment, and relocate, she would do it willingly.

Despite her many unusual gifts, Dr. D., following the santero tradition, has a godfather, a man who has been a santero for more than fifteen years. She turns to him when she needs additional guidance or teaching, which she receives from his spirit guide Clementina.

It is Dr. D.'s sincere desire that each person seek and find the truth for himself or herself. "What I tell people is that fear of looking is always worse than the looking! When you look you get three choices: all of it, none of it, or a piece of it. If you don't look, you have no choice. You are on this earth to make choices in your life."

At the close of my interview with Dr. D., I asked her for a simple description of herself and her work. "Unorthodox but effective," is what she said.

12

──○──

Shirley Calkins Smith

God has given each one of us the greatest gift in the whole universe that could be given . . . God's self is Our self. Within us we have the greatest lover, the greatest comforter, the greatest healer and guide. We are always drawing on that but we are usually ignorant of the process, so we can't consciously direct it.

—Shirley Calkins Smith

Not all mediums are born mediums. While some are born, others are made through hard work and the desire to find Truth, no matter how high the cost. Such was the case for Shirley Calkins Smith, who was born on June 13 in Wilkes Barre, Pennsylvania.

"I've always wanted to help people develop a desire to grow and search for Truth. When I was little kid I really believed I would find the answer, though no one around me had it, so I just kept reading, studying. The first thing I got into was Science of Mind in California. That was fantastic. I sent away for their correspondence course."

At the time, Shirley was about twenty-five and was living in Rochester, New York. She had been raised in the Methodist faith and describes her parents' initial reactions to her new religion as "quite horrified." They remained this way for many years, until they came to stay with her, while their farm was being built, heard the phone ring off the wall, and met with many of the persons she counseled on a daily basis.

It was around this same time that Shirley suffered an indignation

126

that many pioneers in the New Age movement have feared. She was arrested for fortune-telling and taken away in handcuffs. Although fortune-telling laws still exist in many cities, it is very unusual for municipalities to enforce them. In this case, Shirley shared the spotlight with a Sister Ann who charged $300 to change luck and remove curses.

While the actual incident did little to dissuade her from her spiritual calling, it did have an unfortunate effect on her father. She recalls that her lawyer's fee for representing her was $150 and a reading. Her arrest had come only a month after she had started charging for her readings, having worked for five years previously for love offerings during which time her husband held down three jobs so she could persist in her addiction to helping people.

After completing the Science of Mind course, Shirley came into contact with Rev. Marion Newbie, pastor of a local spiritualist church, Divine Inspiration. Describing Reverend Newbie, Shirley says, "I went every Sunday and Wednesday and learned her belief system. I had never seen love flow from anybody in my life like it did from her. I wanted to be able to do that. So I went back."

About eight years ago, Shirley was ordained as a spiritualist minister by the General Assembly of Spiritualists in New York City and has served on their board for a number of years. She has also served as assistant pastor at Divine Inspiration and as vice president for fifteen years.

While support from family members is often a problem, Shirley speaks of that received from her second husband in glowing terms. "My husband was always rather neat because he would tell everybody he worked with (even though he didn't understand it), go see my wife, she'll fix you up. He always told me to go do my thing, which was awfully nice, though I probably would have done it anyway! But there was no conflict there. My parents, after they lived with me and saw what was going on, they really felt pretty good about it." Her mother, who has passed into spirit, even manifests herself now and advises Shirley.

While Shirley was performing the marriage ceremony for her

brother Steven and his wife, her mother manifested and stood behind the couple. Speaking of this, Shirley adds, "One of the things I love most about spiritualism, and I think what drew me to the church, is that I really became aware that there is a presence in the universe that is always there for us and will transform our life if we get in touch with the energy."

While many would believe mediums are born, Shirley prefers to believe they are made. "I think that everybody is mediumistic. I think a loving, caring person is just like a healer. All the gifts are there if we want to develop them."

Shirley has four children, two sons and two daughters, all of whom have demonstrated some psychic abilities. Whether they follow in their mother's footsteps is yet to be seen.

It is her desire to gradually move away from the demands of a church and to establish a spiritual awareness retreat, although it is not known when or where this will take place. To make this happen, her recently printed business cards contain the appellation "evolutionary tutor."

When it comes to the change taking place in spiritualism, Shirley says, "Lily Dale was first called the Free Thinker's Association. I absolutely love that! I feel a little sad that people who are unwilling to grow and change are going to be left behind. I think there are a lot of valuable things we can learn from the past, but I think today the channel for spirit has to receive the blessing first before they can give it. I don't think that used to be the case. I think it was a very selfless thing, and their lives did not show the fruit or the manifestations of the love and joy they could give to other people. I think it's a really wonderful time today but you have got to be willing to grow.

"I think spiritualism is in sad shape because if you get a hundred spiritualists in a room, you will have a hundred different belief systems, and they will all bring their backgrounds with them."

As to the doctrine of reincarnation and its relation to spiritualism, Shirley's views are decidedly clear: "I definitely believe in reincarnation. I also know my own past lives. It answers questions. . . . I do not push it on other people in the readings but sometimes when they are having a very difficult problem I can make a believer of them in one minute because I will get the past life tie that has created that which will make sense with what they cannot make sense of.''

Shirley's knowledge of her own past lives came through the mediumship of Noel Street, who was well known for his books *Dreamer Awake* and *Looking Backwards*, in which he explains his philosophy of previous lives. In a personal reading by Street, she was told of three previous lives and that her work in this lifetime was to be exactly what she is now doing. All this took place many years before she met Reverend Newbie.

Describing her clientele, Shirley says, "There has been a marvelous change. I used to feel a lot of it was for, literally, fortune-telling. But I am not minimalizing. We all have problems with our finances, and how we are going to survive. So that is a valid reason for a reading. But, I think the consciousness has changed. Now the people who are coming are working on themselves and that's a pure joy. They are not there for a fortune-teller, they are there to grow.''

As is often the case with mediums, spirit will bring Shirley information as to the cause of health problems. Of this she says, "I believe that every physical manifestation is the result of your thought and your emotions. We know that spirit doesn't lie and the body doesn't lie, and is an exact replica of your emotional and mental state, so that very often a good reading is itself a healing! Another understanding I have come into this year is that our body is always working in our best interest.''

Once again, like many modern mediums, Shirley does not work with one particular spirit guide but rather reaches out to the Christ, to the highest and the very best of each person she is working for.

It is her belief that in her counseling she is a spiritual therapist and that to a lot of the people with whom she works she imparts "something nonverbal which has very little to do with the words I am saying.''

To maintain her own center, Shirley limits her readings to no more than ten every other day. "I used to read every day, but my whole life was out of balance,'' she said. "Then it was like I was drawing from myself instead of spirit. The most precious thing in the world this year is my time alone because I am making contact with that presence.''

Besides limiting her readings, Shirley tries every morning to do breathing exercises in which she draws in ''that perfect energy pattern.''

As to why many mediums and persons following the teachings of spirit often fail to manifest on the material plane, Shirley believes ''we do not believe we deserve the Kingdom.

''I believe that the soul expresses itself through beauty and harmony. I think we need all these nice things to share with other people. But one of my affirmations—I have to find sneaky ways to get through my own blocks sometimes—is the more I receive the more I can share with other people. I really feel I am working through that thing with money because I believe all money is God energy in action. That's all it is. It's a very mystical thing,'' Shirley adds.

Agreeing with many other mediums, Shirley believes that following a particular diet has little to do with the success she has had in her mediumship.

''Part of me could feel that I may have a Light Center. Another part of me would be perfectly happy with a little bitty one-room A-frame somewhere,'' she says. ''I look forward to traveling more. I just want to grow.''

Distinguishing between being a psychic and a medium, Shirley feels the latter ''brings a spiritual aspect to it.

''I can sit and probably convince somebody of my psychic ability, but with psychic abilities alone you can't help the person. You're just mirroring back what is. Universal laws are super important. One of the workshops I love to do is to teach the principles. This changes your whole reality.

''I sometimes think the word spiritual turns people off. But I think people are so hungry for loving acceptance and right ideas.''

Throughout our conversation, Shirley continually stressed the need for mediums and those serving spirit to take time for themselves to prevent burning out.

"I had severe burnout when I came out here [i.e., to Lily Dale]. I would look out at the water going by and the trees. It was an incredible healing. . . . At this point, one of the things I definitely have in my belief system is that I need to take time for me. It is only out of my wholeness and joy that I can help others. Even if you have the sincere desire to do it, if you don't take time to let that Loving Presence meet your needs first, it can't flow through you to others.''

Since many of my conversations with various mediums had uncovered disturbed and difficult personal lives, I asked Shirley why she thought those serving spirit seemed to have trouble in relationships. Her answer was thoughtful and unique: ''The answer might surprise you. I feel it's a lack of congruity. They don't always have the self-perception or the confidence or the feeling that they are worthy of having a good relationship. I think you are going to find that there is a pattern for people who are 'givers,' that they have a difficult time 'receiving.'''

What is the future of spiritualism? Will its beliefs become commonplace and someday be taught in the schools? Shirley's opinion: ''I think we are the Wayshowers, mirroring back to people. Everyone has the *ability*. I believe we are both the mouthpiece and answerpiece of God. In my workshops I always try to include this concept because we think that to be happy we must achieve something. . . . Everyone is going to become aware they have the *ability*. Right now we have taken a quantum leap in consciousness, and we are stepping from the physical to the heart center, which is the heart and seat of the 'spiritual' man . . . the clairvoyance, the clairaudience, are manifesting more and more. You ask a group now, who has had a psychic experience, and they all put their hands up. Ten years ago, no one would respond!''

Shirley in a nutshell? Here's what she would be likely to say: ''I think the most important thing to me is that from the time I was a little kid I loved to make people feel good about themselves. It's a very simple thing. I just want to help people see a little glimpse of their own magnificence. If I can do that, I feel I have been very, very successful.''

Concluding our discussion, I asked Shirley to share the personal prayer she uses to open each session with her many clients. She shares it with you. Pass it on!

> Heavenly Father, Loved Ones, Cooperatives. . . . We place all our power at you disposal for the production of Good. We ask a very special blessing of love, healing energy, and joy as well as information for . . ., and we know that whatever information is needed for their highest good will be coming through in ways that they can understand. And help us to realize that the same power that holds all the planets in space is feeding us breath, Thy Breath, and that we indeed do create our own reality. Amen.

Shirley is not sure what the future holds, but she has "never felt so unlimited."

13

○

Anne Gehman:
One Chosen by the Spirits

I think there is too much phenomena without philosophy.
I am much more interested in the phenomena if it helps a
person become a better person and to look deeper.

—Anne Gehman

By now, reader, you certainly know that mediums come in all shapes and sizes and that each person is truly a channel at one or another time in his or her life.

While psychic realities are available for anyone to reach out and grasp, why they manifest and why they manifest when they do seem unclear.

A commonality in the lives of many mediums is simply their "knowing" that they always had the gift of spiritual perception. In other words, this was not something they had to develop, like an athlete would his muscles, but rather something they simply had to recognize and use. This was certainly so for Anne Gehman.

Born to a family of Amish Mennonites in Petoskey, Michigan, Anne Gehman has the distinction of being the youngest medium ever certified by the National Association of Spiritualist Churches, having begun her platform work at the age of fifteen. At the age of seventeen she was first invited to speak at Lily Dale. Of the invitation, she says, "I thought it was fantastic!"

Anne describes both her parents as religious people and very spiritual, and of a "psychic temperament." In her own words, "I came by it naturally . . . but I don't think they understood much about it until late in their lives.'' She believes the fact that she was the seventh child—a sacred number in numerology—may to some extent account for her abilities.

"I can't remember ever a time when I didn't hear voices or have visions and see auras. It was just something that was very natural to me,'' she says.

While most mediums delight in telling how their parents and family members thought they were crazy when they saw and heard things, Anne's experience was exactly the opposite, though her parents did find the phenomena disturbing.

She says of her parents, "They were very patient with me and tried to be understanding. I do remember at times when I was eleven or twelve years of age, I had a lot of physical phenomena that occurred around me. We would sit down to the dinner table, and the end of the table would lift up and the silverware would move around. I remember my father praying for me, his huge hands pouncing down on top of my head and his prayer to remove this horrible affliction that I had.''

Fortunately or unfortunately, the phenomena did not stop but rather increased. "I remember one time it was a rainy day and I was sent to my room for something. I sat on the edge of my bed. I had a little Shaker table beside my bed. I would put my hand on it and it would dance around. I thought it was great fun. I didn't know that everyone couldn't do that. I remember the table going up in the air and just then my father walked up into my room to see what I was doing. I think at that time he became very, very concerned and disturbed about what was happening.''

Anne continues, "That was one of the last experiences I recall. I think that I probably consciously or unconsciously tried to stop those things from happening because I felt my father's disapproval.''

At the age of fifteen, the loneliness, fear, and emptiness of being special caught up with her, and she attempted ending her life, a fact she has never been proud of. As a result of this near ending of her physical life, she was seemingly guided to the doorway of a medium, Wilbur Hull, in the spiritualist community named Cassadaga, which had been founded and named by a former Lily Dale resident. It was Hull who taught Gehman the entire philosophy of spiritualism, though at first her strictly fundamental Christian upbringing caused her to consider her new teacher "of the devil."

Anne finished high school with a straight-A average and won a number of scholarships. Instead of college, she chose to enter nursing school, using a four-year scholarship she had won. After graduation, she completed further studies in X-ray and laboratory work, but in her own words "never used any of it and never wanted to."

Unlike many mediums who are gradually led to accept a belief in the world of spirit, Anne has been giving readings professionally since she was the age of fifteen.

When asked where her psychic abilities could have come from at so early an age, she responded, "I am not a reincarnationist in the usual sense. I believe in the recycling of life force and energy. But I am not convinced of reincarnation in the usual sense, not at all.

"Do you know how many Napoleons I have met? And how many Queens of Scotland? I think there is so much nonsense perpetuated. I have really become disturbed at the amount of ignorance that is perpetuated. It really concerns me.

"I believe from the moment of conception when there is the joining together of the ovum and the sperm, there is already an intelligence, a spiritual counterpart, and I think there is continuous growth already within the mother's womb of the total being—body, mind, and spirit.

"I see death as a 'birth' in a sense. There is a great deal of evidence, through spirit communication, that there is continuous growth on the other side. I see no reason, whatsoever, to come back into this dimension of life.

"Eventually, I believe, we are sort of absorbed into the Overall Soul and then draw upon that for different forms of life or aspects of life, and in that way, we may be 'reborn.' We see the recycling of all things in nature, so it is very logical for me to believe that this is also true for the spiritual level of consciousness."

When it comes to the need for a particular gatekeeper, control, or guide in spirit, Anne, like many contemporary mediums, says she does not "feel the dependency on any particular spirit entities as many mediums do. I believe that we have to have independent development in that as well.

"I am always very conscious of two or three different ones particularly. There are certain ones I feel have always been with me. Sometimes I do work in trance, and it is usually the same entity that speaks through me. I remember nothing whatsoever when I work in the trance state."

Anne, like many contemporary mediums, prefers not to be affiliated with any particular church or in her own words, "wear any particular label," though she is an ordained minister with the National Association of Spiritualist Churches and is both a certified medium and healer.

She did have a church in Orlando, Florida, years ago, which was very successful and which conducted a four-year study course, four or five public services each week, and was very social. Recalling this experience, Anne says, "I got very tired of that in certain ways. I did not want some organization to dictate to me whether I could talk about reincarnation or not or whatever."

Although Anne's beliefs in the world of spirit originally alienated her from her parents, in their later life she became much closer to them. Her father passed through transition at the age of ninety-seven and is described by her as "a remarkable man." At the time of her father's passing, she was awakened in the middle of the night, heard her father call "Beatrice Anne," and saw his spirit body. Later that same morning, she received a telephone call confirming her father's passing.

"I have seen some magnificent phenomena in my own home. When my oldest sister passed away, I was with six other persons, none of whom were spiritualists or mediums, they were just visiting in my home. It was late afternoon when right in the center of my sitting room, while we were just talking, suddenly a little cloud began to build up and took the full form of my sister. It was the most wonderful, beautiful thing I ever saw. It was a true, full body materialization in the light. She just turned to me and put her hand out, and I knew she was happy. This was about a year after she had passed away.''

Like many ethical mediums, she is bothered by those who would resort to fraud and gimmickry in order to demonstrate abilities they don't have.

As to why genuine physical mediumship is virtually unknown today, Anne's explanation is twofold. First, the mediums today do not have the type of development that can produce such phenomena. Second, the development of today is more mental and hence better able to deal with the level of education presented.

Can a person be a medium without accepting the philosophy of spiritualism? Anne would answer yes but is quick to add, ''I think there is too much phenomena without philosophy. I am much more interested in the phenomena if it helps a person become a better person and to look deeper. I tend to be very critical of spiritualists, as I think we do not expect enough of our mediums, our psychics, our healers. We accept everything on a very mediocre level. Look around and it's there. It's unfortunate.''

As to the ethics of mediums who feel they must always perform, even when their powers are not there, Anne is again clear in her own belief: ''I don't think any medium is forced to fake it. There is nothing wrong with saying, 'Hey, I don't have it today.' I can remember having people come all the way from California for readings with me. The day they arrived, I woke up that morning and knew I didn't have it. I don't believe one has to apologize, necessarily.

''One evening when I had the church in Orlando, I got up to give the message service, and was a total blank. So I just called upon someone in the congregation.''

As to why this happens, Anne can only say, ''I don't know why this happens. I think being human as we are, there are always times when we are perhaps a little bit out of balance, or there is something in the body chemistry, or the chemistry of thought that just isn't working that day. I think we need to recognize that and be honest about it. There is no reason ever to fake mediumship if you are a medium.''

For Anne, meditation and prayer, rather than books, have given her her greatest inspiration. While she has always encouraged people to read and has made a habit of giving out lists of books, her private spiritual life is truly the source of her life's philosophy.

To those mediums who channel entities or beings who claim to be some kind of nonhuman power, Anne expressed a certain degree of skepticism. Of the recent popularity of such channeled teachings, Anne simply says, "But maybe that's what some people need at this time. I know a lot of people are really moved by it. If it helps them, then fine."

Anne has reticently worked with the police to help find missing people. Often she is given a photograph, an article of clothing, a bloodstain, or a murder weapon. "Usually I start out working with a very skeptical investigator. I enjoy the challenge of that. I have also taught in the Northern Academy of Criminal Justice, teaching them psychometry."

Since Anne makes her winter home in Annandale, Virginia, outside Washington, D.C., she numbers among her clients a number of political personages, and she considers this an exciting part of her work. Since the mid-1960s, this has been an important part of her vocation. She makes no distinction, however, between the rich and famous and the just plain folks for whom she reads. "I think everybody who comes for a reading is very special at that time, whether the janitor from my office building or a congressman, or someone from the presidential cabinet, they are all the same at that time," she says.

In order to preserve her own energy, Anne schedules no more than five readings a day. If there is a great need or an emergency, she may consent to an additional reading but tries to adhere to the five-readings schedule.

Anne is also a member of her local chamber of commerce. When I inquired as to how the chamber had her listed in their directory, "Clergy," she replied!

As to whether or not mediumship can be taught, Anne is very clear in her belief, having taught a number of classes both in Florida and Virginia. "In Florida I had very large classes. There are probably twenty-five mediums in Florida that I trained and helped get started there, many who are certified by National. In fact, if you go to Cassadaga I think half of them are people I brought into spiritualism.

"Where I am now [i.e., Virginia], I do have classes, workshops, and seminars.

"I think we all have it [i.e., potential mediumship] to some degree. I think that it's there; it's a matter of bringing it out."

As to the common problem of many mediums giving readings that are for the most part very general and that could apply to anyone, Anne offers an unusual solution: "I think a lot of it is not letting them [i.e., students] see other mediums work right away. I do not encourage my students to go to places where they would hear other people work. That may sound sort of strange in a way, but I don't want them to see that part of it. If you listen to most mediums, there will be certain phrases they all use. Is that from spirit or have they learned it from one another? I would rather people not be exposed to that but still know what they can do potentially and expect them to do it . . . and do it!"

Anne Gehman, unlike a number of mediums, has a special reverence for her roots in traditional spiritualism. "Look at the progress that has been made outside spiritualism. I think that is really great. The spiritualists have, in a sense, been the custodians of psychic phenomena. And now it is out there. I think that maybe what spiritualists are feeling right now is much like the mother whose child has left home. Now we need a new cause, a new direction. I would like to see us become like the early spiritualists who were really reformers. They weren't interested *only* in religion but were interested in the progression of the entire world. They got involved in politics and all kinds of things. We need to bring that forward. I think there is a tremendous need for leadership. I think there is a need to elevate our thinking, to have something that elevates everyone's thinking."

As to exactly what form this new cause could take, Anne suggested, "One big cause we could work for today is peace. We hear a lot of kookiness out there with the so-called peace movements, but there is something there, a golden thread, a golden strand which we need to pick up on.''

Finishing up my interview with Anne, I posed the question as to what she would do if one day her mediumship was gone.

Her answer, ''If that happened, then I think I would write. I am sure I would continue to teach. I think I would partially retire. Maybe I would start a business. I think it would be fun to have a tearoom.''

As a final note, I asked Anne to describe in a few words what she felt her work was all about. ''Love, that's really what it's all about . . . and service. I think it has to be based upon love.''

Anne Gehman is indeed a very special woman, no doubt born to the spiritual manor where she has lived, loved, worked, and cried. While her journey to date has not always been an easy one, it is definitely one that she somehow chose.

Perhaps, when it comes to the gifts of spirit, we all choose . . . even if in the choosing, we elect not to do so.

14

John C. White: "I Do What Comes Naturally"

I know intuitively that there is more to my life than my physical being, so I am doing this work to confirm my intuitions. I ask for directions from my guides and/or guardian angels and let my intuitive mind receive the answers. I ask because this is a natural thing for me to do.

—John C. White

While it is often said that meduims are born and not made, John C. White is one individual who continues to disprove this premise on a daily basis.

Born in Montreal, Canada, on November 24, 1946, John began his quest for the world of spirit through a course he took in transcendental meditation (TM), the type of meditation, using a mantra, that was popularized by the Beatles' Guru, Mahesh Maharishi Yogi.

After three days of meditating, John began to realize that there was a great deal more to his mind than what he had learned in school. He found himself seeing "very clear mind pictures." A course in Silva Mind Control—a technique for psychic development, created by Jose Silva, that uses visualization and meditation—convinced him that these were intuitive psychic pictures.

"I came to the realization that we all think in pictures," he says. "From there I learned how to do readings, similar to those of Edgar Cayce, through the Silva Mind people, by self-hypnosis."

Photo: Manoug

At the time John began TM, he was working as a musician, and since he was a fan of the Beatles, his attitude toward meditation was, in his own words, "Why not?" While there are no accidents in the universe, John's tripping over the world of spirit began to lead him in a direction he never imagined.

Unlike many mediums who develop their abilities through circles and other group spiritual activities, John has always relied on meditation, first and foremost, as the key to his own development. Of this he says, "Being intuitive is a by-product of meditation. The more one meditates, or the more one is disciplined, the easier the whole thing is as far as your intuition is concerned. Being intuitive, also, has to do with how much energy is available. You can do this work when there is a lot of energy, I mean pure energy. I try to lead quite a disciplined life."

John was raised by foster parents. His foster mother was born in England and was told to come to Canada by a medium in a spiritualist church. Of her personal beliefs, John says, "She is a person who believes in all religions. God was the same but came in different forms. Though she prayed to Jesus, she attended the Mormon Church, the Anglican Church, and was very open."

According to John, when his mother's mother was passing through transition in England, her sister who had already died came to her bedside and told her that her mother was passing on.

John also recalled a little boy named Leslie who came to live with his foster family, and who doctors said would never walk or talk. Leslie is now six foot seven and a half inches tall, is bilingual, and plays several musical instruments.

"She was a healer," John said. "She also healed herself of what the doctors considered incurable cancer." While John had grown up in what could definitely be called a spiritual environment, he did not realize the consequences of his unique surroundings until he began to meditate.

Of this fact, he says, "I probably would not have been involved in spiritualism, per se, if my own church, the Anglican, had taught meditation. Learning how to meditate was, perhaps, the most important event in my life."

When asked how he would explain the mediumistic abilities of others who have not practiced meditation, John suggested the following explanation: "I know scientifically that this ability comes from the right hemisphere. So anybody who says 'No, I can't do this,' or that people are only born with this, what they are actually saying is, perhaps, I don't have a right side of my brain. In Third World countries or in countries where people don't have the educational system we have in the West, they are thinking more out of the right hemisphere. So it is true that for people who may not be as well educated as we are, this may be more normal for them, or they may have more experiences in it."

As to whether John was born with his abilities or whether he developed them, his answer was that he was "born with a very large potential." John's foster parents quietly encouraged his interest in things of the spirit.

After his experiences with TM and Silva Mind Control, John was led to Camp Chesterfield, Indiana, one of the early spiritualist summer camps still in existence. Here he studied for seven summers under the tutelage of Rev. Mamie Brown, who had been a medium for sixty-five years.

Humble about his achievements, John says that he had 10 percent ability and worked hard to create the other 90 percent. John considers his real introduction to spiritualism his experience of genuine materializations conducted by Warren Smith, a well-known physical medium.

Of his Camp Chesterfield experience, John remarks, "The reason I went there was to go to school. They have a great education system, although there is a great deal of fraudulent mediumship going on there. I would go to class every day. It was almost like a finishing school for me. I would stand up and my teacher would tell me to turn on the clairvoyance, to realize what clairsenscience was, to pick up spirit names. I got to refine giving messages in her class. It gave me a very, very strong foundation."

Because of his unique personal experience in learning, John considers his mission not just that of a medium but that of a teacher as well. It is here that he clearly excels. While John *works* as a medium, this is clearly not his purpose in life. He considers his purpose "to become self-realized," which no doubt comes from his early training in Eastern philosophies.

To assist in his self-realization, he essentially relies on the artful blending of three very special traditions: Insight Meditation, Yoga, and Tai Chi Chuan.

He believes that the difference between *his* approach to mediumship and that of most mediums in the West is that the latter depend on outside influences to run their lives. They would, in John's opinion, meditate simply to get and give messages rather than to reach enlightenment.

When I asked John whether some of the Eastern teachers would look down on his work as a medium, he answered, "No. I even know Sai Baba has his helpers. In Christianity they call them guardian angels. In the East they may call them devas. In spiritualism, they call them guides."

As to his own guides, John has several, having met them all during a materialization seance of Warren Smith. Of this, John says, "For this materialization, a bus load of us came down from Montreal. It was quite amazing. They were going through the floor, walking through people. That night he was really good. During that circle, that materialization, I got to know the names of my guides. It says in the Bible that one of the gifts is that of discerning spirit. So I know what it feels like when a specific spirit guide is working around me." Unlike some mediums, John does not have one particular spirit guide or gatekeeper through whom he works.

Because of his exposure to Eastern ideas and influences, John is one of many contemporary mediums who believes in reincarnation, a doctrine not accepted by the early spiritualists and many of the spiritualist organizations.

"I know how to regress people and put them in a past life whether they believe in reincarnation or not. I learned this from a Jungian analyst who teaches this as a therapy. Instead of going to him and telling him of your dreams, you can go to him and he will put you into an altered state of consciousness and work with that," John said.

—————— ○ ——————

John himself has been regressed and while in that state met a Tibetan monk who several years later reappeared to him while he was asleep and took him out of his body. On this occasion the monk took him to the spirit world to visit his grandfather. In his regression, this same monk taught John to astral travel in another lifetime.

Over the years John has continued to maintain a relationship with this monk and will go into an involuntary trance state when he appears to him. According to John, it doesn't really matter whether or not this monk was really his teacher in another lifetime. What is important is that John grew through this unusual experience, learning the difference between astral travel in the spirit world and astral travel in the mental world.

While John may enter a trance state involuntarily, he does not make this a practice when he reads for other persons. Of the need for this, John says, "It's not necessary because if you are in control of your clairvoyant mind and the spirits around you, you can do it in a very conscious state. However, when you are giving clairvoyant readings or working on the platform, you are in a light state of hypnosis. But it is not necessary to go into a trance."

As to whether the trance state of the medium is akin to that of hypnosis, John has very definite ideas: "I believe a way to train yourself to go into trance would be through hypnosis. There would be a certain point when the guide, the control spirit, would take over. I try to be quite disciplined. If you can set up the environment, by changing your brain waves, the phenomena has a possibility of happening. By doing meditation, Yoga, or whatever you do as a 'discipline,' you can set up your environment so the spirits can come and work with you. The more you know, I feel, the more they can work with you."

One of the other questions John wished to shed light on was the distinction between being psychic and mediumship. "I believe that you have a spirit and I have a spirit and that we have 'gifts of the spirit.' I can tune into you right now, to a physical condition in your body which has nothing to do with a spirit. I can tune into people's bodies quite easily. In my early training with Silva Mind Control, that was what they were teaching us. Someone would say a name to you and you would do a physiological reading on the person just like Edgar Cayce did.''

Unlike many mediums who are born with definite psychic abilities, John would say that his gifts are clearly the result of training and leading a spiritually disciplined life. What this means, then, is that it is John's opinion that anyone can, through similar training, develop these same gifts.

Of this John says, ''I realized while doing Hatha Yoga, quite a while ago, that if you can't meditate, if you can't go through your head and calm your body down, you can go through your body, because your body and brain are connected through your nervous system. So if you have a hard time relaxing, you can go through your body, which is what Tai Chi and Hatha Yoga does.''

Like many other mediums, John does not have one but rather a number of guides that work with him. Based on the unique feeling of the energy that accompanies each guide, he is able to differentiate the identity of each. Of this he says, ''I have a philosophical guide when I am giving inspirational speaking. I have another guide when I go into a deep state of meditation or changing my chemistry or energy field. There is another guide I work with clairvoyantly. There is another guide who knows about medical terms. Again, even if I am doing a physiological reading on you, sometimes there is outside information that comes in.''

Also, like many others, from time to time John has questioned whether or not he actually needs a guide. ''Sometimes I am so involved in doing it myself, which was my early training in Silva Mind Control, my attitude was, 'So what do we need guides for?' But then I realized that the information which was coming from my own psychic level had certain parameters on a mental plane. So I got to trust more the information that came from outside of me.

''Then there are the instances in which your grandmother or grandfather may come. Sometimes I have to explain to people, 'This isn't God speaking. This is your grandmother!' ''

Unlike many other mediums, John has also dealt with the fact that he may be reading the unconscious mind of his client rather than actually making spirit contact. On this point he suggests, ''When people come for readings I always tell them, 'Only say names to me if you want me to tune into people. Only say names to me if the people are physically living.' Because if you say a name to me of someone who has passed on, and they don't show up, my mind will automatically tune into your memory of them. So I can tell you all about them but this has nothing to do with their spirit being here.''

How does the client know that this is not what is happening in every instance to begin with? John further elucidates: ''A person may never be able to tell. . . . How a medium may know is that he may sense how he [the deceased] passed on or may get a name, or sometimes a sensation, such as 'lung cancer' or whatever. Sometimes I get a sense of an energy which if I had the instruments I could measure. It's here, it's not here, it's measurable.

''I believe that spirits that talk to us need not always be present. Why can't they 'think' to us at a distance, like ESP?''

When John is teaching others to do what he does, he is certain to emphasize that there are no wrong impressions. In his training, he asserts that one's impressions are always right. What one must learn is how to interpret them.

In an attempt to clarify John's beliefs as to reincarnation, which were for the most part quite different from those held by other mediums, I raised the issue of making spirit contact with one who had already been reborn. Once again, John was quick to respond: ''I believe it was Madam Blavatsky who talked about 'shells.' You can be in touch with the shell of someone. Sometimes, but not all the time, she believes this is what we are doing—talking to empty shells.

''The other possibility is that of the Collective Unconscious of the Jungians or the Universal Mind. I believe that people who are being regressed are actually tuning into that. Some traditional mediums say that another spirit has overshadowed us or that the person being regressed may actually be remembering something they have read. I know that you actually activate the clairvoyant mind when you are being regressed.''

While John would agree that while the spiritualist organizations, most of which were founded in the late 1800s and early 1900s, would not accept his interpretation of the various theories of reincarnation, most individual mediums would! There is growing awareness among many mediums, like John, that a brand-new age of spiritualism is soon to be born.

What can be said without hesitation about John is that he is undoubtedly the most uncommon and atypical medium one might find. He explains this by saying in a matter-of-fact way that it's simply due to his exposure to other belief systems. More likely, though, is that it is simply John.

At the passing of his own parents, John shared the experience of other mediums in making contact with them shortly after their transition. "Two days after my father passed on, I 'met' him upstairs. What I mean by 'met' him is that there was a measurable presence that was 'here.' I remember my first reaction was, almost comically, 'What are you doing here?' He would come quite often. . . . really strong enough so I could tell it was him.

"When my mother passed on, I remember feeling her energy at her casket. Again, I said to her, with a sense of humor, 'Why don't you come back later. More people are coming!' She loved animals very much so ever since she passed on, whenever I am doing readings for people whose animals have passed on, all their animals come; and I am able to tell them what animals they had. I feel that this is her contribution."

As to how many readings per day he can do without burning out, John was quick to respond and added his particular brand of humor. "Living here at Lily Dale, it's like 'walk-ins.' Not Ruth Montgomery's walk-ins . . . but it's like walk-ins. Of course a lot of people come here to get their fortune told and others want to actually communicate with someone they love who has passed on. I keep myself in good shape. Again, the ability to do this has to do with how much energy is available. Here I've done up to fourteen a day [each reading is half an hour]. I can do eight to ten easily. Since you become an extension of each person who comes for a reading, if you are having a good day, and people come in with a lot of energy and are open, you can do more. Some people sit in front of you and almost put you in a trance. With some people it's like pulling teeth. It depends on who is sitting in front of you."

John's clientele has ranged in age from twenty-one to eighty, although he will occasionally read for children brought in by their parents. In all his readings John "is very much aware of the power of suggestion" and therefore screens everything he says to people after making a quick calculation as to "How will this affect this person sitting in front of me?"

Of this, John says, "I call this putting good records inside people's heads. I want to put good records. Since the future is a by-product of our thinking, which is the only reason I can see into the future, if I see something that may cause a person concern, I always look around to see what we can do to help eradicate that or change a life-style. I would never give a negative reading."

John also admitted that there were some people, despite his vast training and clarity, for whom he could simply not read. "There is no medium alive who can read for everybody!"

Why this is, John does not know. It may be their attitude. It may have to do with the combined energies. To date John recalls only four out of many thousands. One such person, he recalled, was having problems with the IRS for nonpayment of taxes and wanted John to solve his problems.

"The spirits will only come if they believe you are sincere," John said. "If you have a person sitting in front of you who is not sincere, they are not going to show up."

As to the question of diet, in general, John admits that it is an individual matter. While some mediums can eat or drink whatever they like and still read for others, because of his self-purification through meditation and Yoga John no longer grants himself this same license. John eats very little red meat, a preference which evolved by itself, possibly as a result of his meditation practices, and does not drink.

As for the future, John would like to lecture and teach more and write a few books to share his unique understandings as to "how people can learn to develop their own intuition."

At the time of this writing, John is also considering the possibility of starting a church or center in Ontario.

To sum up John White is no easy task. Perhaps John did it best in these words: "I feel I can take anybody from the street and teach them. Quite a long time ago in spiritualism, people used to sit in dark rooms and hope that phenomena happened. But now we know that we can develop our clairvoyant ability. Over the years I have gathered a number of techniques. I know how to get it out of people . . . through trigger mechanisms. . . . I know how to make it happen when it's not happening. I get a lot of joy out of doing that.''

There is absolutely no doubt in my mind that John White is a very old soul living in a wonderfully young body. He exemplifies the oft-quoted adage ''Many are called but few are chosen.'' Clearly, he is one of the few.

15

———o———

Patricia Hayes

*We can all live with love and peace, with direction and
purpose in our lives. There is a new wave of psychic and
spiritual interest. This wave is expanding into a tidal
wave that will sweep the hearts and minds of all people.
We are all lovers and healers. It is our divine nature,
and we are in the midst of maturing that divine nature.*

—Patricia Hayes,
Inner Sense Journal

Twenty-three years ago if one asked a medium such as Arthur Ford
to explain exactly how he did what he did, the answer would more
than likely have been, "I don't know. I just do it!" or "I don't
know. It just sort of happens." But that was the Age of Pisces,
when such words as *esoteric* and *occult* were the mainstay of everything connected with metaphysics, and especially spiritualism.

But now we are in the Age of Aquarius, and everything that was
hidden in the ocean of the unconscious is being revealed. No longer
does one need to join a secret order or go to a mountain retreat to
study Yoga. On the shelves of a local supermarket or drugstore one
can easily find books filled with the "how-to's" never spoken of in
the age that has passed.

When such internationally known personages as Shirley Mac-
Laine and the Beatles turn toward spiritual things and openly share
their experiences, we must readily admit that the world has indeed
changed, whether we like it or not.

And so it is that new wine appears that can no longer fit into old

bottles and with it the whys and how-to's of *almost* everything come to the fore—even of mediumship.

"Find a need and fill it. Find a hurt and heal it." Words like these of Robert Schullers begin to take on new meanings. When they do, there is usually a person, or persons, who begin a quest toward understanding and are not satisfied until they have taken the watch apart and put it back together again.

One such person is Patricia Hayes, whose School of Inner Sense Development in Roswell (Atlanta), Georgia, founded in 1974, transforms sensitive people, from all walks of life, into highly skilled channels for healing.

Before discussing exactly how Patricia and her husband, Marshall Smith, accomplish what would seem like a miracle to the truly uninitiated, we must first go back in time to Patricia's own introduction to the world of spirit.

As is often the case, Patricia's personal odyssey began shortly after the death of her father in 1963. She and her mother had flown up from Florida to Pittsburgh to attend the funeral. While putting the family house in order, three days after the funeral, she and her mother began to hear the sound of musical tones playing the melody of the tune "How Dry I Am." As there was little furniture left in the house by this time, and certainly no music boxes, neither she nor her mother could imagine the source for the sound they were hearing. Remembering that her mother and father did have a musical decanter that played this tune on the bar in their home in Florida, Patricia thought at first that perhaps her mother had brought this with her to Pittsburgh. When her mother assured her that this was not the case, they decided they would search the entire house, including the cellar.

Throughout most of their search, the tune persisted, until suddenly it stopped. At this point, the two did what anyone else would have done under the circumstances—they called the police! The police eventually came, but since the music had already stopped, they found nothing, no doubt assuming the report was simply the product of the minds of two hysterical women.

Since neither Patricia nor her mother had any interest in spiritualism at the time, it never occurred to them that the source of this phenomenon was most likely Patricia's father, who was attempting to assure them both of his continued existence.

At the time of this occurrence, Patricia's home was in Vero Beach, Florida. Shortly thereafter she moved to Miami, and it was there that she encountered a minister in the Swedenborgian church, Rev. Ernest Frederick, who suggested that she and her mother have a reading by a psychic who had just arrived from Puerto Rico.

It was this first psychic reading that totally changed Patricia's life. In it she was told things she had never shared with anyone, personal facts that no one could have possibly known.

Recalling this first experience, she says, "I was absolutely amazed. I had considered myself a very private person. He told me many things I had never told anybody. He told me things about my marriage, about my family when I was growing up. I decided that moment, if it was the last thing I did in my life, that I would find out how this was done. I would find out if it was a trick, or if it was real, how it could be done. This is what started me on my search. From that point on I started experimenting with people."

Patricia was then a psychology and behavioral science major at the Fort Lauderdale branch of the New York Institute of Technology. Her natural curiosity led her to read anything she could find and to start to systematically experiment with what would later be called *psi* abilities.

After being on the path for about two years, she attended her first Spiritual Frontiers Fellowship meeting one evening. Arthur Ford singled her out and said she was the kind of young person who was needed in the movement. As to why she was singled out by Ford, Patricia said, "It was probably my energy. I had a real strong energy field and really, truly wanted to know!"

By this point, Patricia had five children, ranging from newborn to seven years old, who all grew up with various psychic development groups that met in her home as often as five nights a week. Of this time in her life, Patricia says, "One of the experiments was to get the kids asleep so we could go on with our work. We would send them quiet, loving thoughts *upstairs*."

It was at this same time that Patricia encountered her first real experience with the healing power of prayer. Her daughter Kelly had been scheduled for an operation to correct a badly placed urethra, which she had been born with and which caused her continual high fevers. At the suggestion of one of the older group members, a prayer vigil was instituted and continued for six weeks, which resulted in her complete recovery, without surgery.

Fortunately for Patricia, her husband at the time, Bud, while not involved in her work to the same extent, was nonetheless part of the group and open to the ideas she was pursuing. Of this period, she recalls, "What I was doing at that stage was writing papers in college and using people as guinea pigs, in a sense, to find out what methods worked and what didn't. My whole trend of development and thought in this was really for results, to find out if there was a method."

But we have gotten ahead of our story. The night Patricia attended Ford's lecture it ended with she and her mother going out with him for a sandwich. It was none other than Ford himself who suggested to Patricia that she and her family should become involved with Spiritual Frontiers Fellowship, which he had founded a number of years before.

Bud, Patricia's husband at the time, became the area chairman for S.F.F. in South Florida and a friendship was begun with Ford that would last until his passing in 1971. Whenever Ford traveled to the Miami area for a lecture, he would stay with Patricia and Bud, and came to love her family and groups as if they were his own.

In 1968, Ford moved to Miami, and Patricia was given the opportunity of a lifetime and became his personal secretary. By this time she had already begun serving S.F.F. as national youth director, a position that required her to travel all over the country to organize S.F.F. conferences.

So skilled was Patricia in her work that S.F.F. used one of her books—a method of teaching intuitive and spiritual development, *Our First Thousand Groups*—as an organizational tool for their own growth.

Patricia served as Ford's secretary for about three years, taking his mail, handling his telephone calls, and traveling with him as needed.

When I posed the question to Patricia, "Was he a father to you?" she answered openly: "He was more a grandfather to my kids. He was always teaching me. He was always telling me to sharpen up my typewriter. After he had died, I went to see Enna Twigg in England and had a sitting with her. She absolutely wasn't going to go into trance because she was tired and didn't do that anymore. Well, Arthur came right through her and talked about the second key on my typewriter. That if I don't get it fixed . . . it was terrible to send out sloppy writing. He was that type . . . very stern and strict."

It was not until 1974, after Arthur's death, that Patricia finally discovered the key that led to her founding the Arthur Ford International Academy of Mediumship in his memory in Miami. Of this major breakthrough, Patricia recalls, "I was riding home one night. I was a passenger. I received a vision which was the method of mediumship we have been using since 1974. I saw the charts we use, the total method in whole. When I got home, I wrote it all down and called people, because I had been involved with people all over the country by that point. I said, 'Look, I got some research. A method just came through and I need some testing. I want you to come down here and we're going to test this out and if it works, you've got a method of mediumship you can use in channeling healing to people.' So we did it. There were sixteen people from all over the country, a cross section, in that particular group. The exact method he gave worked with fantastic results. We continued to research that for six more months before we knew we really had something fantastic, a new method."

After continued testing, Patricia was convinced that her method would enable her to take "anybody who has developed a degree of sensitivity, a degree of caring for other people," and further enhance and develop their psychic ability.

"People who really want to be involved in a helping profession, but yet do not have society's credentials to do it, are the types of students I work with today," said Patricia. "When we interview them for the school, the main thing we are looking for is integrity and character. When you can teach people method, you give them some powerful tools.''

Throughout her career, Patricia has, for the most part, attracted students to her various training programs by word of mouth rather than by advertising. It has always been the fact that her students get results that have kept her programs at the forefront of similar developmental programs. While others may promise, her techniques deliver.

In 1980 Patricia began to realize a need for a more central location for her activities and found it in Durham, North Carolina. As she felt the energy of water necessary for her continued spiritual healing activities, she chose to establish her retreat center on a lovely lake in the foothills of the Georgia mountains, north of Atlanta.

While many persons study with Patricia to become professional mediums, this is not the sole purpose of the instruction. Patricia comments, ''Mediumship is a way of life anyway. It's channeling, using your higher qualities, beginning to be aware of quality in everything you do. I am very much a practical teacher. If it is not practical, then what good is it? Healing can be very practical to the person who's helped.''

Although Patricia has also taken her teachings to various business organizations, she admits that this is not one of her favorite things.

The source of Patricia's knowledge can be expressed in a single word—meditation. ''Back when I started, twenty-five years ago, there were not a lot of teachers around. The ones that were in India you had no access to. I learned a method of meditation that Arthur had taught me years ago. I used to meditate once a day for a good hour when the kids were asleep in the afternoon.''

As an adjunct to meditation, Patricia has also relied on the ancient Indian art of psychic breathing, *pranayama*, which can be used to increase the intuitive faculties. Of this she says, ''There is a little book called *Science of Breath*, by Yogi Ramacharaka. The first three years I got involved with this, I used it religiously and practiced. I recommend this book all over the place. Because it's short, people will read it. And if they do those methods of breathing, they find out they will get results.''

Around 1973, Patricia found herself writing after her daily meditations, but not with the intent of producing automatic writing. Rather, she was simply trying to capture what had come through in meditation—when something or someone began to take over her pencil and write on its own. This ability greatly increased over the years and now serves as the primary method for Patricia to channel various works, such as *The Gatekeeper,* which she authored in 1980.

While Patricia's teachings have evolved primarily out of her own experience, she has made it her business to read all the Eastern philosophies and did at one time study Silva Mind Control, which she says was "fine, but not my particular interest . . . a kind of different thing.''

It was not from any one teaching that she gained the techniques that she now uses, but rather from her interaction, experimentation, and observation of what took place in the various groups she leads.

On this point she comments, "I gained a lot of experience from working with groups. I would see things in people and would express that to them and watch what that would bring out. If you were to ask me what my greatest gift is, I would have to say, 'Bringing out the best gifts in other people!' Everybody has their own niche or special skill and that happens to be mine. A lot of people wouldn't like that particularly, they would want one of their own. Sure I do readings and therapy. But if you ask me what I do best, it would be to put people in touch with their own abilities.''

As is often the case with the working of spirit, when the disciple is ready, the master will appear. For Patricia, her ability to channel coincided with her visit to the Great Pyramid of Giza. She had gone to Egypt to write a book on the investigation of psychic energy. While returning on the airplane, she began to channel what later became her book *The Gatekeeper.* Of this trip she recalls, "When I went over there, the energy was so strong. My energy was activated. I was extremely psychic. This happened one other time when I worked with dolphins at the University of Miami. When I worked with the dolphins I found myself totally, totally psychic. I could see thought forms, I could read people's minds. This was because I was working with mental communication at the time.''

While Patricia began her teachings with instruction in all aspects of mediumship and channeling alone, in recent years she has developed a totally new system of psychotherapy for personal growth and change, based on the relationship of an individual to his or her energy field. This new therapy she calls Ro-Hun, after the name of the guide who first channeled this method to her.

When using Ro-Hun, the therapist, through his own sensitivities, is able to identify negative thinking patterns and emotional traumas that have been stored in the client's electromagnetic energy fields, which, tradition holds, surround the physical, emotional, and spiritual bodies. Consisting of two hour-long sessions, with one or more follow-up sessions as needed, Ro-Hun therapy offers a unique way in which to get in contact with and correct deep-seated blockages that may even have their origin in other lifetimes.

Ro-Hun therapists are trained in a year-long internship program, followed by continuing education and annual recertification. For the most part, students seeking to become Ro-Hun therapists have already completed the sixty-hour Mediumship Development Training originally offered by the Arthur Ford Academy.

The way in which Ro-Hun Therapy came into being in the first place is intimately tied to Patricia's development. In her own words: ''When *The Gatekeeper* came through, in three months it was written. There was a character in that book that came through called Dr. Ro-Hun, which I didn't then have any knowledge of. It was just a name. The Gatekeeper came through and said he wanted to bring through this information on holistic health. I was not even interested in holistic health. When I read that book I marvel that they could even get the information through me.

''Dr. Ro-Hun was the second one through and I remember saying to the Gatekeeper I wouldn't have much patience with him. I'm glad that he isn't working with me all the time. He had a very research type of stiff mind. I like a flowing type of telepathic approach.''

According to Patricia, Dr. Ro-Hun told her that he was over on the fifth dimension and that he was researching particular thought patterns. He said that his name was chosen to symbolize a particular vibrational energy. "Ro is my sound and Hun is my profession." he told her. "We choose our names differently than you do. We choose the first sound of our name for the frequency of vibration and the second sound for our chosen mission. Ro will be recognized by others on the same frequency and Hun is my profession, which is the study of health."

About six months after *The Gatekeeper* was published, Dr. Ro-Hun again came through to Patricia and began to dictate techniques that now serve as the basis for Ro-Hun Therapy, in much the same way that Arthur Ford had given Patricia the techniques and charts that she uses to develop mediumship.

Of his initial instructions to her, Patricia recalls, "He came through with the exact method of therapy and said, 'If you begin to experiment with this therapy and use it exactly as I give it to you, for we have researched it on this side, you will find miraculous results. Most of the therapies and most of the things that are out there today have been watered down, a little bit of this and a little bit of that. Use this exactly and begin your research now!'"

Since Patricia is first and foremost a scientist, she did not announce Ro-Hun Therapy until she had the opportunity to begin testing the various techniques herself. "I didn't even want to tell other people about it until I experimented with it. First, because he said that if you didn't know what you are doing, it could be dangerous since you are working with the energy field."

After a lengthy time of experimenting on her own with various cases from germ phobia to acne, Patricia once again, as she had done when she had received the special instruction in mediumship development, called together a group of six students to share with them what Dr. Ro-Hun had taught her.

Of this early experimentation, Patricia comments, "I was following *exactly* what he said and making sure I did it *exactly* and measuring the results. We had a one-week follow-up, a one-month, and three-month, and a six-month."

For those readers who may still be confused as to exactly what

Ro-Hun is, Patricia has offered the following clarification: "Ro-Hun Therapy is based on the theory that we are 'energy.' Within our chakras [energy vortices], many times thought patterns get locked in there. Somebody could have told you, or you could have watched your father take advantage of women, and you could have thought that was you. So you will take in that thought pattern and it becomes a part of your experience. When you get into this, it is almost like a psychic surgeon uses surgery. You are cutting emotions, the energy. What happens is the energy begins to bubble up, loosen, almost to form an ice block and then images begin to come, past images. And they come to the client, and they come to the therapist. The therapist's energy is locked in with the patient's, so the therapist must be psychic in order to interpret and redirect this energy to bring about a healing."

As of this writing, there are only fifty-six Ro-Hun therapists who have been certified and are practicing in the United States. Recently, a number of psychiatrists who expressed an interest in Ro-Hun were required to complete the basic course in mediumship development in order to develop the skills needed for Ro-Hun. Patricia refers to this requirement as "boot camp."

In the last four years, Patricia has become more and more selective as to who will be admitted to this special training. "If we keep it pure, the therapy will be pure," she is quick to say.

Due to the intensive nature of Ro-Hun training, at this time the cost for the initial one-week training, including room and board at the Delphi Mountain Retreat, is $1,200. The three additional one-week trainings, which are spaced out over the course of a year, cost $800 each.

After completing these courses, students may be certified and can begin their own practice as Ro-Hun therapists, generally charging fees of $300 for the three basic therapy sessions.

While Ro-Hun therapy is a "no contact" energy therapy, the clients nonetheless actually "feel" what is taking place within their bodies, which, according to Patricia, is "a mind blower for a lot of people."

"The therapists we have love their work," Patricia is quick to add. "I would honestly say, Ro-Hun is work. When you are doing Ro-Hun Therapy, you are using everything you've got—your body, mind, and soul. Your hands are moving very quickly. You are in total psychic attunement with that person. You might sit over a position and you will be so in the flow that you will not feel your body for an hour and a half."

According to Patricia, the Ro-Hun process releases thought forms that have substance, but not as we know matter. Unlike other therapies that take months, or even years, to bring about change, Ro-Hun brings immediate changes in intimate relationships, in how people relate and communicate with people they haven't seen in a while and with their families.

"When I am able to get something loose, and you start talking about it and go through the release process, so to speak, the energy field of that person goes just like a 'poof.' There's a poof," Patricia added.

When I suggested to Patricia that her work might be a combination of psychic surgery and the old mesmeric techniques that everyone tried to disprove, her response was simply, "Exactly."

"Ro-Hun is not a marathon of pain. A lot of people in the beginning think that getting the garbage out has to be painful. When you get some of those lower chakras unblocked, the energy starts to flow up to the higher ones. It puts a person in touch with his own spiritual condition. And this is where I think Jung left off. In other words, they can begin to feel that spiritual vitality. When I reach the higher self, I am home free!"

Patricia now believes that if you want to know why the outer world is like it is, you simply have to practice Ro-Hun a while. "It's all in there," she says, referring to the blocked energy patterns.

The key to success in Ro-Hun Therapy, Patricia says, is "really caring about people and wanting to help." She adds, "You are not going to open up your deepest thoughts to me unless you can feel my total love and my total caring, and you can feel it in the energy at the time. That's why traditional therapists couldn't touch it, because they are working on the conscious level."

While Ro-Hun is similar to past-lives therapy, which can yield information about the repetition of certain emotional patterns, the latter does not give the insight, or better yet, the emotional release that Ro-Hun does. It is dealing with the thought pattern that has created the past *or* present life reality that is crucial. This Ro-Hun both elucidates and releases.

According to Patricia, it really doesn't matter how many lifetimes ago an emotionally blocking event took place. As long as that thought pattern has persisted, it must be recognized and released.

Sometimes the client, although recognizing the blockage, refuses to let it go. When this happens, it is the task of the Ro-Hun therapist to work with that refusal to let go on the part of the client until the release actually takes place. This, no doubt, is what makes Ro-Hun Therapy "hard work."

"The therapists are trained not to listen to the client's words, but to be sensitive to the energy," Patricia added. "When I say, 'I feel free,' I can either *feel* it or just *say* it. The therapist is trained to feel the shift in the energy."

Little by little, various psychologists and psychiatrists are beginning to learn of the Ro-Hun work and ask for introductory lectures. Recently, Patricia spoke to such a group in Hawaii and had twenty-eight of the forty present sign up for the program.

Of Ro-Hun, the entity, Patricia says, "He is still studying. He continues to give us what I call advanced processes. It is interesting, because he only gives them after we perfect one and learn to work with it. Then another one is given. This is very practical in a way. If you gave somebody everything at one time, they wouldn't know the value of what they were working with."

Of the phenomenon of channeling in general, Patricia's only comment is that "some people are so involved in hearing 'his' wisdom, they forget that they have their own." This, Patricia feels, is also the problem with gurus!

On why there has been so much automatic writing of late, Patricia offered the following: "I feel there is an united effort by those on the other side. I'm not just talking about the other side, though, because there are channels of healing here too. There is a united effort. Look at the practical aspects. Information is coming through many people by automatic writing. It's basically all practical, at least the information I have channeled.''

As to the question whether or not Patricia feels her work is a natural evolution of spiritualism, she responded, ''Yes, I do. I feel that part of the education is going to come through books, through writers, through beginning to educate as they [i.e., readings] entertain a little as they intrigue people. . . . When you write a book you are a channel in a sense.''

Recently, Patricia and her husband published a new book, *Extension of Life: Arthur Ford Speaks*, which they cochanneled. In this unusual work, Ford presents a series of messages concerning the survival of consciousness after body-death. According to Patricia, Ford told her before he passed away that if there was any way in which he could make contact with her, he would. He seems to have kept his promise.

In bringing our discussion to a close, Patricia shared the following observations: ''People are in a new readiness. Look at what Shirley MacLaine has done. There is more of a need for channels today because there are more people questioning; there are more people asking for answers. For everyone who asks a question, there has got to be someone out there they can come to.''

What Patricia said she was looking for in the future was not the doubling of her students but rather the production of a better quality student, which in her definition means a more caring person. Originally, those who came to her many classes were seeking to simply become psychic. Now, since the channeling of Ro-Hun, the ''goodies'' have been taken out, and it's just plain, hard work. ''Today, mediumship has gone beyond the spiritualist camp, and it is out there, and mediums are serving different roles,'' Patricia said.

When I asked Patricia what she thought the future was for such spiritualist camps as Chesterfield and Lily Dale, ''part of our history'' was her answer.

When I asked Patricia to describe herself in a few sentences, this is what she said: ''I care. I feel great purpose. I have a real curious mind and don't think I know everything. I'm open to learning. If I feel something, I act on it, and stay in strong touch with my feelings. I'm not in this for where it's going to take me. I'm not interested in fame. I'm just interested in these things. I'm happy, so I'm free. Because of that I am free to truly be able to probe some of the things I want to probe and to try and get some answers. I've always had this thing that if I find something out for myself, the first thing I want to do is to share it. I've also always had the true knowledge within me that if I can do it, so can anybody else. And I can see the beauty in people. It's very easy for me to look beyond the surface of the misery and really see the light.''

16

Robert W. Johnson: From Agnostic to Spiritualist

There is no particular group to which God belongs.
Though others would like you to believe this
  when they sing
    their particular songs.

God cannot be contained in a manmade tabernacle
  or church.
For God lies in truth within man,
  that is where
    you must search.

—Robert W. Johnson,
"GOD, TRUTH AND SEARCH"

While many persons are led to spiritualism and mediumship after participating in such spiritual practices as meditation, sometimes a person who has no spiritual life whatsoever finds himself cast into the realm of spirit without any advance preparation.

One such person is Robert W. Johnson, whose conversion to spiritualism after thirty years of agnosticism is indeed a strange story.

"I was agnostic until I was thirty," says Bob with an intriguing smile. "It was all right for you to believe in God, but leave me out of the thing. I was married at age twenty and from about twenty-two things were really not going that well. While I had a very good knack for getting jobs, I didn't have a knack for keeping them."

168

Photo: Ronnie Ginnever

According to Bob, he and his wife, Alice, were in a real tight financial bind. They were about to be dispossessed from their home. He didn't know what to do.

Although he had been born into the Catholic faith, he had never believed in nor practiced it. Yet for some reason, on this occasion he was drawn to visit the Shrine of Our Lady of Lourdes in Litchfield, Connecticut. Of this Bob says, "I didn't know what to do. I wanted to see if I could figure this thing out. I didn't go because it was a shrine, but because I had been there years before and found the place very peaceful and quiet. I thought if I could get there then perhaps I could get at least one answer. I went and it was peaceful and quiet. I thought if I could get there then perhaps I could get at least one answer. I went and it was peaceful and quiet but I really couldn't get any answers."

After spending a great deal of time walking around, Bob concluded that his situation was impossible and that there was truly no way out. As he was thinking this over and over, he began to hear a voice outside himself saying, "What seems impossible is not impossible!"

Bob looked around. There was no one there, not even another person in the distance. At the time he noticed he was standing next to a statue—a statue of St. Jude, patron saint of hopeless cases.

"Who do you tell you heard a voice?" Bob thought.

He went home and on the way decided to tell his wife, who said, "Bob, if you heard a voice, you heard a voice!"

With this Bob realized that one of his problems was that everything had to be logical, black or white, and that throughout his entire life he had never allowed gray areas to exist in his thinking!

He said to Alice, "Do we have any money at all?"

"Ten dollars," was Alice's reply. She had been saving it for a book.

Bob said to her, "Why don't we take this ten dollars and send it in the name of St. Jude someplace?"

They picked Graymoor, a Catholic retreat in Garrison, New York, and off it went in the name of St. Jude. Whenever they got two, three, or four dollars together, off it went in the name of St.

Jude. By the end of the year, strange as it appeared to Bob, he and Alice were current in their debts for the first time.

Looking back, Bob says, "I don't think it was the money itself. It was just a step to faith. We actually had enough money to put a deposit down on a house. It was like the pits up to the light! But I still wasn't sure that this had anything to do with spirit."

Bob figured that things had turned around simply because he had changed his thinking. He had also changed his job. Instead of selling bread, he was now selling cars and had become an overnight success.

As the years went by, every once in a while, Bob would ask Alice if she sent any money to St. Jude. When she said she had forgotten, Bob told her to do so. His sales had dropped! One time, Bob even drove all the way to Garrison to personally drop off some money. If something works, why not use it?

One day Alice read in the newspaper about an upcoming workshop on ESP (extrasensory perception), which she knew Bob was interested in. Although the workshop was being held in the Dutch Reformed Church in Brewster, New York, Bob was assured that it had nothing to do with spirit or God. The instructor, Donald Battey, was just renting a room. "All right," he said to his wife. "Send the money and I'll go."

When Bob arrived at the class, he found himself face to face with Battey, "with this big cross on his chest." Bob said to himself, "Oh boy. Here it goes. More of this religious stuff."

Since he had already prepaid the course, Bob, in his own words, was "cheap enough to stay." While in the main, the course proved unfruitful, toward the end of the day instructor Battey announced that they would now work with psychometry, the psychic faculty of mentally inducing perceptions of people from objects they have worn or handled.

Bob recalls his experience as follows: "I took a ring from this woman who was sitting on my right and held it. I started seeing these pictures—a house on top of a cliff. I saw waves breaking down at the bottom of the cliff. When I explained to the woman what I saw, she said, 'That's a house in Maine. I was there last week. I was thinking of buying that house. Because of what you saw, I'm going to buy it!' I said to her, 'If you want to do that lady, go ahead. That's just my imagination.' "

After this class, a woman came up to Bob and asked if he was interested in participating in a Spiritual Frontiers Fellowship study group. Again, as soon as he heard "spiritual," his answer was "Not particularly."

Her response was, "We meditate there." Since Bob had never meditated and was assured they would teach him at this group, he agreed to attend. The night of the meeting, Bob drove some twenty miles. At this point in his life he found it somewhat devastating to enter the house only to realize that he was the only man in a group of ten to twelve women.

When the actual study period began and a book, *Search for God*, was brought out, Bob was again devastated but resolved he would simply sit the evening out and never return. (The book was on Edgar Cayce, but Bob didn't know it at the time.)

After the study period was over, the meditation period was announced, and Bob was told the lights would be turned out, after which each person would say their mantra and begin to meditate.

"What's a mantra?" Bob asked.

"A word or phrase or sound that makes you relax," was the response.

Recalling what happened next, Bob says, "They turned the lights out and I was sitting there in the dark thinking, 'This is stupid. I don't know how to meditate. Nothing is ever going to happen. It's impossible . . . impossible? All right, I'll use St. Jude as my mantra.'

"So I was sitting in the dark going 'St. Jude, St. Jude, St. Jude' over and over again. I was starting to get bored with this thing when all of a sudden, like watching television, I started to see pictures rolling, rolling so fast I couldn't recognize them."

Suddenly, the picture Bob saw began to slow down, and he felt himself begin to move out of the living room in which he sat, through the two French doors, and out into the street. He moved along the street to a *cul de sac* and proceeded toward a house. He rose from ground level and went through the attic window. Once there, he looked around, noting the arrangement of the chairs, a day bed, and a stairwell with light down below. What caught his attention was an unusual light fixture without a globe. There was just a shade stuck on it. The walls had plastic brick that if poked would buckle in.

The next thing he knew, he was back in the living room. The lights had been turned on and everyone was commenting on what they had seen in their meditation. For the most part, those gathered had simply seen various symbols, angels, castles in the sky, mostly beautiful things! Bob's reaction to all this was simply, "That's their imagination!"

When Bob started telling the group about the attic he had seen, you could have heard a pin drop. Unknown to him was the fact that this very group met every other week in that very attic room.

When Bob returned the following week, he saw the attic in person, exactly as he had seen it in his meditation. While he was now willing to admit that there might be something to meditation, he still refused to connect what he did with the world of spirit or God.

Although far from being a believer, Bob nonetheless set a discipline for himself of meditating daily, and he continued to attend the study group every week, for a period of several years.

On one occasion, a flash of white light that he had often seen appeared and stayed, and he felt that he was in the presence of something very great. This was the beginning of what might be called Bob's conversion from nonbelief to belief.

Although up to this time, Bob's ability as a clairvoyant had been increasing in leaps and bounds, after the white light experience his abilities suddenly stopped, without prior notice or explanation. No longer could he see anything while in the meditative state.

How did Bob feel when he suddenly lost his gift? He recalls, "I felt all right, but nobody else liked it. People looked forward to me telling them certain things." Unlike many persons who would abandon their pursuit, Bob continued his meditation and attendance at various groups, even though he was no longer able to do readings for others.

Finally one day, while in group meditation, he was told by spirit to open his eyes, which he had just closed. When he did this, he saw across the room a cloudlike white haze that moved toward him and entered into him. In his own words, "It was almost as if my stomach was being pushed into my backbone." According to Bob, this experience did not hurt but was rather like a pressure.

When he came out of the meditation, he had decided not to mention this to anyone in the group when his wife said, "What was that?" She had also felt a compulsion to open her eyes and had seen the haze move across the room and enter into Bob. Up to this moment, Alice had never seen spirit forms, auras, or any manifestation. This was a first for her.

Though Bob had had yet another real psychic experience, and one which had been seen by Alice, he was not yet aware of the exact nature of the entity who had passed into him. It was not until a few weeks later that the real significance of this experience was made known to him.

Bob recalls his second close encounter as follows: "It was a couple of weeks later that they first came through. The first thing they said was that this body, meaning me, was not possessed. From that point, they appeared in the next group again and explained they were angels and messengers of God and that they had come to teach. It just went on from that point to now years later."

As to the exact nature of these angels, Bob says, "They don't give their names as particular entities. You can call any one of them and the number is vast. You can call any one of them Angel Constantine which means constant messenger. The reason they don't give a name is that they say we as human beings have a tendency to call on names rather than to call on God."

In order to evoke the presence of the Angels Constantine, Bob first says a prayer and then enters into meditation, during which time they appear and speak through him.

The prayer Bob uses to evoke their presence is as follows:

> Our Father who Is and lives throughout the universe, we honor your Holy Name.

We pray that your kingdom be recognized soon upon this earth, as it is throughout the universe. Give to us today that which we need to sustain our bodies so that we may carry forth your truth. Forgive our ignorance of the ways of others as we forgive those who are ignorant of our ways. Let us not walk the path of Life in Darkness but shed your light upon the Path so that we may clearly see that the Kingdom, the Power, and the Glory are yours, Forever.

Bob says of this particular prayer that it may have no special significance. He simply feels comfortable with it and has used it for many years now.

Of the appearance of the angels, Bob states, "I never expected this to happen. It would be the last thing I would imagine. I didn't just start doing people. Once a week I would go to this group and then we would come out and give some teachings. Eventually it came to the point that one night a young girl asked a question and they said that the answer was personal and she should meet with me privately. And that's how that started." And so it was that Bob the agnostic car salesman found himself the channel for angelic beings.

Once he enters the trance state, after reciting the prayer and entering meditation, he remembers absolutely nothing of what questions he has been asked, nor what answers or teachings have been given out. Although his readings are generally an hour in duration, his recollection of them is as if they were simply a few minutes long.

Since Bob has no recall of what has taken place, he says he enjoys hearing the tapes of his client's sessions when they wish to share them with him. On first hearing these tapes, Bob says he "felt funny," but now he has accepted his unusual gift. Unlike many other mediums or psychics, Bob does not go to others for readings but rather feels that anything he may want or need will be supplied.

Once Bob was a guest on a television show and subsequently got the opportunity to see himself at work. After viewing the segment in which he was in trance, he says he "liked it. It was like watching me, a twin, same features, same structure but used differently. It was really fascinating."

Bob finds he can do only four readings per day and finds it necessary to schedule an hour between each one for relaxation. On one occasion, he found himself scheduled to do five or six readings, one after the other. He describes this experience as having been "weird," saying "everything just shot by. I can't do that." No doubt, his time/space perceptions had been greatly disturbed.

Upon questioning, Bob suggests his unusual abilities are due to work he has done in prior lifetimes. The reason he chose the path of the agnostic was that he had done this same kind of work in other times and had been severely persecuted as a result. (One of Bob's previous life recollections is that of being burned at the stake for his beliefs.) Hence, his soul chose to deny the reality of God and spirit until he reached a stage in his development in this lifetime when he could again handle the experience.

Bob has no personal recollection of the exact nature of the angelic beings that speak through him, since he is always in deep trance. According to Alice, there are about fifteen different entities, all male: This is the case "simply because I am male," according to Bob.

Of their nature, Alice says, "They have explained they are a Holy College. More exact definition would be a tutelage. They won't say how many are in [the tutelage], but it is a large amount. Most of them have not incarnated, but there are a few who have. They have said that he [Bob] is the only one they work with as a group. Some of them as individual entities do speak through other mediums, but he is the only one they speak through as a body."

In the beginning of his channeling the tutelage, a great deal of poetry came through that was used as a way to give messages. Bob, personally, has no interest whatsoever in poems or poets.

Of the changes that have come to his life as a result of his mediumship, Bob says, "I am not the same person I was. My whole understanding of the world is different than it was. My whole handling, my expression to the world, is different."

In order to further the direction his life was taking, Bob eventually affiliated with the International Church of Ageless Wisdom in Philadelphia, which had been founded by Beth Hand, and was in time ordained as a minister. In 1978, because of his work and dedication to the church, he was elevated to the position of canon, was consecrated bishop in March 1984, and served on the synod, the governing body of the church.

Like others who have chosen the work of spirit, Bob's relationship with his family has changed from what it was originally. He was asked to coofficiate at the Catholic wedding of a niece a few years ago which he considered both a great honor as well as some recognition of his work by his family.

"It is not that they would participate," Bob was quick to add. "Over the years, they have come to understand that it's good work."

Recently, one of Bob's brothers passed into spirit. As is usually the case with Bob, when someone close to him passes on, near the time of their transition he sees them walking down the street as if they were alive. This happens to him while he is conscious and often in full daylight.

Unlike other mediums, Bob does not see auras as expressed in color, but rather he sees an energy field.

Of this Bob smiles and says, "I guess in my own right, though I don't practice it, I am psychic. All of a sudden I know and I feel."

Of the distinction between psychics and mediumship, Bob says that the former are using their own facilities and are always conscious of what they are sensing. The latter, Bob says, is more in the nature of spiritual guidance.

Again, unlike fortunes, Bob's readings do not tell a person exactly what's going to happen in the future. Rather, they offer guidance that provides the listener with the tools to solve his own problems. Sometimes the origin of a problem may even be another lifetime. According to Bob's and the tutelage's philosophy, the future is not preordained. One is simply sending out vibrations to create that future. Change the vibrations and the future is changed accordingly.

On Thursday evenings, Bob and Alice, who is an ordained minister, hold a weekly service at the Beth Hand Chapel in Highland, New York, which was founded by them. During his service, Bob will teach, followed by a meditation during which he often will go into trance and present a general message to those assembled.

Like others who have gone before him, Bob has maintained the primacy of meditation in his personal devotions. At about eight o'clock each morning, he sets a half hour timer, and enters the meditative state as he has done for many years now. When the need is felt, an additional meditation period may be added in the later afternoon or evening. His habit of using a timer, both for himself and when he reads for others, is one of long-standing and, like his prayer, simply works for him!

While Bob, like many other mediums, once toyed with the idea of having a large spiritual center where people of like mind could congregate and work together, he eventually reached the conclusion that in the finality the work of spirit is very individualistic and essentially one-on-one.

When asked how his work differed from that of other mediums, he answered, "I don't really call myself a fortune teller, a psychic as such. It's real spiritual. When I say spiritual I don't mean anything phoney or out of this world. I mean it's good, solid advice how people can become spiritual themselves . . . how to make the spirit which is *in* you, work with you. While other people talk about guides, the tutelage says that the ultimate guide is your own spirit!"

To date, Robert has channeled two books, *Mystical Thoughts for Meditation: He Sends You Knowledge* (1980), which is a collection of inspirational poetry, and *The Letter of the Law and the Lore of the Letter* (1981), a description of the esoteric meaning of each letter of the alphabet.

Again, like other mediums, Bob confessed to not following what he himself was told "unless Alice forces me to." Nor does he believe it necessary to follow a particular diet to do the work that he does.

As to whether anyone could learn to do what he does, Bob answered as follows, "No, I think everybody has gifts. I don't think that everyone should try to do something like this. They should try and find out what their gift is. I think we are all somewhat psychic. I think we are all somewhat healers but some of us have more power

in that area than others. I think that one of the reasons I am doing
this, and continue to do it, is that when I come out of trance, I have
no curiosity. I think too many people have too much curiosity."

At the end of our meeting, I asked Bob to describe himself. He
said, "I guess my thrust is that I truly want to see the best for
people. Hopefully, they will find out *who* they are, and start living
with that being *which* they are, rather than *what* other people want
them to be. In other words, that they become their own being.
That's my thrust, that's what I want. I want people, not necessarily
to believe in this God or that God but believe that there is this
tremendous, tremendous power that can really, really work through
them and be used. Not just have someone tell them about God but
have them experience it."

17

Gretchen C. Lazarony: It's Just a Family Tradition

*You are a Spirit. You have no limits. You can do any-
thing. What you have to teach people is to believe it . . .
to know that they are a spirit and not a body. The ability
is there. You just have to regain it. . . . Yesterday is a
canceled check. Tomorrow is a promissory note. Today
is ready cash.*

—Gretchen Lazarony

There is an old saying that what goes around comes around. Sometimes, though, something just "is" and seems to persist from generation to generation without the need for explanation. Often called
traditions, these habits and inclinations seem to exist in spite of
themselves. Such is the case of the strange flirtation between
Gretchen Lazarony's family and Lily Dale.

Born on August 1, in Corry, Pennsylvania, Gretchen is a fourth-
generation spiritualist on both her mother's and father's sides of the
family. She is proud of the fact that her mother and father actually
met at Lily Dale.

While Gretchen was raised in the spiritualist tradition since childhood, as were her parents, the church she first attended was of the
Methodist faith. "There were no spiritualist churches where I grew
up in Pennsylvania," she says. "But summer was always Lily
Dale."

Her mother's father, himself a spiritualist, lived a quarter of a

180

mile from her home and assumed the role of both father and grandfather when Gretchen's own father passed to the other side when she
was only ten years old.

Of her introduction into the world of spirit, Gretchen simply says,
"I know that I've always been able to do what I do. When I would
go to mother and tell her what I saw or what I heard, she would
encourage or say, 'What else did you see?' She just accepted it as
perfectly normal. Unfortunately, a lot of children get told, 'Oh, stop
imagining things' or whatever."

While both Gretchen's parents in her estimation could have
worked as mediums, they did not. Her mother was a teacher, and
her father an electrical engineer. Gretchen also has a brother, a
couple of years older, who she says "is very able" but has also
chosen not to work as a medium.

Gretchen grew up in Spartansburg, Pennsylvania, moved to Cassadaga, Buffalo, and Fredonia, New York, and in 1967 acquired her
own house in Lily Dale. Since to Gretchen spiritualism had always
been a way of life that was totally accepted, she couldn't imagine
that people couldn't do what she did as a medium.

It was only when she started school that she learned not to talk
about what she saw. On one occasion while visiting a girlfriend, she
began to describe a man she saw in the room who had had his leg
amputated, but who died anyway. It was only when her young
girlfriend became hysterical and ran to get her mother that Gretchen
realized she had said something wrong. It seems the person she had
seen was the oldest brother of her young girlfriend, a change-of-life
baby: He had died some seventeen years before in exactly the manner Gretchen described. So exact was her description of what had
taken place that her girlfriend's mother kept Gretchen from visiting
her daughter for many years. According to Gretchen, incidents such
as this continued to plague her "until I learned to keep my mouth
shut!"

Gretchen was married when she was twenty and has two children,
a boy, Jack, and a girl, Shelley. It was not until her children were
grown, though, that Gretchen decided that she would become a
professional medium and sought to register herself as such. Both of

her children were encouraged to develop their own gifts of spirit, in the same way that Gretchen had been encouraged by her parents. Of this she says, "The first time I knew that my son had any ability was when he was three or four. We were driving in Fredonia and he asked me who the lady was who had gotten into the car. He described my mother perfectly who had died when he was six months old."

Of Gretchen's mother appearing to her after her passing, Gretchen says, "I think probably I've heard more from her since she died than after I was married!"

Gretchen's daughter is herself married, while Jack, her son, has just graduated from high school and will most likely pursue a career in chiropractic, studying in Toronto. When I asked if Jack had any healing ability, Gretchen responded, "I believe a great deal. Although he doesn't do much with it, he is aware of it."

Like her parents, Gretchen met her first husband at Lily Dale. She was working at a tea shop at the time. Although she did not work actively as a medium while she was married to him, he nonetheless accepted her work. Gretchen and he were divorced in 1975.

Her second husband, according to Gretchen, accepted her ability, "but didn't know what to make of it. He was from a Presbyterian family. He was also very intuitive but didn't admit it much, or work with it much." He was killed in an automobile accident.

On that occasion Gretchen was driving her husband to work when they were struck by a car that ran a stop sign. Her husband was killed almost instantly; she was taken to the hospital, where she almost died. She remembers seeing herself outside her body and hearing the nurses talking and saying, "Don't worry, she'll be dead before two!"

"I thought," Gretchen said, " 'That's me they're talking about. The hell you say!' I remember sitting in the hospital room and looking at that body in the bed over there and directing healing. I was put on healing lists at spiritualist churches all over the country. I could see that healing energy flow into the room, and I just sort of channeled and directed it into my body."

Gretchen remembers watching the doctors as they did the surgery to rebuild her jaw, an operation that took more than six hours. She also remembers seeing her husband with her and knowing that he had crossed over. She recalls seeing her husband come into her room a number of times before she was actually told by the doctor that he had passed on.

It took Gretchen three months to recover from the accident. Speaking of its effect, Gretchen says, "It made it very real to me that you are a spirit. You are *not* a little piece of meat. You're a spirit. I knew that because I was sitting there tugging on that body lying on the bed. And I knew that if that body died, I wasn't going anywhere."

A year later she married her present husband, with whom she has been for seven years now. As Gretchen's husband is in the contracting business in Florida, they divide their time between the two places, but following the family tradition, it's always Lily Dale in the summer.

Once Gretchen reached the decision to go professional with her mediumship, she encountered mixed reactions from other family members, for even though they had been raised in the spiritualist tradition, "it was not generally accepted." Fortunately, Gretchen had her husband's total support for her new career, so off she went.

But Gretchen is unique in yet another way. Besides being a spiritualist, she is also a Scientologist, as is her husband. Of this most extraordinary combination, she says, "I am a spiritualist but I am also a Scientologist. It's a perfectly normal outbreak of spiritualism. Spiritualism . . . you deal with the spirit. People are spirit, they are not bodies. We deal with the spirit. This is what scientology does. It is simply dealing with individuals as spirit."

In 1979, Gretchen had read the book *Dianetics*, by L. Ron Hubbard, the late founder of Scientology. "I knew the man had a lot to say. He knew exactly what he was talking about and I wanted to know more about it," Gretchen added. Like spiritualism, Scientology has been surrounded with controversy and criticism from its inception.

Before deciding to become a professional medium, Gretchen had attended college in order to become an interpreter but was interrupted by marriage and having a family. Now that she is a medium, though, it is almost as if she could do nothing else. On this point, she is quick to say, "I can't imagine not doing it. I really enjoy it. It's very rewarding when someone comes who has lost someone dear to them, to be able to bring to them absolute proof that that being still *is*. Or perhaps to answer a question. Somebody has been missing . . . yes, they are alive or now they are dead."

Regarding the need for a particular spirit guide, Gretchen is one of the many who feel that this is definitely not requisite, nor is it necessarily desirable. She says, "I don't have any guide, thank you. I tune in to the individual, picking up situations they are involved in, perhaps situations with family or friends. Their spirit people do come in. Somebody who was close . . . relative, friendship ties, etc.

"My personal opinion is that you're *you*. When your physical body is gone, you are still *you*. Just because someone's in spirit doesn't make them any more knowledgeable or any less than someone who has a body. I have been in contact with several people in spirit.

"I am always willing to listen if somebody comes in with something to say, but no, I do not have a particular group nor do I believe any one *has* to!"

Gretchen adds "If you *think* you have to have guides, you do! No, I don't, thank you. One girl asked me about my guides and I told her I didn't have any, and she said, 'Well what do you do, go straight to God?' I said, 'Well, why not go right to the top?'"

As to the relatively recent phenomenon of mediums channeling various disincarnate superbeings, Gretchen holds very definite ideas: "I think P. T. Barnum said it. People can believe what they choose. They always have and will continue to do so. Why would someone who no longer has a body . . . why are they still interested? Why are they going to stick around for some of the basic garbage that people ask or want? I think if you think about it logically, perhaps you ask questions."

Like many of her contemporaries, Gretchen does not go into a trance when she reads for her various clients. Of this she says, "I prefer to be conscious and aware of what is going on."

Whether she employs clairaudience, clairsentience, or, in her

own words, "just knows," it makes no difference. As Gretchen
would say, "as long as it's accurate, who cares?"

How many readings she can do during a day without reaching
psychic overload depends on the quality of the person or persons
with whom she is working. Consecutive readings for a number of
persons who are negative seem to take much more energy than those
for positive persons who actually contribute to the readings.

"I make it a practice that if a person is not one hundred percent
satisfied with the reading, I don't want his money," Gretchen says.
"But I've never had anyone not pay me."

Gretchen makes it a habit to schedule her own appointments. If
she feels that the person making the appointment is not the kind of
person she wants to read for, she simply will not make an appointment. "Nobody makes appointments for me. I know when I am
talking with that person whether I want to do that reading or not."

Does Gretchen follow her own messages from spirit? Her answer
made sense: "You need to know who the message came from. If my
mother gave me advice on business, no way! If your Uncle Harry
was a crummy businessman, and he died four years ago and comes
and tells you to sell your business quick, because it's going down-
hill, are you going to believe him? You have to know *where* the
message comes from!

"I think I pay more attention to something I *just know*. It doesn't
necessarily come from a particular entity. It's something that's just
there and I know it!"

It's Gretchen's belief that just as the material man has five limited
senses, the senses of spirit are unlimited, because spirit itself is
unlimited. Hence when the knowledge is there, you either listen or
are sorry.

When it comes to the conflict between spiritualism and reincarnation, Gretchen's belief is that there really is no conflict. "I don't
think there is a problem. You're a spirit. Spiritualism says you're a
spirit. There are National Spiritualists, people belonging to the General Assembly—like any orthodox religion, there are Baptists,
Methodists, Presbyterians—they are all Protestants. The language
of spirit is telepathy."

Unless a reincarnating spirit has become so immersed in its new identity, it could still make contact with another person through telepathy, even though it is no longer in the world of spirit, according to Gretchen. Hence, it would be possible for someone to make spirit contact, under some circumstances, forever, though the contact might not be of the same quality one might enjoy before a soul has chosen to reincarnate.

Speaking of the various opinions held by spiritualists, Gretchen commented, "It's something you can't really prove. Some people who have read Jess Stern's books on reincarnation, like *The Girl with the Blue Eyes*, would say that's *proof* of reincarnation and other people would say that's merely a *good medium*. You can't really prove it!"

Adding to these thoughts, Gretchen continued, concerning her own previous-life memories: "I haven't looked for proof, no. I do have names and dates, yes. In one lifetime in particular, I could probably trace it but why? I'm just not interested enough to do that. It doesn't really prove anything. Your life is now and tomorrow. Yesterday is interesting, but that's all it is. What's important is now and tomorrow. That you can control. Yesterday is done."

One of the things Gretchen speaks freely of is her sharing with other mediums: "I suppose like anybody in any profession you have to have people who do the same things, so you can basically relax and talk. We do talk shop because unless you are with another medium or someone who understands, you can't talk about that aspect of your life. One of the things I miss in Florida is the companionship with other mediums. If I was to sit down and talk to somebody else like I talk to some of my friends here, they'd think I was crazy. They have no reality on it."

Gretchen says among her medium friends, the split is about 50/50 in terms of those who believe in previous lives and those who do not.

Like others in the same field, Gretchen's children come to her from time to time to ask her opinions of various personal situations. She recalls that when Jack was younger one of his friends was not permitted to come play with him because they lived in Lily Dale.

"The devil will get you when you go through the gates," they told him.

"They had to deal with that," said Gretchen. "It was a bit irritating to them, I know, when they were growing up. I could usually tell when they were lying about something important, because there would be a little flash in the aura. I would just know it!"

While various mediums often attach special meanings to the auras of their clients, which they can readily see, Gretchen's views on this matter are indeed unique.

"I have always seen auras my whole life," she says. "It's been my observation that it's about as important as the color of your hair. What does a blue aura mean? It means your aura is *blue*."

It is the clarity of the aura, not the specific color, that Gretchen feels is significant. The clarity and the strength of the aura mean something, according to her way of thinking, but she does not read auras as others would.

"Sometimes it's just being aware of the emanation. It's an energy field. Any organism has an aura. The atoms are in motion. In auras, we are basically talking about the 'body,' the body aura. How significant is that? It is significant as far as the body is concerned, but it doesn't have anything to do with your spiritual development because *you are not a body!*"

Gretchen has not chosen to seek ordination by any particular spiritualist church, though she has been certified by the N.A.S.C. While she has been offered numerous ordinations, it is her belief that to accept this without making the commitment that comes with the day-to-day operation of a church would be wrong. "It's a way of life. It's something you need to be fully committed to. I don't choose to make that type of commitment," she says. Asked whether having a certificate of ordination would make her work any different, Gretchen quickly responds, "All Catholics aren't priests."

While there have been attempts on the part of various spiritualist organizations to better educate their clergy and healers, according to Gretchen such programs are meeting with resistance "because people don't want to put in the time and effort to really *know* what they

———— ○ ————

are doing." In her words, "They want the reward without the effort. This is a fast-food world, unfortunately!"

Other than abstaining from the use of alcohol while she is working with clients, Gretchen does not follow or advocate any particular dietary habits. "Alcohol inhibits your perceptions," she says. "It seems to get the body in the way of it. When I work I am outside the body. I don't stay 'in' the body, I step outside."

When I asked Gretchen exactly where she saw herself going with her mediumship, she suddenly became very quiet and then answered, "I wish I knew the answer to that. I don't know."

"I am doing what I enjoy doing. I am doing what my life has made easily attainable to me at this point. I have the abilities I have. I'm here, so I'm working as a medium. I don't know where I'm going."

While Gretchen admits that she could not imagine herself not working as a medium, she experiences an uncomfortable feeling as she looks ahead in time. She doesn't believe she can be truly happy or satisfied with what she might be doing unless she uses the abilities she has. "Like anything else, if you have abilities you want to use them," she says.

Gretchen is also bothered by the fact that to the extent that she and her work become better known, her privacy shrinks. "Here in Lily Dale in the evening, if I want to sit on my porch and relax, I can't unless I hang a sign in the window that says, 'No readings.' I can't walk around in the afternoon and have people recognize me without running after me. Even if I go down to Fredonia, Jamestown, or even Buffalo, people will recognize me and come over and chat about that reading or what you told me. . . . I don't like that! I like my privacy. I'm a private person and much prefer to keep a low profile."

Especially bothersome to Gretchen is what she feels is the overemphasis on the body to the detriment of the teachings of spirit. An example of this would be the exhaustive attention placed on the physical body by various exercise programs and diets.

"I'm afraid I don't think it's enough," she says, referring to the current interest in spiritual things. "I'm afraid I don't think it's going to do the trick. I feel very pessimistic about where this world can be going if we don't very quickly regain our perspective.

"This is another reason why I am a Scientologist, because Scientology is spreading worldwide and is actively working to say, 'You are a spirit. You are not a body.' Spiritualism is not an evangelical movement.

"I know people talk about the 'good old days.' They were what they were. Times have changed. The good old days were good days, but they were different days. You can't go back to that. The world has changed. We don't need to go back to that. We are dealing with today. What worked sixty years ago won't work today."

While Gretchen cannot imagine ever selling her house or not spending summers in Lily Dale, since she and her husband's families have been there so long, she is not satisfied with spiritualism as a philosophy because "it's not expanding."

"I think this is because people have accepted just so much, and think that's it. There are cycles. You start, you change, you stop. Spiritualism started, it changed. But it hasn't changed for a long time. Unless there is change and growth, you're stagnant. The world is going. If spiritualism isn't going, even if it's just standing still, in a sense it's going backward . . . because the rest of the world is going on."

As to whether spiritualism is a philosophy or a religion, Gretchen would suggest the latter. "It's a religion," she says. "It simply proves that you are a spirit. You don't have to accept it on faith. Spiritualism proves it. That's the difference between spiritualism and most other religions."

Bringing our discussion to an end, I asked Gretchen to describe herself as others might. Here's what she said: "That I was honest, accurate. That I provided guidance and help. That I enriched, helped, or encouraged a lot. Basically, that someone was glad that they had been in contact with me."

Being born to the manor is not always an easy task. For with it comes responsibilities to all creatures here below. For Gretchen, the mantle of spirit was woven the day the Fox sisters heard their first rappings. While where her journey may ultimately take her is yet unknown, that she *is* traveling is without dispute. *Omnia tempus revelat* might best be her motto.

A NOTE
FROM THE AUTHOR

———o———

The three interviews that follow describe practices that represent a departure from the normally accepted practice of mediumship in which the medium would make contact with spirit guides of the client or use his own guide or guides in spirit to bring forth information in the reading. Normally, such a reading would answer specific questions posed by the client rather than address a group of persons in order to present a particular teaching or philosophy.

While the history of spiritualism has seen mediums who taught while in trance, the last decade has seen the emergence of what has been called channeling rather than mediumship as a major trend in the evolution of spiritualism.

The late Jane Roberts, who channeled the entity Seth and who authored many books describing Seth's philosophy, did much to bring this particular trend to popular prominence.

While technically speaking it may be said that everyone who is a medium channels information from someone or someplace to someone, those who practice this *new* work would prefer to be called channels rather than mediums. There is a marked difference in the type of material that is brought forth by these daughters and sons of Aquarius. Considerations such as selling a house or finding a new love interest or a better job now play second fiddle to the discovery of the truth of one's being.

That the entities or beings channeled have decidedly distinct personalities and histories, usually greatly removed from that of their mediums, suggests a need to reexamine Carl G. Jung's concept of the Collective Unconscious or the ancient Indian concept of the Akashic Records in this new context.

One thing is certain: The phenomenon of channeling will by all indications continue to increase in the years to come, bringing with it an assortment of philosophies of being like no others in history. What this will mean for us as individual spirits—or to the history of religion or spiritualism—cannot yet be seen.

Surely the axiom "The greater the light the greater the shadow" is more than relevant in this instance.

—Zolar

18

Linda Willows

There is a "teacher" within each of us. First learn to meditate, to learn to reach the source within you, to learn to reach the place in you that has the teaching, that has the wisdom, that has the Truth. When you have a question, you can go within to find the answer. Sometimes on that journey to the place of Truth within each person, they will encounter a spiritual teacher or a guide. But they haven't encountered him because that's their purpose. They encountered him like a friend on the Road to Truth, both walking the same way. That guide or teacher may be well ahead of you and will turn around to help.

—Linda Willows

Linda Willows is bothered by the overuse of the word *psychic*, which she thinks is a remnant of the 1960s and 1970s. She would prefer to call herself a channel—an appellation that can be shared with her mother and sister, who also can do what she does.

"By channel I would see it as a vessel that has the ability to allow something to move through me. So I allow the intelligence and the energy of RW, who is the teacher who speaks through me, to use me as a channel for his teaching," says Linda.

Linda has in her own mind been doubly blessed for she has had two remarkable teachers, her mother, Eunice Zimmerman, who she considers "philosophically always expanding" and RW, her "spiritual teacher." "I consider myself very fortunate to be in life where

I can get to talk to Eunice," she is quick to add. She has never called her mother Mom, but prefers to call her Eunice, since she is "not an average kind of woman."

She and her sister were educated by Eunice in what Linda would call a "philosophy of life" that perceives life as "continuous." As young girls she and her sister were so deliberately exposed to all religions that at the ages of eight and nine, respectively, they chose to call themselves universalists, certainly a heavy handle for two very young women.

"We studied the Bible, the Bhagavad Gita. We studied many of the teachings. She brought Socrates to us. I think she laid the foundation that made the rest of the work possible. But I also acknowledge that souls choose their parents," Linda adds.

At the ages of seven and eight, Linda and her sister were taught by their mother to sit in meditation. "Whatever she did, she did for us," says Linda. "She really stirred the heart feelings of devotion. I'm grateful to her and hope I can do it for my children."

Linda would explain her unique ability by the fact that she was raised totally without belief in the limitations of the five senses. "It was totally normal for me," she says, "to experience telepathy with RW, which I experienced first as a presence, a golden light, and a certain physical sensation, like a wind."

"It was as if I was in some open space and greeted by something familiar," she adds. "I very happily felt this presence and thought nothing of it. I didn't think it was unusual or strange in any way and that started when I was a teenager, maybe fifteen. I did a lot of traveling. I really started when I was very young and was often alone."

Linda's early life was spent as a ballet dancer and member of many dance companies. It was in this capacity that she traveled extensively throughout the United States, Canada, Mexico, and Europe.

"I used to be, both in meditation and in waking consciousness, aware of RW as a presence and would receive thoughts from him. Not clairaudiently, I would 'hear' a thought. Although I can remember times in my life when just on waking in the morning, I would experience just hearing something. As if someone were standing right here and whispering it. That I also just accepted.'' It was between the ages of fifteen and eighteen that all these impressions were received by Linda.

"When I was on tour with the dance company, wherever I went I started a meditation or self-development group. This was what I wanted to do with my life, even though I was dancing. The dancing was a way of always being with people and is one of my greatest loves as far as creativity. But I always had a group.''

About this time, like many others who have become channels, it was through daily meditation that Linda first began to hear RW, who told her that it was time for him to communicate through her—she does not lose consciousness when this occurs. Again, Linda simply accepted what she was now being told, recalling that as a little girl she had been told she would become a medium. "I met someone who was a psychic when I was a little girl. She said that someday I would be a medium. My vision of a medium was an old lady. I don't remember who it was. We went once to see someone; Eunice wanted to take away the mystery of psychic phenomena. I was about ten years old at the time.''

It was not Eunice who taught Linda how to make contact with RW but rather RW himself. From initially being perceived as a familiar sensation, sometimes seen as a light, RW gradually emerged in Linda's consciousness. Of this she says, "He instructed me how to go about being a channel. That's how it started. I wasn't taught by anyone in this world, nor do I believe anybody should be! RW told me what to do. He said to sit in meditation.''

Originally, Linda set aside a specific time each day to meditate. Since she has children of her own, she no longer adheres to a set schedule but still meditates whenever she can. "Meditation is a way of greeting the soul at the beginning of each day. It is *essential* to self-realization.''

On those days when she is doing a reading or channeling, she does not meditate until afterward, since the channeling itself takes a great deal of energy.

In the beginning she could channel for only two or three minutes at a time. She was instructed by RW to channel every day, two minutes, three minutes for an entire year. "It was like a muscle I had to build up—a concentration muscle!" she says of this.

Currently, in her workshops and classes she will channel for up to an hour and a half. When she first comes out, she feels a surge of energy for about half an hour, though her speech is often disconnected, as if just waking up in the morning. Since while in trance Linda often feels very warm, when she comes out she will often reach for a sweater.

After the exhilaration wears off, Linda will suddenly feel very tired. How tired she will feel depends on whether the reading was difficult or easy, as determined by how able the individual or group was in receiving RW's message. If the individual or group easily comprehended RW's message, she will feel less tired than if it was like "talking to a wall." In other words, she must have a sense that the energy, i.e., RW's message, is being received for it to have been a truly good channeling.

Of the difference between her channeling and meditation, Linda makes the following distinctions: "When I channel it's almost like going into meditation except that instead of going into the pathway you use for meditation, I go straight up. I have a very specific place in my consciousness . . . it's very hard to describe . . . that I go to and hold. It's as if that place has a doorway, not a real doorway, but symbolically, it's a place where I can greet RW."

Linda begins the process of channeling by offering a prayer in which she asks that she may be a clear channel for the Truth, and that her words, her life, and her actions may be a channel for the love and truth of the Christ source. She asks that all personalities may be set aside and that above all else, she will be clear in her perception of RW's message.

Besides actually channeling RW, Linda can also speak with him telepathically. Linda uses this less tedious method, for instance, when she happens to receive a phone call from someone in need. At times like this, she feels certain mental sensations that tell her that RW is nearby.

Of RW himself, Linda has been told that he is a spiritual teacher who has had many lifetimes on earth. He has no desire to reincarnate and prefers to disseminate his teachings through Linda.

As to what the initials RW stand for, this is known only to Linda and those close to her work. Of this question, Linda says, "This is not really significant to anyone else. He has said that the soul really doesn't have a name, like we think of names. It might have a sound or a light, or a sound that represents it which is the vibration of it. The only use for names is that we humans like them. It helps us identify. In a lot of cases we need the name because it helps us remember past associations with a person or makes us feel more comfortable or safe, which is alright! So he has put forth a name of the way I used to feel when his presence was there. RW represents a need of my personality for recognition."

Like others who channel, Linda finds it difficult to describe who and what RW really is. "I think of RW as a specific 'being' as you and I are a separate 'entity' . . . though I don't like the word 'entity,' as it's associated with hauntings and spirit things. I don't call him a 'spirit' because I don't like what's happened to that word, though spirit is a beautiful thing. I see spirit as energy, as light, not floating things. I think of him as a being of intelligence, wisdom, and love, a teacher."

As to the relationships between RW and similar beings, such as Seth, Linda shared an instance in which a member of her group asked RW if he knew Seth! "RW answered, 'Yes, I do. I know of his work and I know of him.'"

Commenting on the difference between the teachings of Seth and those of RW, Linda believes that the essence of their teachings are similar but that Seth's expression is far more complex than that of RW, though she admits that she "still loves reading it. RW has a way of making the complex seem simple," she says. "I love that. That's very helpful to people. You can get really bogged down with a lot of the esoteric and metaphysical books. I've read many of them."

Linda would further clarify the difference between Seth and RW by saying that while they belong to different centers of light on the other side, they "are both transmitters of the same light. It just transmits slightly differently in terminology, because it comes through different vehicles," Linda adds. "That's how I see it."

When I asked Linda if anyone else channeled RW, Linda's answer was simply, "No, no . . . never."

What if someone in California suddenly started channeling RW? "I wouldn't believe it. I would question it," she quickly replied.

As to whether RW could simply be a fragment of Linda's own personality, her comments were not unlike those of other channels: "I think that like every other channel that has ever existed, I have my moment of self-doubt, but I do not doubt RW or his existence. When I look back and see the work and I see that if you take the material . . . not what I said . . . but what RW has spoken, the material speaks for itself. I had a lot of doubt in the first years. But now there is nothing in me that doubts that I channel or that there is an RW being. What I doubt is me."

At the moment, Linda is in the process of assembling RW's teachings for publication. This has caused her to reflect on the great wisdom and simplicity of what has come through since she began fifteen years ago.

Although originally it took Linda some time to enter the state in which RW would manifest, it now takes her at the most a few minutes to feel his presence. When RW actually takes charge, Linda's voice and appearance change slightly. Of this process, Linda says, "If my consciousness were a vehicle, I drive it up, by which I mean a finer frequency. I use a specific mental technique to change the vibration of mental energy. First, I prepare the physical vehicle. I prepare the emotional vehicle by putting aside any feelings or lack of stillness or tranquillity in me. That has to be in perfect balance or it's like a weight, and I can't lift up out of that. So I have to gather the physical energy, the emotional energy. I work with the heart energy."

Linda says that if she trusted herself she could induce this state in about sixty seconds, but since she wants to be certain that she is truly clear, it takes her about five minutes to complete the process that opens the way for RW's appearance. Initially, it took about fifteen minutes.

She equates this process "with walking through your house before you go to the door to let someone in. I want to make sure that everything is just so. If I leave something unattended to, the physical or the emotional, I don't want it to interfere or bother what's going on."

Linda then moves her energy up through all the levels and centers, directs the energy from between the brow, and consciously channels and moves it, as a spiral, to form a link between herself and her source.

At this point, she feels that her consciousness has become pure thought. She moves up into the channel she has built and reaches a certain point where she can greet RW and is aware of his presence.

Of this she says, "It's like I create an elevator. I have to go up to him. He doesn't come down to me. I go up to the level he's on. I get off the elevator and stand there with the door open. He's holding the door open for me. Then he goes down the elevator and uses my vocal cords, my heart center, my arms, and connects to the person who becomes the external object. During the reading, I am standing there at the elevator in the chamber, holding the elevator door for me, when it's time to come back."

While RW does not generally read for individuals but rather teaches, occasionally information will be given out that a particular person may need to hear for continued soul growth. For instance, a person who is ill may be told the spiritual reasons "the energy got that way."

Fortunately for Linda, her work as a channel has had the support of her husband, though he has neither asked for nor received a reading of his own. Linda recalls telling him about her work on their second date. "I already was a channel when I met him and I realized that I could never get involved with anybody who didn't accept that, at the very least. They didn't have to be together with me on it. But I had to do what I had to do. So on the second date, we were in the car, and I said, 'Bob, there is something I have to tell you about myself.' I was very dramatic. . . . I was always very dramatic. He was very upset and thought I was going to say that I was with child or something."

Linda went on to tell Bob that she was a medium, channeled RW, did readings, and so forth. Bob's reply was, "Oh, is that all? That's interesting!"

Although Bob is a skeptic by nature, he nonetheless continues to support Linda's dedication to RW and his teachings. I doubt if Linda would have it any other way.

As to the split that often occurs between one's life as a medium and the problems of the real world, Linda says the following: "I really use RW for my spiritual growth and as an acknowledgment of a presence that helps me remember to stay awake and conscious. I don't tune in a lot or look into my future and all those things. I'm really not interested in that. In fact, I almost oppose it. I never look for insights as to what will happen next week or tomorrow. I'm concerned with now. I think if I did that it would be missing what's going on here. Maybe it wouldn't be right for me to do it anymore."

What Linda tries to do is to integrate RW's wisdom into her daily life so that each moment may be lived fully awake. In this sense, then, RW is a philosopher, a teacher, and not an entity who concerns himself with such petty concerns as buying a new car or learning when an estranged husband will return. In Linda's opinion, answering these questions would be a waste of RW's ability.

Linda commented on the rash of channelers who have appeared over the last ten years: "We are just entering a very particular Age. I think for the last twenty years or so we have been at the threshold where everything is at an extreme, everything is very tense, from weather to politics. I think that souls on earth are responding to an inflow of Christ energy into the earth plane. I think we each respond in a different way, according to the vessel that's receiving the energy. Some people respond to it maybe by writing or creating art, or even having children. Some people respond to it in a way that may be familiar to them which might be channeling. I believe I've channeled in other lifetimes. This is not the first time. It's like an old skill."

How does one know that what she is channeling is indeed true and not directed by forces of darkness? Linda has very definite ideas: "I wouldn't go near this line of work, normally. I really think it's very, very dangerous. I would never, ever encourage anybody to do this. The way of knowing that you have a purpose in life is not psychic ability, not trancing, ESP, or telepathy, or any of that. RW calls that the effect of something else. It can be the effect of ego or it can be the effect of true, sincere spiritual work. It's up to the individual to know they have to be responsible for that.

"In very many cases, there is a great degree of ego and the need to be special. We are all born with a little bit of the need to be *special*. And our secret desire is to be special enough so that God sees us, so we are recognized by Source. So we look in the wrong places for that recognition. All the work that takes you *externally* for recognition, whether it's trancing or anything at all, is the wrong way."

For Linda, the only recognition is that of the soul for God. One should not even wait around for God to recognize Self. It's Self that has to recognize God. This has nothing to do with trancing.

All the sensationalism, interest, and glamour in the world of spirit is by itself of little validity. "OK, yes, they're there," she would say. "I don't see any glamour at all to a soul just because it's passed on. Some people think just because it comes from *there* it's wise, it's good, or it's truthful, or it has knowledge we don't have. There are people over there just like 42nd Street. It's a range, and it could be *anybody* coming through. All they have to do is call themselves something, or a name, and you believe it!"

Of this tendency to just accept whatever comes through from the world of spirit as truth, Linda says, "I think this is really, really dangerous!"

Linda believes that good channels come about not because a person is seeking to become one, but rather as the by-product of the search for truth.

Linda is also quite adamant in her personal belief that mediumship techniques should not be generally taught. "I am very opposed to this," she says. "I think this is very dangerous. People can be taught a technique and walk away and be in touch with discarnate spirits in a week. I think it is very easy to be caught up in mistaken identity in spirit. I think one can unknowingly open the lower centers through psychic development and have to do an awful lot of work to close it up later. Really what you want to activate is the heart, the throat, and the head.''

I asked Linda what she would do if RW one day came to her and said that this was her last contact with him. She was quick to answer: "I would be really sad. I don't know where he would go since his presence isn't here or there. So I don't see him as something I could leave.''

Again, like many contemporary mediums, Linda has not sought to be ordained a minister. While such might afford her a veil of protection, by becoming a minister of one particular sect, she would in her opinion be "saying no to all the others. I wouldn't want to be linked up with dogma of any kind,'' she says.

Bringing our discussion to a close, I asked Linda to speak about where she would like to see RW work in the future and why it might be special. This was her reply: "First, I don't think that anyone's work is special. I think *special* is a dangerous word! I want RW's teachings to be in books so that they're there for others to read it and know it. I feel that RW's work fulfills what he sees is one of the major purposes of conscious life . . . that is to inspire! 'To inspire what?' is the next question. I think his work inspires thought. It inspires change. It inspires action in perceiving yourself, and your life, and your feelings, and the world around you in a different way. I feel that most of us live our life with a plastic globe around our head. We see the inside of the globe. And the globe is painted with what we have experienced and been told. On the outside of the globe is reality, which exists despite what the inside of our globe tells us.

"The RW work helps us to pierce through, to get out of that globe and have a true vision of *who* we are, *why* we are, *where* we are going, and *what* it's all for.''

In short, Linda sees the goal of all RW's work as what might best be called the illumination of the soul. She is not interested in having the world beat a path to her doorway or sit at her feet while she channels RW's teachings.

19

———o———

Julie Winter:
Not Just the Girl Next Door

You are all connected to many realms other than this physical focus. All of you. And the animals. Everything, everyone. The part that appears in the physical world has to beat in a certain way and has a particular set of sounds, of beat-frequencies. You think the rest of it isn't there because you can't bump your nose on it. But it is all there, all the time, all interwoven; but only a portion of it is physical.

—Micciah

The world of spirit has little respect for people, places, and things; in the same way, the law of gravity cares not what has been thrown out of a window. Law, natural or spiritual, exists and works its magic despite what we as humans may say or think about it. It would not be law if it were not so.

When it comes to choosing exactly *who* and *what kind* of person will suddenly find themselves crossing the threshold between this world of matter and the world of spirit, someone or something seems to have the final say.

So it is that people like Julie Winter come to do the things that they do. They don't question. It just happens.

Julie was born in New York City on February 11, to parents who were liberal and artistic intellectuals. Her father died when she was five. Julie describes her family as ''hypereducated,'' made up as it

was of doctors, lawyers, and various professionals. While she was Jewish by birth, she was never raised in the Jewish religion and attended Sunday school only twice in her life, at her own request, when she was six years old.

During summers Julie visited Wentworth, New Hampshire, and sang in the choir of the Congregational church. Of this early period, she says, "I was psychic when I was a child. I assumed that everybody was psychic, which I think everybody is. I always had a *sense* of things that were known but not said. I assumed that it was social protocol that there was one set of information that was communicated and one set that was not."

It was around the time her father passed through transition, though, that she first became acutely aware that she was different. "When my father was very ill, when I was four, I would wake up in the middle of the night and would look at the doorway of my bedroom. I would see him standing there, complete in his blue and white seersucker bathrobe, but I could *see through him*. It was as if he were three-dimensional but not solid! He was always there. I would wake up in the middle of the night and look. For a period of months, he was always there. Never my mother. I didn't think anything of it."

In retrospect, Julie would now say that what she was seeing was the astral, or light, body of her father, though then she thought nothing of it. "After he died," says Julie, "I had a sense that he was around me but I never saw him."

When Julie was about ten years old, she read *The Unobstructed Universe*, by Stewart Edward White, a book about mediumship, which made perfect sense. During her teen years, Julie played with a Ouija Board "on and off." A mother of a friend of hers had purchased the board and dabbled with it.

When she was seventeen, Julie left home and went off on her own. After attending the City University of New York, she transferred to the New School for Social Research and began to study acting.

In one of her acting classes, she befriended a woman who asked when she was born so that she could cast Julie's horoscope. Recalling this experience, Julie says, "What really intrigued me about it was that some of it was so accurate and some of it was completely inaccurate. She had done it for the right time and the right day but for the wrong year!"

So piqued by this experience was Julie's interest in astrology that she began to inquire where she could learn all about astrology. By a series of coincidences she was led to Weiser's Bookshop in New York City. There, in the basement, she discovered more books on astrology and other mystical subjects than one could ever imagine existed.

From astrology, she went on to study Yoga, tarot, palmistry, and numerology. After seven years of study, she began to practice astrology professionally.

In the interim, she also became interested in healing and studied Science of Mind at the First Church of Religious Science in New York City, becoming a practitioner in 1972. This activity was followed by studies in core energetics and hypnosis.

In 1975 Julie was teaching a class at the New School when she met a student who did channeling. At this time, while she had read everything she could find, including the early books by Jane Roberts and Eileen Garrett, she never imagined that she would herself become a channel.

After experiencing a personal session with this student, Julie decided to see if she could channel. She recalls, "I sat down on the rug and began to chant. I opened my mouth and this loud voice came out, 'We greet you.' I channeled for about maybe half an hour and then took down notes."

This took place in September 1975.

While it is sometimes difficult for her to describe in words, Julie says of the mechanism of her channeling, "It doesn't quite feel like stepping aside. It feels more as if the fabric that makes me solid is becoming less and less dense. If you drive a shift car when you go into fourth you stop feeling the gears are engaged when they open; it feels more like that than if I am stepping aside. I am conscious of everything I am saying. I don't go out."

While someone might expect this experience to entail a certain degree of fear, for Julie the moment was one of excitement. "I was thrilled. I had read all the literature, psychiatric as well as occult," she says.

Being somewhat of a scientist, Julie made an agreement with herself that if the information that came through her was "supportive, useful, and seemed to be nurturing and loving," she would continue. On the other hand, if the information that came through was in any way "clinically bizarre, authoritarian, or controlling" in regard to other people, she would stop.

Slowly, she began to tell her friends about this phenomenon. She asked one friend, a physicist who was interested in the occult, to work with her by posing questions to see if she could get information about things she did not consciously know.

At the time of her first channeling experience, Julie was engaged in a combination of things, including astrology, counseling, and teaching classes in healing. Slowly at first, she began to integrate her channeling into the other work she was doing. "I began to include it as part of my work," she says, "first experimentally. I included it in the classes I was teaching. I said, 'I would really like to try this out with you and see if you think of it.' I always invited comments and feedback and was constantly questioning, 'What is it?' and 'Where does it come from?'"

Starting with her first channeling experience, Julie has been aware of the fact that she in some way makes contact with a particular entity.

"My current understanding of it," says Julie, "is that it isn't a being. It's a realm into which I tap. The combination of that aspect of reality and the aspect of my greater self produces what seems to be a very personable 'entity.'"

Julie continues, "It appears as an *entity*. Somewhere along the line, one of my students said, 'Do you have a name?' And the reply was, 'The *sound* that is closest would be Micciah.'"

When Julie is channeling Micciah, her voice takes on a unique accent that she explains by the fact that her voice bumps. It is not that she is channeling an East Indian, Middle Eastern, or Eastern European departed entity. In fact, until someone asked Micciah for a name, Julie simply called him Sam.

What has Micciah said about himself? Julie replies, "That that [i.e., Micciah] is a realm of teaching and healing. By altering my ordinary state of consciousness I can overlap with that realm. In that way I can receive impressions I would not ordinarily have."

What bothers Julie about the channeling of others are claims that they are channeling "a perfectly realized being. This is God speaking through the humble mouth of 'blank' [meaning the name of the person doing the channeling]. Therefore, 'blank' is not responsible for any of the information that is channeled." This kind of work, in her opinion, is an outrage. "I take responsibility for anything I channel," she is quick to add.

Unlike some mediums, Julie is aware of everything she is saying, although she is in trance when Micciah speaks through her. Immediately thereafter, she can recall all that has been said but may lose some of this memory a week later. Her agreement with herself is not to change anything she says while in trance, although consciously she may disagree with what is being said.

While most of Julie's students have easily accepted the phenomenon of Micciah, she has been very careful in her use of this work when counseling or in conducting therapy sessions.

Of this she says, "It is a prime target for fantasies of omnipotence. To be really clear that the channeling work, if used as part of therapy, is used with specific kinds of boundaries, I keep checking with people. 'Do you feel angry? . . . Do you want me to fix things? . . . Is it mixing you up that I can be *me* and another entity? . . . If I am that magical, does it make you angry that I can't just make you well?' That balance has to be addressed."

In January 1985, Julie and video artist Jon Child began to produce their own half-hour television program on which she channels Micciah. This program appears in New York City on a cable network, and in California, Oregon, Vermont, and Louisiana.

At present, Julie does three private channeling sessions a week, usually scheduled for every other day. Each session lasts about an hour and is divided into a half hour of actual channeling and an equal time to process the information that has come through.

In addition, Julie teaches seven groups each week, some of which also have channeling sessions. This brings the total number of her channelings for a week to about five. Of this she says, "That's *all* I want to do. Unless it's an absolute dire emergency or someone is very ill, I do not do any more. Period. The end."

When asked how she felt during and after channeling, she replies in a single word, "Ecstatic!" Trying to describe what actually takes place, she says, "I don't feel taken over. It feels as if my physical body becomes lighter. It's as if I could put my finger through my arm."

Unlike others, Julie does not say a prayer or do any special breathing exercises. In jest, she says, "I just cross my fingers. No, I often hold a crystal. I take my bracelet off. I don't like to channel with anything on my wrists."

On a few occasions, while teaching others, Julie has been told by Micciah that this particular person, in order to be grounded, *needs* a particular ritual. Generally, though, Julie simply holds her crystal and does a short meditation before she goes into trance. In this she asks that she will be clear, truthful, and spontaneous. There are no magical words used, nor does she repeat the same meditation each time she channels.

After her client leaves, or when a class has been completed, she washes and drinks water. "I can lose a couple of pounds in a channeling session," she says. "I am just covered with perspiration."

Julie has not yet had the opportunity to enter a laboratory that could measure what takes place neurologically when she channels, though she is open to any such scientific testing of her abilities if offered by reputable scientists. She has offered to make herself available for such testing, on her television program, but to date no one has accepted this offer.

As to the distinction between the words *medium* and *channel*, Julie says the following: "I think the word channeling is overused and underdefined! Just forget it! I don't use the word medium at all, unless I'm fooling around and say I'm a 'medium rare.' Everyone and their basset hound are channeling. People run up to me in ladies' rooms and say, 'I hear you're a channel. I'm a channel, too.' I don't feel contemptuous of people channeling, just the mushiness of the language."

Julie would explain the entire process of mediumship and channeling in terms of models. For instance, Arthur Ford and other early spiritualists had spirit controls and that became a model for other mediums. In jest, Julie would say, "They fell in love with their model!" Hence, whenever someone was instructed in becoming a medium, they were taught how to contact their spirit guide or control.

Julie does not like the word *channeling*, thought to have been coined by Jane Roberts in the Seth books, but does not yet have another word to describe what she does.

On occasion, Julie will hear someone's name while in trance. When this happens, she may feel the physical presence of some kind of entity that may bring with it a memory of a passing. For instance, if the entity passed from an injury to the chest, she may actually feel the pain that the entity felt at the moment of transition. When this happens, she can converse with this entity, "but it's like talking from room to room."

She explains, "Micciah may say, 'Do you want to have information about this?' If the person says yes, he'll say, 'Just a moment, please.' It's then like shouting, 'Can you please ask. . . .' Then I listen. I have to listen very hard and I get information back."

While Julie would say, "I hear, I see, and I sense," she does not actually see the spirit entities in their earthly garb as experienced by some mediums. Julie does see energy and colors that are auric in nature. Hence, Julie is neither a medium nor a spiritualist, though she would respect both models. She simply describes herself as a "healing therapist."

Of Micciah, she says, "I describe Micciah as a nonphysical energy entity with whom I work in collaboration, which is as close as I can get."

The issue of responsibility and ethics in channeling is one about which Julie has very definite ideas. In Julie's mind, not only must the entity be responsible to bring forth only that information that can be used positively for the greater good, coming from a place of love and not fear, but the channel as well must take full responsibility for what is being said through her. For instance, it is not enough to predict natural disasters without also providing information about how they can be avoided or how those in possibly troubled areas can be alerted. To do otherwise is to simply be a fearmonger, which is contrary to the Christ principle and to the spirit of the Aquarian Age that says, "You are *both* your brother and his keeper!"

As to why the phenomenon of channeling is suddenly in the forefront of psychic phenomena, Julie says, "I think that things are falling apart at the seams. I suppose you could go back and look at the cycles and the proliferation of this kind of information at different times in history. I don't know how much you could tell. Now people are being desperate and Auntie Nellie is being served up with the oatmeal. I think that what's happening is just another model. Why do we get other models? I don't know."

As to whether or not everyone can learn to channel, Julie says, "I think everyone can learn to open themselves and get out of the focus of this waking trance. I don't think that everyone is going to do it as I do it. Some people do it through their painting, acting, carpentry; some people do it in other ways."

Besides her popularized channeling that is broadcast, Julie conducts both a healing class, which was begun twelve years ago, and a training course for healers, begun six years ago.

In addition to her study of astrology, Julie initiated the healing class, enabling her to attain more satisfactory results from the work she was then doing. It meets each week for an hour and a half. During the summer, while on vacation, Julie works out different topics for the September through June period. Recently the entire group worked on what she terms "Inventing the Sacred" or "Breaking All the Rules." The question discussed was "What becomes sacred in ordinary life?" Of the healing class, Julie says, "There is process work. There is meditation. There is talking."

"I think the greatest social change is a change of consciousness," Julie would say.

Julie's training program, begun with four therapist colleagues in 1980, is called Helix, "because it's between hell and something or other in the dictionary." Essentially a four-year program, it was set up for people who wish to practice as healers or therapists. A high percentage of people Julie has worked with, however, are artists who wish to practice healing as their art.

Those participating in Helix, once accepted into the program, attend an eight-hour meeting on the first Sunday of each month, biweekly two-hour meetings, and at least one process weekend per year. In addition, there are readings and other assignments. Twice yearly, those in the program are evaluated as to the quality of their commitment, both spiritual and personal, their ability to be with people, and their integration of the conceptual and practical.

Though Julie has been fortunate inasmuch as she has always had the support of the men and women in her life, she often has little time for her personal life. She says, "It's my fault! I work a lot of hours."

Like other therapists, she can get calls for assistance at any time, though she says most of her students and clients "are very respectful of my time and do not call me unless in deep waters."

Of this she says, "I really think the test of someone's work is who they are as a person. That split between you as a teacher, you as writer, and you as a human being is an artificial one. The test is who are you when you get off the podium."

As to what the future holds for Julie and Micciah, she has no long-range plans and "never has."

"I have a big house in the country I use for all my Helix students one weekend a year," she says. "As soon as you want a center, you get into real estate whether here [i.e., New York City] or in the country. As soon as you are into real estate, you are into advertising as to how you support the center. I don't like centers. In spite of the fact that I have started a lot of groups, I am not by and large a 'group' person."

Julie also feels that organizations tend to go through and act like astrological cycles. They start out of anarchy and the fertility of chaos. Then they form loose organizations in which the people are really dedicated. The more organized it gets, the more saturnine it gets. Then there is the breakdown, and it falls apart. Julie does not want to be a part of this.

While many persons who do the kind of work Julie does, day after day, often doubt their effectiveness, Julie's self-assurance permeates every aspect of her work. "My feeling about myself is this is what I came to do," she says.

Bringing our discussion to a close, I asked Julie to describe herself as if writing her epitaph. This is what she said: "That I am loving, direct, a humanist, sometimes comical, foolish, irreverent, generous."

Trying to place a single handle on the work of Julie Winter is an impossible task. Though seemingly contradictory, she has succeeded in artfully blending all that she learned from Science of Mind, astrology, and psychology. While the fact that she channels cannot be denied, she has not been so foolish as to place it above all her other beliefs. Rather, she seeks always to find and share the divine spark George Washington called conscience.

Her struggle to remain creatively independent and not to become just another face on the "psychic self-help circuit" permeates everything she does and says. Her clarity, sincerity, and integrity are indeed extraordinary.

Perhaps the only way to describe her is to paraphrase yet another characteristically unique individual—Ralph Waldo Emerson—who said that the thunder of what you are speaks so loudly I can't hear what you are saying.

20

○

Pat Rodegast:
Teacher, Healer, and
Emmanuel's Friend

*Consciousness cannot help but create itself. You just, by
the very nature of your being, expand and create. Who
you are at any given moment, whether it be prebirth,
physical, or after physical life, is your creation.*

—Emmanuel

By now, reader, you are no doubt beginning to see the repetition of
certain threads and patterns in the fabrics of the lives of those who
have been called by spirit. One such thread is the use of various
sorts of daily meditation as a springboard for making spirit contact.
This should not be surprising, for the master spiritualist of all
times—Jesus—gave the instruction "Enter into thy closet."

Pat Rodegast's first experience of channeling took the form of
transcendental meditation.

Pat was born on March 17, in Stamford, Connecticut. While
Pat's parents were not involved in New Age concepts at all, she had
a grandmother who was into astrology, Yoga, and health foods, and
was "very religious." Describing her eclectic family, Pat says,
"She [i.e., Grandmother Smith] was a Baptist. My mother was an
atheist. My father was an absent Episcopalian. There was no formal
religion in the family except my grandmother."

Pat's grandfather had had a psychic experience when he "died"

after contracting pneumonia. While he never spoke of this experience, after his death Pat discovered letters he had written to Sir Oliver Lodge in England regarding his experiences. Of these, Pat says, "He had died and seen a river. He wrote to him [Lodge] because he could never speak it. He was a lawyer and yet physically could not speak of this. He just could not."

While Pat did not have any psychic experiences as a child, she had what she called a "knowing that there was more to life than what was presented to me in my family."

According to Pat, she would say things to herself like, "'Someday I'm going to die and I'm going to know the answer.' And then I would say, 'But I know the answer. It's love.'" She was five or six at the time this took place.

Recalling her childhood, Pat says, "Everything that I would say . . . like in the morning when the dew was on the grass . . . 'I bet the fairies had a party last night.' It was like 'Oh God, Pat!' There was no sympathy, no empathy for sensitivity. Period. This was New England upbringing! There was an absolute put-down on anything that wasn't intellectual in my family."

When Pat was about sixteen, she decided on her own to become confirmed in the Episcopalian church, which met with a predictable degree of familial disfavor.

Graduating from high school during the Depression, she found herself without the necessary funds to enroll in college, so she entered the job market at the age of sixteen as a service representative for the telephone company. Later she held various secretarial jobs and attended the American Academy of Dramatic Arts in New York City. After pounding pavements looking for theatrical work, Pat finally obtained a winter stock position in Sarasota, Florida.

Pat married and attended the University of New Hampshire, where she furthered her acting career. When her husband graduated, they moved to Jefferson, New Hampshire, where once again she worked as a secretary. Pat had two children by this marriage.

It was not until many years and two marriages later that Pat was led to meditation. Of this she recalls, "I was living in Westport [Connecticut]. A friend of mine where I was working had been murdered. At that time, people at work were going to see a psychic. It was one of those things that everybody was doing—I wasn't going to go, I thought it was pure hoke. But I didn't know where else to turn because before my friend was killed and after I had all these strange feelings I couldn't explain.''

So Pat went to the psychic, Marci Seidel, and was told that the only reason she herself was not a medium was that she didn't believe in it. She suggested to Pat that she meditate. When Pat asked how she should meditate, she was told to try TM, then in its heyday due to the endorsement of such notables as the Beatles and Mia Farrow.

Following Marci's advice, Pat and her daughter, then fourteen, enrolled in a TM class, not knowing that this would change their lives. Of this Pat says, "In about a month I began to see *things*. It happened real quick! I got to the point where I would just go to the *place*. I didn't have to use the mantra at all.''

The *things* that Pat started to see were spirits, which she originally perceived as some kind of shadows that would not go away. She says, "I was so excited. That was the beginning. I had done psychometry and seen stuff.''

In order to further her development, Pat became a student of Marci's and attended her classes, which included sitting in developmental circles. From then on, she began to allow her abilities to grow more and more, having received verification of them as she went along.

"I was a real faithful TM meditator for a couple of years. Morning and night; twice a day. It works. It really works,'' she says.

Then Emmanuel appeared and totally changed Pat's life.

If Pat hadn't done TM, would she still have been led to the means whereby she could channel Emmanuel? She answers, "Probably, but I don't know. Oh, sure. The soul has a plan.'' Of the first time that Pat "got tuned in,'' she says, "It was scary. The first time I got tuned in, I was elated for twenty-four hours and then I crashed. Oh, my God, now what do I do?''

While Pat was practicing psychometry before Emmanuel made his appearance in her life, it was really meditation, and meditation alone, that enabled her to develop to the point where she could tune in. Of this she says, "Meditation was really the thing for me."

A couple of years after first seeing "shadows," Pat began seeing a "gold light" in her peripheral vision. She best describes this experience in her own words: "I said . . . wow, what's that? I was almost afraid to look for fear it would disappear. This was my inner vision. And then it took about a week . . . seven days. . . . It sounds very corny, but it really did. The vision just sort of walked around me like that. I was still afraid to look at it. Then finally it stood in front of me and I said, 'Who are you?' And he said, 'I am Emmanuel.' He spelled his name. Then I said, 'Are you going to be with me?' And he said, 'Yes.'"

About the same time Emmanuel first appeared to Pat, she joined the Center for the Living Force, a spiritual community in Phoenicia, New York, then directed by Eva and John Pierrakos, where she studied bioenergetics. This, Pat says, "was a lifesaver for me. I needed grounding."

It was the influence of Eva Pierrakos, herself a channel, that enabled Pat to comprehend exactly what had taken place when Emmanuel appeared and to keep this experience in the proper perspective. "If anybody is doing this kind of work they have *absolute* responsibility for clearing themselves of all their garbage, or as much of it as they can. It's essential. The spirit can't talk through anything more than he's got. If you have an investment in 'stuff,' you can't hear the truth! I'm still clearing myself. I will forever do it, have sessions. For me, it was essential."

How did Pat feel when Emmanuel first appeared? She answers exuberantly: "Delighted! There's something about Emmanuel that doesn't allow me to be afraid. Doesn't allow is a funny way to say it. There is a wonderful . . . love . . . that's there. As soon as that appears, or that connection is made, I feel absolutely safe. So I felt wonderful. I didn't know what we were going to do but I figured everything was OK."

As is often the case when one initially makes spirit contact, Pat was at first afraid that one day Emmanuel might not show up, especially when she was sitting before a number of persons.

Emmanuel's response to Pat was, "We never go anywhere. It's you that bounce up and down. If I'm not here, it's because you're not touching me. It's not that I'm not touching you!"

It was not until *after* she began to channel that Pat read everything she could get her hands on about channeling, including, of course, the Seth books by Jane Roberts. Before she began to channel, she says she read nothing "because I didn't believe it."

As to the question whether anyone else ever channeled or could channel Emmanuel, he himself answered on one occasion by saying, "What makes you think my *only* name is Emmanuel?" According to Pat, Emmanuel is an "area of consciousness and we name it what we name it as it comes through us."

It is Pat's belief that a spirit guide and the channel make up the entity, the consciousness. "I don't think we are just telephones. We are part of the process, the channeling. That's why if you are not clear as a human being, you can't be clear as a channel. How can you? That's who you are!"

To Pat's way of thinking, Emmanuel is clearly part of her higher self, or whatever you want to call it, and part of the greater reality where we ultimately all belong. It's sort of a bridge. Spirits are bridges, the ones that touch us.

Until recently, Pat remembered absolutely nothing of what she channeled of Emmanuel. A few days before our meeting, she was told by him that she must now begin to remember rather than maintain the separation.

Of her actual experience of channeling, Pat says, "When I do private readings, I don't remember. It's personal, it's wonderful. I don't need to remember. I don't need to be burdened. I go into a trance, not so deep, which is real interesting. I'm *there* when it's happening. I laugh when it's funny. I cry when it's sad. I get the benefit of the whole thing. I sit in that wonderful space of love, incredible! But I don't remember."

According to Pat, she really did not know what Emmanuel was doing until she and her friend Judith Stanton started gathering information for her first book, *Emmanuel's Book*, which was published in 1985.

As to how the book came about, Pat says, "Ram Dass suggested it. Judith Stanton, the woman who compiled the book with me, had used some of Emmanuel's material on death in his Death and Dying Retreat. He said, 'Tell Pat if she ever wants to write a book, I will be glad to write the introduction.' That was the beginning."

She continues, "In reading the stuff that we took off the tapes . . . [as] we compiled it, it was revelation to me. I would say, 'Wow! Listen to this.' This is great 'cause I had no recall, no idea of anything that he was doing, or the continuity of it. Now I am beginning to realize that he has a thread of purpose. I am not quite clear about it yet."

Of the other beings who are currently channeled, Pat believes that they "all say the same thing in their own vocabulary, thank God!"

"Anything that comes from fear, I don't give credence to," she says, referring to the predictions of doom and destruction promulgated by some entities. "I may die in New York, but I still don't believe it. Emmanuel says anything that comes from fear is predicated on illusion and can only do harm. Even if what you are doing is good works, if your motivation is fear, you are feeding the darkness."

Pat believes, as does Zolar, that the only cataclysm that is approaching is a spiritual one. Clarifying this point, she says, "Emmanuel says that humanity is ready for the next step in awareness, that's all! People talk about earth changes and shifts, and he says the earth has been doing that since it was born. I just have no patience with doomsayers. I think people get off on being scared. Emmanuel said the nuclear buildup that people have been so afraid of is the best teacher you could have because it makes people stop. He says there is not going to be a nuclear war. School isn't ready to get out yet! He calls this the school room."

Upon reflection, Pat says that *after* Emmanuel appeared she became very conscious of her responsibility, her truth, and her integrity. Before Emmanuel, she says, she was "in behavior, where most of us are." After Emmanuel's appearance, she moved toward "beingness, where your truth and integrity really are." She would also say she moved from the psychic to the world of spirit.

Did Pat ever imagine when she first began to meditate that she would now do what she does? "Never . . . never," she replies. "When I started doing it professionally, I never thought I would do workshops. Never thought I would do a book. It just sort of all evolved. People would say, 'Do you have a [business] card?' 'No.' That's one reason I trusted. I never pushed it. I just allowed."

Although Emmanuel appeared about twelve years ago, Pat started doing workshops only about three years ago, which she considers is when she went "professional."

What has Emmanuel told Pat about himself? "That he's a being of light. That he's been alive and that he and I were together. That he was a physical person and his last incarnation was in the 1500s. He gave a description to someone about the kind of life and he sounded like Siddhartha, or Buddha, or whatever. But he hasn't said that."

While reincarnation fits well into the Emmanuel teachings, his definition of karma is very different from that of most persons, according to Pat. "He says we are not here to balance books or pay back. We are here to live our lives. So when he says karma, he calls it just the workshop we form for ourselves in this lifetime. If somebody says, 'Do I have a karmic debt with . . .?', he says it doesn't matter.

"There is no such thing as chronological time for spirit. In the eternal now, you are here. So do here! Don't worry about 'I did that to them so they have to do it to me,' or vice versa. That's excess baggage. That's just another structure."

Recently, Emmanuel has been talking about the difference between structure and form. Consciousness creates its own form, but if you try to put it into structure, you limit it and take away its vitality.

About a month ago, while Pat was enjoying the bliss of expansion by dwelling on the fullness of her cup, she heard him say to her, "You are to teach the Gospel of Unknowing, the walk of Faith." Emmanuel explained the Gospel of Unknowing: "You've got no history and we create the future with every breath. We're *here*. It's *now*."

Over the years, Pat's work with Emmanuel has evolved in different directions. At present she works with a psychologist, Barbara Glabman-Cohen, with whom she conducts workshops to train other therapists to apply Emmanuel's philosophy in their own practices, as well as with Judith Stanton and a healer, Barbara Brennan.

Recently, Pat has been conducting a year's course in Philadelphia, Pennsylvania, for registered therapists. According to Pat, the first thing Emmanuel told those assembled was that "your brain is great for getting you from here to there, helping you remember your name and your address. That's all. Put it aside!" Pat says she couldn't help thinking about the eight years of schooling of each of those assembled. "I thought they would shoot me," she says.

When he will channel through Pat is always Emmanuel's decision. "I am conscious of moving back," she says. When not channeling, Pat just works as Pat, having been trained as a helper and having had a lot of therapy herself. "*My* own sensitivity, as well as my channel, helps me to work with people and their process," she says. "So it's both. And I love that. It's nice."

When Pat works with healers, she also works both as Pat and as a channel for Emmanuel.

Like most channels, she has never done fortune-telling, nor would she ever consider it. Of Emmanuel, she simply says, "He's a teacher. He's a teacher! He's wonderful and has saved people years of psychotherapy. He goes right to the pain, right to where it needs to be gone to!"

Of those who do fortune-telling rather than promulgate personal responsibility, Pat says, "That's putting consciousness into structure. You can't do that. It dishonors it."

Going further with this idea she says, "We create it as we go. Free will, you know. I know for myself if you told me that I was going to be doing such and such a year from now, I would goof it up either by working toward it or by not wanting to do it! If I am to teach the Gospel of Unknowing, you can't know!"

Pat has accepted the mantle of responsibility. She says of this, "I tell you, I am very careful about being clear. I am grateful for that."

How does it feel to have a friend like Emmanuel? "Wonderful," is Pat's reply!

Where is the Emmanuel work leading Pat Rodegast? This is what she says: "I don't know where. I can tell you where I *hope* it's leading. I hope it's leading . . . this sounds grandiose . . . I want Emmanuel not only in the Halls of Medicine, where he's moving, and in psychotherapy, but also into politics and law. *My* longing is the Peace Movement and eliminating fear in the world. This is my dream. Of course, this is where I want Emmanuel. It seems as though it is beginning to move in that direction through the auspices of wonderful people who are doing wonderful things. When you sit back this far and watch the plan, it's incredible!"

While Pat used to do six readings a day, she no longer does that. Over a year ago, Emmanuel told her to stop doing private readings. And she did, except for emergencies.

Since she has begun doing workshops, she no longer finds it necessary to fulfill everyone's expectations. Pat used to try and structure each workshop herself, but now she lets Emmanuel do it.

She says, describing her workshops, "We used to be very rigid. The last few workshops, we have had absolutely no idea what's going to happen in the next *minutes*. We have all gained workshop savvy, having done them enough now. What is wonderful is that I have finally learned I don't give the workshop. We don't give the workshop. The workshop does *itself*!" Pat travels and does a workshop almost every weekend.

Pat says of these workshops, "It's fun. I never know what's going to happen, what I am going to learn!"

Does Pat miss doing private readings? Absolutely not! "It got to be arduous. I got to be booked a year in advance! I am real clear: I *do not want to be a guru*. I do not want anyone's dependency. And Emmanuel is wonderful with that!"

Does Pat have a devoted core of followers who have been with her since the emergence of Emmanuel? You bet! "We call them "Emmanuel junkies." Just some . . . just some real sweet people who when they can attend, they do. Sure, he's addictive in a way. That kind of energy is addicting, that kind of sweetness and truth and safety."

At the moment Pat and Judith are gathering material for a second book, mainly taken from a series of seminars that were presented at the Universalist Church on Central Park West in New York City.

For this series, Emmanuel chose the subject matter, including a course entitled "The Many Aspects of Self." According to Pat, this particular seminar dealt with "self, self and others, self and the world, and self and God." Tapes of the seminars are currently being transcribed.

Another series was entitled "Seasons of the Mind . . . Youth, Middle Years, and Old Age." When I suggested to Pat that these were great titles and that Emmanuel should consider a career on Madison Avenue, she laughed. Still another series was entitled "Tea and Current Events with Emmanuel," during which actual tea was served.

While Pat has no "shoulds" in her philosophy, by choice she has been a vegetarian for about eight years now. She says of this "that it evolved. It started out as just 'no beef.'"

What would Pat Rodegast do if one day Emmanuel said, "I'm leaving!"? Her answer struck a familiar chord: "I would feel very sad. I'd honor it. I'd try to understand and accept and know what my next step would be. I would be sad."

Emmanuel's message for us all? "Don't be afraid. All there is *is* love. The only reality is love. All the rest is illusion. That's the message!"

What makes Pat Rodegast tick? This is what Pat would say about Pat: "I serve loving truth through my channeling of Emmanuel and through my own intention, my commitment. What I want to do is to comfort people who suffer and who are afraid. I think that the voice of Emmanuel certainly is the voice of love, the voice of truth, and also the voice of hope and healing."

21

How to Develop Your Own Mediumship: Part One

When mediumship is truly understood, both less and more will be expected and obtained through its agency than has been the case hitherto. Less will be expected from those in spirit-life who give the bulk of the messages ordinarily received, but more will be demanded and welcomed from higher celestial sources, because aspirations will reach higher, and the science of spiritual telegraphy will be better understood.

—W. J. Colville

By now we have examined enough lives of modern mediums to see that "when the disciple is ready, the master will appear."

Although it has been said that only one person out of a thousand can become a truly competent medium, the path to development lies open to anyone who wishes to pursue it, and who is willing to take whatever time and effort are necessary to bring it about.

Like anything else in life, mediums are both *born* and *made*. Surely anyone who has been drawn to this tome, and to other Zolar writings, has been in some way called to the priesthood. Will you answer this call in this incarnation or must you die and be born again?

Remember the words of the great master, that many have ears and do not hear, eyes and do not see. Whether you will read what has *not* been written in these pages and what has *not* been said, depends not on Zolar but on you alone. In the final analysis, it is always your own decision to seek contact with the world of spirit or to turn away in fear.

By now you have learned that mediums are not extra-special people but rather simply people who have heard the beat of a different drummer and have risen to the call of the drums and fife they alone may hear. It has always been this way since the very beginning of time.

But let us now recall what has been said by those who so freely have shared their gifts of spirit so we might ourselves partake of this grand experience.

Meditation

First and foremost, almost all mediums agree on the significance and the importance of regular daily meditation. This single practice, above all others, is no doubt the very shaft that drives the wheel of development.

While meditation takes many forms, it is essentially the act of entering into one's closet and listening to the voice of God and spirit. To do this successfully, three steps must be followed.

First, meditation must be practiced daily and must truly become a habit of mind. There can be no excuses, no "but if's" if someone wishes to make progress in the world of spirit. At least once a day, at least six days a week, one must stop and turn within.

Second, meditation must be regular and performed at the very same time of the day and in the very same place. If 7:00 A.M. is the time you have decided upon, you must make sure that at this hour each day, promptly, you begin this practice.

If you choose to meditate in a *particular* chair in a *particular* room, you must use this chair and this room throughout your meditative practices. Of course, should you find it necessary to travel and leave your appointed place of worship, you must of necessity adapt to another place and perhaps another time. But to do so will hinder rather than aid you in this very special practice.

The reason one must adhere to a rigid schedule is simply one of conditioning the mind and body to *expect*, to *anticipate*, this very special moment of contact. Many persons who have begun to meditate have failed to realize the importance of regularity and have as a result failed in their attempt to make spirit contact.

Why is this so? The answer is simply that the mind and body must be programmed like a computer. This is why the ancient mystery schools and monastic orders always conducted their prayer services and meditations at the same hour each day, never varying from their schedules.

This means then, that you must carefully select *when* and *where* you begin your meditation, changing the time and place only if absolutely necessary.

It is not just you who must be programmed to enter into the world of spirit, but your surroundings, and most important of all, your friends in spirit! You cannot expect your friends in spirit, your guardian angels, of which we all have at least one, to come to you without some kind of notice. While many persons believe that spirit guides will always come when called, this is so only after we have made and bonded our contact with them.

The world of spirit, from what we have been told by those who have passed over, is not unlike the world of matter. There are jobs to be done, lessons to be learned, and daily tasks assigned by the grand architect of the universe. Since this is so, our spirit guides must be given advance notice as to when and where they must appear in the same way that you keep an appointment book.

Imagine, if you will, your spirit guide or guides writing in his or her appointment book the fact that every day at 7:00 A.M. I must be with Zolar, my brother, sister, son, daughter, or grandchild.

It is for this reason that often spirit will not make an appearance when the meeting time of one's meditation has been changed or the sitting of a particular spirit circle has been moved to another time or location. Regularity is the only key that can truly fit the lock of spiritual enlightenment.

Third, meditation will be successful only to the extent that one can relax the hold of physical body and its five physical senses. Picture if you will the mind and the body as two children sitting on a seesaw. When body is up in the air, mind is down on the ground. This is the position that most of us occupy throughout our waking life, the position in which we are acutely aware of the things of the body—pain, noise, hunger, stress.

For the mind to take charge, the seesaw must be tilted in the other direction. Body must drop to the ground so that mind can be elevated into the air. There is no way in which both mind and body can be up in the air at the same time. This is the mystical understanding as to exactly how meditation works.

Just as we have five physical senses, corresponding to the body, so do we have five astral senses corresponding to the mind or soul. Among spiritualists, these are often called the five "claires": clairaudience (hearing), clairvoyance (seeing), clairsentience (feeling), clairgustience (tasting), and clairalience (smelling).

Just as one can feel with the body, so can one be trained to feel with the mind. This is really what is done by those in spirit who are no longer hindered by a physical body.

To recap, for successful meditation, one must practice at the same time and in the same place each day and begin by totally relaxing the physical body.

How to Meditate

While there are various techniques given to produce the meditative state, by far the simplest is one that appears over and over again in the sacred writings of all religions, and that was employed by Arthur Ford.

In its simplest form, this technique consists of relaxing each part of the body in turn by visualizing (seeing with the mind's eye) and simply letting go.

This single technique, if practiced daily according to the above rules, will do more to enable a person to make spirit contact than any other method Zolar has discovered. A series of exercises will make this disembodiment possible.

Exercise One

Find a comfortable chair and perhaps a footrest or stool. While this exercise can be done while stretched out on a couch or bed, beginning students will often find themselves falling asleep, which is contrary to the intent and purpose of the exercise.

If you have to do something after your meditation, obtain a clock or watch and set it to go off for a particular time after your meditation. If you do not do this, the thought of having to get somewhere or do something will arise in your mind and interfere with this practice. Make yourself comfortable, with the spine as straight as possible but not so rigid that you will be unable to relax. Let your breathing become as deep as possible and simply flow in and out. Later on, we will give you special exercises for this.

Close your eyes and simply let yourself fall into the folds of the chair. With your eyes closed and while continuing to breathe freely, imagine you are looking at the large toe of your left foot. In your mind's eye, see this toe exactly as it appears when your eyes are open. As you see it with your mind's eye, imagine a mist or steam passing out and feel it begin to relax.

If you have done this properly and truly relaxed this toe, you will feel the beginning of a tingling sensation, as if it were falling asleep. Now go on to the other toes of the left foot, one by one, relaxing and picturing each in your mind's eye.

Once you have succeeded in relaxing your toes, go on to the rest of your left foot. When this is totally relaxed and only when you feel that this is so, you are to repeat this process with the toes of your right foot, starting with the big toe.

Complete the same process with your entire right foot. When done, return to your left ankle. Visualize and relax. Now the left calf, now the left thigh, and up the entire left leg. Now go back to the right side, and relax the right ankle, the right calf, the right thigh, and entire right leg.

Continue relaxing each part of your body in turn, alternating from the left to the right side and ever moving upward—hips, stomach, chest, back, neck, hands, arms, shoulders, and on up to the very top of your head.

If you have performed this exercise correctly, you will begin to experience a tingling sensation in each part of the body, which will eventually extend throughout. Should you not begin to experience this tingling sensation, you must keep relaxing and visualizing that particular part of the anatomy until you do.

Beginners often get stuck on one or another part. Don't be discouraged by this if it happens to you, even if it's with the left foot. Simply practice each day, at the same time and in the same place, until you are able to thoroughly relax yourself from the tips of your toes to the top of your head. Easy? Yes, that's all there is to it, but you must be faithful.

Always remember the picture of the two children on the seesaw. One is mind, and one is body. What you are doing is lowering body so that mind can rise. Despite what you may have been told, despite what you may believe, this is the truth and the only way!

You must practice this exercise at least *once each and every day* for as long as it takes for you to energize the astral or psychic body, which is really what you are doing. This single exercise is the key to all the other work you will be doing.

Special Breathing Exercises

In the East the special use of the breath has always played a role in psychic development. One does not just breathe in order to live, though that is what most of us do.

Ancient mystics and priests discovered that breathing in a special way somehow actually quickens the psychic perception and can truly bring one to the world of spirit.

If you remember our interview with Patricia Hayes, who was

formerly Arthur Ford's secretary, both she and Ford put great store in the use of breathing exercises to assist one in entering the trance state. In fact, you will recall that Ford was first taught such special breathing exercises by Paramahansa Yogananda.

What is not commonly realized by most people is that breath contains a special property or kind of energy, called *prana* by the Indian yogis.

It is not simply the necessity for oxygen that makes one have to breathe, but rather the need for this special kind of energy, *prana*, the same energy that is found in electricity.

This is why the ancients believed the soul actually entered the body of the newly born with the first breath. *Anima* in Latin means both soul and breath.

Just as some people live to eat, rather than eat to live, so do others simply breathe to stay alive rather than use their breath as a vehicle to carry their soul to the world of spirit.

Begin to watch your breathing, and you will learn many wondrous things. For instance, when you are nervous and excited, your breathing will be faster, and your pulse rate will follow accordingly. When you are naturally relaxed, such as after you have performed your daily meditation exercise, you will find your pulse rate and breathing much slower than when you began.

What we are saying is that through the proper control of your breathing, you can actually *become one with the energy of the cosmos*.

In his autobiography *Nothing So Strange*, Ford says the following concerning proper use of the breath by those who would become mediums:

Students of psychic development soon find out that rhythmic breathing has a peculiar effect in producing a peculiar kind of energy. What this energy is, is a debated question. Whatever its intrinsic nature, however, it is felt as a current, a definite force, a vitalizing agent. And it stimulates psychic development. Indeed, without it psychic development is impossible.

Again, like meditation, while there are various methods of breath control, called *pranayama* by the Indians, the following exercises are those that appear most frequently in the writings of those who have actually made spirit contact.

Exercise Two

Ascertain your normal heartbeat by placing the first three fingers of the right or left hand over the opposite wrist. Be sure that you use your first three fingers and not your thumb, which has a pulse of its own.

Once you have established the count, you are ready to begin this exercise. Sit comfortably, and begin to breathe *in through your nose* while mentally counting one, two, three, four, five, six in accord with your pulse beat.

When you have reached the count of six, *stop breathing in*, and hold your breath for the count of one, two, three. Then slowly *exhale*, again to the count of six. Rest for three counts and then begin again.

Let us repeat. Breathe in for six counts, hold your breath for three counts, breathe out for six counts.

This exercise is to be repeated preferably three times a day, commencing with five minutes for each session. After a week's practice, you should attempt to extend each practice session to at least ten minutes each. This means you will be practicing three times a day for ten minutes each.

This particular exercise is the most basic in the mastery of breath control. Some students have found it easier to count from one to nine, breathing in on the count one to six, and holding the breath for seven, eight, and nine; then exhaling for the count one to six and resting for seven, eight, and nine.

Once you have practiced this exercise for a few weeks, you may wish to start increasing the duration of each cycle. This can easily be done by breathing in for eight counts, holding the breath for four counts, exhaling for eight counts, and resting for four counts.

The exact number of counts (which again should correspond to your pulse rate) is unimportant as long as the proper ratio is maintained. The incoming and outgoing breath should be the same count while the retained breath and the resting breath should be *half the count* of inhalation and exhalation.

If you are a smoker, you may find that even a count of six is too much. If this is the case, start with four counts and increase from there.

Again, for best results this exercise must be practiced daily.

Exercise Three

Once Exercise Two has been mastered, this exercise is to be used whenever possible. Called the Grand Psychic Breath, this exercise, like meditation, releases psychic energy that can be used to make contact with our spirit friends.

Sit comfortably, and with the fingers of the left hand, gently press closed your left nostril, and breathe in through the right for a count of six. Hold your breath for three counts, then gently close the right nostril and exhale through the left for a count of six. Rest for three counts. Now gently close the right nostril, and breathe in through the left for six counts. Hold the breath for three counts. Now gently close the left nostril, and exhale through the right for six counts. This completes one full cycle.

Let us repeat again. Breathe *in through the right* and *out through the left*. Then breathe *in through the left* and *out through the right*.

This exercise should replace the second, once it has been mastered, and should be practiced whenever possible throughout the day. Again, like the meditation exercise, if it has been practiced correctly, the student will find that each part of his or her body will begin to tingle and come alive. This is an excellent exercise to practice when one is depleted of energy or before practicing the meditation exercise.

Exercise Four

Once Exercise Three has been mastered and the flow of psychic energy (*prana*) has been felt, while continuing to breathe in the manner instructed, the student should attempt to direct this energy to the various chakras, or psychic centers, in the body.

These centers are as follows:

the forehead
the back of the head
the base of the brain (often called the medulla)
the hollow of the throat
the solar plexus (located between the navel and the breastbone)
the sacral region (the lower tip of the spine)
the reproductive area

The Use of Sound to Contact Spirit

In the previous exercises, meditation and breath have been used to relax the physical body while quickening the psychic and spiritual centers.

Although there may be mediums who do not consciously perform these exercises, close physiological examination of them during the trance state will show changes in the pulse rate *that correspond to those we are developing* through these exercises.

From ancient times, sound has been used to produce a meditative state and to stimulate various psychic centers, especially the pituitary and pineal glands.

These two very special glands are located in your head. The pituitary is found about one inch behind the root of the nose. Behind it, in almost the exact center of your head, is the pineal gland. While these two glands produce various physical effects on growth and other functions, their *psychic counterparts* have much to do with spiritual development. Just as everything in the universe consists of both matter and energy, so do each of the so-called endocrine glands have a spiritual or psychic function.

The following exercises cause a connection to be formed between these two glands, which then allows the passage of energy through the *antahkarana*, or psychic bridge.

Exercise Five

Sit in a relaxed position as previously instructed. On the note A natural, sound the mantra RA-MA seven times. This is to be done by drawing out the AH sound, i.e., RAAAAAA . . . MAAAAAA for as long as you can. Take a deep breath through the mouth or nose, and then begin to sound RAAAAAA and then MAAAAAA, until the very last ounce of breath has been used up.

It is very important that the breath be entirely consumed by the sound of RA-MA. Before chanting each time, be sure to take a deep breath, which is to be entirely used up by the chant.

Repeat this seven times. Rest. Repeat nine times.

A variation on this exercise is as follows: While performing the above exercise, picture in your imagination a bright yellow light, slightly tinted with green, like bright sunlight falling through the leaves of tall trees. Once this picture has been formed in your mind, project this light up to the center of your head *while continuing to chant RA-MA.*

This exercise and its variation should be practiced at least once daily, along with the breathing exercise and the daily meditation. (By now you are probably starting to say, "Hey, Mr. Zolar, I don't have time to do all this!" If so, you don't have time to become a medium, either!)

Awakening the Love or Throat Center

The throat center, which corresponds to the thyroid gland, is located directly behind the Adam's apple, forward of the spinal column.

It is here that divine love first begins, later to be passed on to the heart center. This center *must* be awakened if one is to make contact with friends in spirit. In the finality, it is only love that can bring them to us and enable us to reach them.

Exercise Six

Once again, begin by sitting in a relaxed position. After centering your attention on the throat, imagine a bright orange light covering this area. Take a deep breath, and as you exhale completely intone the mantra THO (pronounced as in "throw"). This mantra is to be sounded on F sharp above middle C. Repeat this chant five times each day while continuing to visualize the color embracing the throat center.

Some Useful Visualization Exercises

The following exercises have been found useful in creating the correct psychic state so that our spirit friends may make contact with us. Not everyone who practices these exercises will enter the trance state. But as has already been discussed by various mediums, it is doubtful whether it is actually necessary for one to enter a deep trance in order to work as a medium. Many mediums simply tune in and repeat orally what they hear clairaudiently or feel clairsentiently.

While one can desire to enter the deep trance state, interviews with various mediums indicate that it has to come about on its own accord and in its own time.

Just as not all mediums have a particular gatekeeper or control, such as what Fletcher was for Arthur Ford, so does it not seem necessary to enter a deep trance state in order to perceive our spirit friends. Children, for instance, often see spirit friends or spirit playmates without becoming entranced. It is easy for them to do this since they have not been programmed to believe that they cannot and that what we call death is the ending of life.

In the last analysis, it is always our beliefs, our thoughts that bring us freedom—or bondage.

Exercise Seven

Once you have succeeded in totally relaxing yourself through meditation and breathing, imagine above your head a great white orb, like the sun, as wide as you are tall. See this globe in your mind's eye as pure, white light. You must clearly see this light totally without any qualities or markings whatsoever. Practice seeing this light at least three times a day, for one month.

Exercise Eight

After practicing Exercise Seven for an entire month, once again visualize this globe of white light floating above your head. This time, feel yourself being drawn up into it at the same time that it is descending down into you. Imagine that you are standing in this center of white light.

Making Contact with a Loved One in Spirit

In order to begin to draw the energy of a loved one, now in spirit, to you, you must set aside a private space in your home as something of a shrine—a location in which you can place a photograph of the loved one, a crystal glass filled with water (which you will change every seven days), a white candle, and a small flower vase. The photograph should be of the loved one only, with no one else in it.

Once a week, you must change the water in the glass, replace the flower or flowers, and light the white candle. Just as meditation must follow a strict schedule, these practices should be done on the *same* day of the week at the very *same* time of day. The candle may be allowed to burn itself out.

Every day, you must take this picture from its very special place with you to your meditation chamber and do the following exercise.

Exercise Nine

After completing your meditation, and while you are still relaxed, open your eyes for a moment and look at the picture of your loved one. After gazing at the picture for awhile, lay it aside and again enter into meditation. After you are completely relaxed once again, visualize the face of your departed friend. See and feel it as clearly as if that person were standing right in front of you. Mentally call the name of the person, over and over again, as you continue to see his or her face. Now try to feel yourself actually merging and becoming one with your loved one.

Practice this exercise at least once a day for six days. On the seventh day, replace the water and the flowers, and let a white candle burn once more.

After completing this exercise, the picture should be returned to its special position next to the water and flowers. Remove it from this position only when you meditate each day, and replace it when you have finished your meditation.

This concludes the exercises that you are to do *by yourself* in order to make spirit contact. In the next chapter we will present various methods to be used "when two or more are gathered together."

22

—o—

How to Develop
Your Own Mediumship:
Part Two

*The mediumistic faculty in all its forms can be cultivated
by sitting in the spirit circle, which tends to perfect and
spiritualize the magnetism of the sitters by their mutual
action on each other and by the influence of the spirits.*

—Mrs. Emma Hardinge Britten

In the previous chapter we presented a number of exercises that
should be done by one who seeks to make spirit contact. The nature
of these exercises are akin to the training an athlete undertakes prior
to entering an actual contest. Just as boxers will run to build lung
capacity, and football players lift weights, so must the developing
medium build psychic or spiritual muscle.

Once you have attained success in these exercises, you are ready
to join others who are likewise seeking to become mediums.
Developmental groups, or "home circles," as they have been called
since the inception of spiritualism, can often be found by attending a
spiritualist church or various lectures sponsored by Spiritual Frontiers Fellowship. Appendix 3 lists several spiritualist camps and
organizations that you can contact for information about churches
and lectures in your area.

If you are unable to locate a home circle where you live, you may
simply wish to start one, guided by the instructions that follow.

Kinds of Mediumship

Before studying the traditional instructions for sitting in a circle, we must distinguish between the various kinds of mediumship and their manifestations.

Lloyd Kenyon Jones, in a booklet entitled *Development of Mediumship*, lists the following as the best-known and most satisfactory types:

1. The direct voice medium, who secures the voices of discarnate spirits so these may be heard by all others present.
2. The materializing medium, through whose powers the discarnate forms materialize, becoming just as solid and real to the eyes and the ears of the persons in the seance room as mortals would be.
3. The etherealizing medium, who secures the astral or etherealized figures that are apparently phosphorescent, that do not appear solid like the materialized forms.
4. The transfiguring medium, around whose physical being are built forces to give a resemblance of the spirit that is manifesting through the physical body of the medium.
5. The trance, test, or control medium, who is controlled and through whom the spirits speak.
6. The healing medium, who may produce none of the manifestations above-named, but who brings healing forces to others.
7. The independent, slate-writing medium, who secures writings on slates that are not touched by the hands of any living person.
8. The spirit photographer, whose sole gift is to photograph materialized forms in a cabinet, or under conditions similar to those produced by a cabinet.
9. The painting medium, through whose mediumistic powers beautiful paintings are made upon canvas or other materials, without the touch of human hands.
10. The physical manifestation medium, through whose force musical instruments are played, or articles of furniture moved, or physical objects suspended in space.
11. The automatic writing medium, through whose hands dear ones in spirit write with pen or pencil. This type includes the planchette and the Ouija Board.

12. The inspired medium, through whom the spirit forces work in an inspirational manner, such as in oratory or music.

Having this basic knowledge of the different types of mediumship, we can now proceed to the home circle, which has served as the primary tool for mediumistic development since the phenomenon first appeared.

The Home Circle

By a home circle we simply mean a group of persons who meet on a regular basis with the express purpose of making spirit contact.

Like meditation, it is important that this circle meet at the *same* time and in the *same* place each week. In fact, to as great an extent as is possible, the group assembled should be limited to the *same* persons as well, and include only those persons who are sincerely committed to making spirit contact.

While there is a great deal of debate as to whether or not developmental circles must be held in the dark, such experts as D. D. Home, whose life and works were discussed in an earlier chapter, would clearly answer in the negative. It was Home's belief, as reported many times by Sir William Crookes, that nothing could be made to manifest in the dark that could not be made to appear in the light. Again, if your personal inclination is to require darkness or semidarkness for your seance, this should be followed. On the other hand, if you are inclined to sit in the light instead, do so, for your spirit friends come both in light and darkness.

An advantage of sitting in the light, as pointed out by Home, is having the evidence of one's eyesight as to what is actually being seen, which can outweigh the absence of certain phenomena. In darkness one is not always quite sure as to what has been seen. Also, darkness always makes it possible for fraudulent mediumship to take place. In any event, you must choose for yourself.

Zolar would suggest that initial meetings be held in the light. If after a few meetings phenomena do not appear, proceed to semidarkness and wait once more. If development still seems retarded, proceed to total darkness.

Remember that, once developed, a medium who speaks on the platform of a spiritualist church usually works in the light while giving messages. The ability to work in the light is well established.

As to the actual layout of the seance room, as far as possible it should be quiet and away from any disturbances. If there is a telephone in the room, it should be disconnected or removed so as not to disturb the circle.

If you have any domestic pets, especially dogs and cats, they should also be removed from the room prior to sitting. Very often they will see and hear spirit long before those assembled and may react adversely.

It is also important to control the temperature in the room. If it is somewhat cool, you may want to raise it, for as the seance progresses, the temperature often drops, which may make it uncomfortable for those assembled.

You may also wish to place around the room some fresh flowers. It is also useful to place crystal bowls of water, both in the center of the table, if one is sitting around one, or on the floor at the center of the circle.

Think of the seance as building a battery. Each person who is himself a conductor of subtle energies must be placed in exactly the right position for the maximization of energy. This is why it is important that the circle meet on time, with the same persons present at each meeting.

In the beginning, one should meet no more than three times a week, at exactly the same time in the evening in exactly the same room. Again, note that regularity is absolutely necessary to produce the highest results.

The chairs that are used should offer firm sitting. Dining room or straight-back chairs may be preferable to those that are especially soft. Each person should sit with the spine as straight as possible and with both feet placed on the floor. The legs should remain uncrossed, with the hands resting palms downward on the knees, unless other instructions come from spirit.

If there is already present one person who has shown a fair degree of development of the gift of materializing mediumship, a cabinet will be needed. This can be a closet off the seance room to which the door can be left open, with some dark material such as a blanket hung in front. The cabinet enables the energy of the materializing spirit to be concentrated and made visible.

If this particular type of mediumship is being practiced, the other sitters should form a semicircle in front of the cabinet.

If those in attendance are working toward voice mediumship, it will be necessary to have a trumpet, one made of aluminum or fiber. This can be suspended by a string or ribbon and hung in the center of the circle. There should also be on hand a tray of water into which the trumpet can be dipped, should manifestations begin.

The circle itself should be composed of no less than four persons and no more than twelve. If at all possible, there should be an equal number of men and women, who will seat themselves alternately, male and female, around the table or in a circle.

Once a seating arrangement has been established, it should be written down and maintained from session to session. It may be that along the way two persons are inclined to change seats or be instructed to do so by spirit. If this happens, this new seating should be noted and utilized next time. The medium or, if there is not a medium present, the person most sensitive should sit at what might be called the head of the table or center of the circle.

Conversation before the circle, when sitters are gathering, should be light and free from criticism and discord. Remember that holding a circle is akin to the act of worship, for God and spirit are one.

When each sitter has arrived and has taken his or her seat, the seance is ready to begin. If it has been decided to sit in the dark, lights can now be extinguished. The actual size of the circle is, of course, determined by the number of persons present. It should be kept as tight as possible and should initially last for no more than an hour.

It is always good to begin each sitting with a prayer, which can be spontaneous or read from the many prayerbooks that are available. *The N.S.A.C. Spiritualist Manual* contains a number of such useful invocations. It should be noted, though, that there is no magic in any particular set of words. Rather, what is important is that the attitude of those assembled be clearly directed to the magnificence of the work that is about to begin.

After the prayer or invocation has taken place, the sitters should join hands and sit in silent meditation until the energy of the group has been raised. If the sitting is at a table, the hands of each person may simply be placed palms downward, with the small fingers of the hand of each sitter touching those of the person next to him on both sides. The table, which should be made of wood, serves as a conductor for the energy that will be released by the circle.

Once the circle is complete and the seance begun, there should be no movement about the room. Those in need of drink or restrooms should take care of these needs *before* the seance actually begins. Many a good seance has been destroyed by someone having to get up and excuse themselves. This is to be avoided at all costs.

Sometimes, once spirit has been contacted, a particular person may be asked to leave the circle without explanation. If this happens, the person so chosen should not feel hurt or slighted but recognize the fact that he or she is assisting those who remain in the circle to maximize their development. This does not mean that this particular person cannot develop, but simply that their unique energy field may not be in harmony with that needed by the other sitters.

On some occasions, those sitting may feel compelled to sing popular or inspirational songs, or to chant, as we have instructed in an earlier chapter. If this occurs, those in the group should follow their inclinations. Spirit loves music in all its forms.

While anyone who attends a seance is desirous of manifestations, it is possible that they may not appear for a number of sessions. It is here that we separate those who are truly sincere in their desire to become mediums from those who are just curiosity seekers. Even if there is no manifestation, the same persons should continue to meet for as long as it takes spirit to make an appearance.

Remember that spirit works according to God's time and not man's. While man may wish to have something happen right now, this may not be the desire of spirit. Rather we must simply sit in silence and wait.

As spiritualism follows natural law, there will be manifestations, according to the biblical promise that "where two or more are gathered together in my name, there am I in the midst of them" (Matthew 18:20).

Manifestations

If one or more of the sitters proves to be mediumistic, manifestations can occur at the very first sitting. These may take many forms, including traditional rappings in different parts of the room and the appearance of various lights or flashes. While not all the persons sitting may see the lights due to the position of their seats, all are likely to hear the rappings.

Once the rappings are heard, those sitting can begin to question them by the use of a spirit alphabet as follows:

One rap indicates "No."
Two raps indicate "Doubtful."
Three raps indicate "Yes."
Four raps indicate "Don't know."
Five raps indicate "Call the alphabet."

Should five raps be heard, it will be the duty of the circle leader to begin to call out the alphabet, one letter at a time, until a rap or table tilt indicates a particular letter. Though time-consuming, if used correctly, this method makes it possible to obtain a complete message with little or no special skill required on the part of the sitters.

If one is sitting for trumpet manifestation, one of the first indications of the presence of spirit is the movement of the trumpet in the air or on the floor.

In the event that a member of the circle becomes controlled and the beginning of trance mediumship manifests, the person may begin to groan and moan. This should not upset those sitting as it is a natural occurrence and must happen before genuine trance can take place. There must be enough confidence in one's friend in spirit, and in God, to know that no harm can come to anyone in the circle no matter what may appear to be taking place. Our friends in spirit always work through love. Love never produces harm.

If someone does become entranced, or controlled, and begins to speak in a different voice, those present in the circle may begin in turn to ask questions, for which they will no doubt receive answers in due course.

When this occurs for the first time, it often takes the controlled person some time in which to come back into his or her self, after the seance has been concluded. Again, do not be alarmed if this is so. You may assist this person by lightly tapping the medium's hands or delicately splashing a little cool water on the person's face.

Sometimes during the seance those assembled may feel touches on their face, hands, or legs, or on other parts of their bodies. On some occasions, the smell of flowers or perfume will be present, or the sounds of rustling garments will be heard. The appearance of vaporous shapes or forms may suggest the need for a cabinet in which to capture them next time.

In the case of materializations, which usually occur in the dark, no light should be turned on until it is mutually agreed that the seance is concluded. To turn the light on prematurely often causes the energy that has been released to flow back into the medium with great force, producing a shocklike feeling.

When spirit voices have begun to be heard, they themselves will inform those present when the seance is to be ended.

Slate Writing

To develop what is called independent slate writing, the seance room is arranged in the usual manner, with the exception that a small table should be placed in the center of the room to hold the slates.

The slates are simply two small, double-sided blackboards with a small piece of chalk or chalks placed between them. The two slates should be tied together with string or cord. Those sitting in the circle should place their fingertips on the edge of the slates during the seance.

Sometimes before the chalk begins to move, those sitting in the circle will feel a sensation of cold air blowing over their hands. Those who are more sensitive may perceive this as a wavelike motion or pulsation, while others may feel slight electric shocks. If slate writing is to manifest, messages will begin to appear on the inside of the slates, with no human hand touching the chalk.

Slate writing is a special form of mediumship that usually appears as a result of the combined development of the circle rather than as a result of the abilities of a single person. One should enter the circle not with a particular manifestation in mind, but rather being thankful for whatever might appear.

There is no way of knowing for sure what particular manifestation a particular group of individuals present might best be suited for. One must simply pay attention to whatever appears.

Automatic Writing

No discussion of spirit phenomena could be complete without mention of the popular Ouija Board and the planchette—the tools with which automatic writing takes place.

It is impossible to estimate how many thousands, or perhaps millions, have played with the Ouija Board and the planchette, a small triangular table mounted on three legs that is placed on the board, on which are printed the letters of the alphabet, the arabic numerals 0 through 9, and the words "yes," "no," and "good-bye."

This modern counterpart of a very ancient device, allegedly used by the Greek philosopher and mathematician Pythagoras in the sixth century B.C., came into great popularity during World War I, when many interested in spirit sought to contact loved ones who had been lost in the war.

The Ouija Board derives its name from a combination of the words meaning "yes" in two languages, French and German. For the most part, those who play with the Ouija Board are doing just that—playing. In the hands of sincere seekers, however, the board can be useful in promoting spirit contact.

To operate the board, one or more persons lightly place their fingertips on the planchette and, mentally or aloud, ask a particular question. After a short while, the planchette will appear to begin to move and will often spell out an answer. Since it is necessary to see the letters to which the planchette points, the board is always used in the light.

While use of the Ouija Board has been called everything from the work of the devil to just good fun, its workings have been greatly misunderstood. To many, the information that comes through the board is spurious, silly, and meaningless. In some instances this happens because those using the board have done so for too long a period of time and have actually exhausted the subtle forces that are released by this process.

Again, it is all-important that the use of this device be approached in a positive manner.

If one removes the planchette (named after a noted French spiritualist) from the Ouija Board and replaces the front leg with a pencil, it is transformed into a device commonly used for automatic writing.

In automatic writing, which is currently of common use among many mediums of note (you will recall that Patricia Hayes uses this technique), the planchette is placed on large sheets of paper. The person desiring to develop this form of mediumship simply rests his or her fingers on the planchette and waits for it to move. While it may take many evenings of sittings before the planchette will begin to move, once it begins it will usually continue.

At first only scribbling will appear. However, if one is persistent, in time the formation of letters will appear, and messages from friends in spirit will begin to come through.

Although, like the Ouija Board, the planchette can be used with others, it is particularly useful to one who wishes to develop this particular type of mediumship alone.

A mistake that is often made by those who wish to develop this skill is to write too long and too often. In the beginning, no more than one or two evenings a week should be used. These should be at the same time and on the same days. In this case, though, each session should be limited to no more than thirty minutes.

The best way in which to get results is to simply let the mind go blank and to allow whatever or whoever wishes to come through to do so.

In the past, a number of famous books have been written by and through spirit in this way, and I expect that even more will come forth as the influence of Aquarius intensifies as we move closer to the twenty-first century.

Lloyd Kenyon Jones, the author of *Development of Mediumship*, suggests the following cautions for both the Ouija Board and automatic writing:

1. All desire to hasten the receipt of messages from dear ones in spirit should be avoided.
2. The sittings should be of short duration and only on one or two evenings a week.
3. All questions asked should be sensible questions, and not along the line of typical fortune-telling.
4. Only one question should be asked at a time, and that very clearly and simply.
5. When the answer indicates that the information cannot or should not be given, that question should be dismissed and not asked again.
6. Unless the experimenters refrain from asking silly or unreasonable questions, they will not get satisfactory results. Our loved ones in spirit are very earnest. Why should we not respect them sufficiently to be serious with them?
7. When the message from the dear ones has been finished, there will be a definite indication that no more should be expected; that indication must terminate the sitting.

It should also be mentioned that some persons are able to do automatic writing by simply holding a pencil in their hand. While a planchette is a valuable tool for development, it is indeed just that, a tool.

The Use of Hypnosis

Many reading this chapter will recall our earlier discussion about the use of hypnosis or mesmerism to produce the trance state. As hypnosis requires a trained practitioner to induce the trance, we cannot say much here about its use in this way.

Certainly one has the option of seeking the assistance of a trained hypnotist. For the most part, though, we would not recommend this method, as in order to be hypnotized one must momentarily yield his or her will to that of the practitioner. Whether such yielding produces positive or negative spiritual results has been a matter of great discussion among occultists. Each individual must decide and choose for himself or herself.

Final Thoughts for Those Seeking Spirit Contact

As has been seen from our discussion to date, sitting in home circles is no doubt by far the easiest way to develop mediumship.

One must always be mindful of a fact that young, developing mediums often forget, namely, that there is a breadth and width to everything in the universe save the deity itself. This means that one can even overdo one's desire to become a medium. The vital life force that is required to produce spirit manifestation has limits and boundaries just like anything else. It must be *used* in order to be developed, but it cannot be *abused*.

Too frequently, beginning mediums become so excited at their success that they seek fame and fortune far too soon in their careers. When fame and fortune come before one's ability is firmly established, such often give rise to the temptation to fake one's abilities when genuine results do not manifest. It is this temptation and its consequences that have given spiritualism a bad name.

To close this chapter, again no better advice could be found than that of Lloyd Kenyon Jones:

We must not think that every person in the earthworld will be a spiritualist. We must remember that in the different religions there is beauty. Even though they may disagree with us, they are worshipping the same God. They are His children. They have as much right to their religious convictions as we have to ours. Condemn no person because he is a Catholic or a Methodist or a Christian Scientist or anything else. Each of us can see according to our own understanding and our own training and experience.

A hundred people located at a hundred different points around a mountain might all see that mountain differently, but they would be looking at the same mountain.

And so there are many different creeds worshipping God. They worship Him from different points of view, but it is the same God. Each one is as precious in his vision as any of the others. Each is His child.

As mediums understand and preach this doctrine of tolerance and love, they will bring credit upon their religion and upon themselves. Mediumship will mean more in the world than it has in the past.

If you are mediumistic, then you have much to be thankful for, and it is worth the time and the effort to try to bring out the powers that are within you, so that you may carry comfort and happiness to at least a few mortals. If during your earthlife, you have helped only a few, you may feel satisfied that your life has been for a great purpose. It has been worth living. Keep these ideals of spirit communication and mediumship before you at all times, and then you will not commit the error of feeling that one child of God has more right on earth than another child of God.

To be a medium means that a certain obligation has been placed upon you. Perhaps that obligation will demand your persecution— your suffering. What if it does? If you are really living for the truth in which you believe, the truth you love, then no sacrifice on your part should ever be too great for that truth. Your truth must be the dearest, nearest and sweetest thing in your existence. And when this has come about, you will find that you have moved many steps forward in making yourself an acceptable instrument through which the loved ones in the spiritworld may bring assistance and comfort to sorrowing, erring humanity.

23

The Laws of Spirit Mediumship: One Hundred Questions and Answers for the Investigator*

1. *What is spirit mediumship?*

The definitions accepted by the National Spiritualist Association tell us that "a medium is one who is sensitive to vibrations from the spirit world, and through his or her instrumentality those functioning in that world are able to convey messages and produce the phenomena of spiritualism."

2. *Do you believe that mediums are such from birth, or can they be developed?*

Experience has taught us to believe that our best mediums were such from birth, for psychic incidents of their childhood lead us to believe that such is the case. However, the spirit teachers tell us that each and every individual has some latent mediumistic power which

---

*These questions and answers, long unavailable to the seeker, were channeled by the late Rev. Lena Barnes Jefts, who at one time directed the School of Spiritual Truth in Miami, Florida.

can be developed by determined effort. We cannot always have the phase which we desire but must be content to develop that for which we are best fitted.

3. *Why is it that the loved ones of spirit must come through a medium rather than communicating directly to their own on earth?*

Could you send a telegram without the instruments? Can you pick music out of the air without your radio? The medium is the instrument through which these vibrations must come and unless the individual is a developed medium they are not liable to receive the message correctly. It is just as sensible to say that there is no music or sound passing through the air because you are not able to hear it with your physical ear as it is to say that your spirit mother cannot communicate because she is not able to do so through you directly.

4. *Is the development of mediumship harmful to a person?*

No, rather to the contrary, for many are greatly benefited mentally and physically by such contact.

5. *Do you believe that a person is liable to become obsessed by evil spirits if they try to develop mediumship?*

Absolutely not, the erroneous statement that one in becoming passive and receptive to spirit entities may attract an evil spirit who will lead them to do wrong creates much misunderstanding. The law of attraction governs these things, good attracting good and evil attracting evil. This is a natural law and we cannot get away from it; if an evil spirit can lead you to do wrong, it is the evil within yourself which makes it possible. To the good and true medium only the good can come.

6. *What are some of the things essential to good mediumship?*

A practical understanding of the philosophy and laws of mediumship, a sincere desire to give out only the highest and best, and a wish to be of service to mankind as the incentive for developing that mediumship. A true and sincere mediumship is the holiest gift ever received by mankind.

7. *Who was the greatest medium ever known?*

Jesus of Nazareth. The Bible is full of instances regarding his marvelous mediumistic powers.

8. *What great natural law controls all phases of mediumship?*

The law of vibration. All things in the universe are vibrating and their rate of vibration determines their nature. Each medium has a vibratory wave length and upon the strength of that medium, the conditions brought by the sitters, and the knowledge of the laws of communication displayed by the manifesting spirit depends the entire success of the phenomena presented.

9. *What would you advise as the best means of developing spiritual mediumship?*

I would suggest joining a developing class if possible under the direction of a good teacher. If you are not able to do this then form a small circle of sincere investigators and sit by yourselves. Three, five, or seven people of mixed sexes is best. Be practical, punctual, and conscientious, and do not become discouraged too easily if you do not receive manifestations right away.

10. *What are the best times and conditions to sit for such development?*

Any time that your mind is at ease and you can absolutely relax. You should appoint a certain time for your sittings and let nothing but sickness prevent you from keeping that appointment. Harmonious conditions are necessary for development and that is why you should choose very carefully those with whom you would sit. In your interest and anxiety to develop, do not overdo and sit too often or for too long a time.

11. *You say not to sit too often or too long—why? What effect would this have?*

Your body and brain are of matter and are attuned to the slower vibrations of the material plane. When you seek constantly to attune yourself to the higher and much more rapid vibrations of spirit, you are apt to shatter the delicate mechanism of that brain and cause disaster to the physical body. To become a fanatic on any one subject is to become unnatural, and the spirit teachers do not want us to do that. Let us always be natural and practical in our mediumship, realizing that it is not necessary to be weird in order to be a spiritualist.

12. *How often should one sit for unfoldment?*

Once a week in your class and perhaps twice a week for a short period of concentration or inspirational writing are enough.

13. *Is one apt to receive messages that are not uplifting or of a high moral character from those in the spirit world?*

What you seek largely determines the nature of what you receive. If John Smith of earth was a thief and not in the habit of telling the truth, he would be no different in the spirit world until he had learned the laws of progression and worked out of those conditions; therefore, he would not be apt to give you a very moral or uplifting communication. Your own mental and moral status determines the nature of spirits you will attract.

14. *Why is it that some spirits become confused when asked to give a message regarding time?*

In the spirit world, time is not divided into hours, days, weeks, and years as it is of earth, for time is eternal. The spirit entity may see something that is about to happen, it may be near or far off, and not being familiar with time as we see it, they sometimes make a mistake in judging the length of time before this will come to pass. The spirit guides are much better qualified to judge time for they are in constant contact with earth conditions, and even they sometimes make errors.

15. *Do you believe it necessary for a medium to be educated aside from his or her psychic development?*

Absolutely, yes. We might as well face facts and realize that one of the reasons why we have not attracted more of the higher and more intelligent minds into our ranks today is because of the illiteracy of many of our workers. Our mediums should be able to contact the thinking minds of the world in a manner that will be a credit to the cause, presenting a pleasing personality, using proper literary form, and being able to present the work always in a manner that commands the respect of the hearer, even though they may not accept it as truth. While education alone cannot make a psychic, it goes a long way toward making a psychic a success and a credit to the cause.

16. *Has the mental and moral status of the medium anything to do with those whom they contact from the spirit world?*

To a certain extent, yes. The law of like attracting like is a natural law, and it functions on both spiritual and material planes. If we are of a high mental and moral standard, is it not quite natural that spirits of a like nature can manifest harmoniously in our vibration? As before quoted, "Upon a medium's own ideals depends the heights to which her or his message shall ascend."

17. *What do you believe to be the most important teaching derived through mediumship?*

Those rules and precepts that enable us to understand better our lives both here and hereafter; those laws that teach us our relationship to the Brotherhood of Man and the Fatherhood of God; that marvelous counsel that bids us live in harmony with ourselves, with natural law, and with all mankind while we are yet upon the earth plane.

18. *How do we receive our spirit guides?*

They are attracted to us through the action of natural law. They can see our need of them or we perhaps through our instrumentality can be used by them to help mankind, thus aiding their development or progression as well as our own. Again the law of like attracting like is manifested, our weaknesses, our good traits, our work or interests in this life always attracting those of a like nature or desire from ''across the border.'' Upon your own mentality and spirituality depends the kind of guide that you will attract.

19. *The Bible tells us of spiritual gifts. Do you consider mediumship as such?*

Most certainly. There are many gifts of mediumship which are not recognized as such: any work of earth in which the spirit forces assist is really a phase of mediumship. Our greatest artists, musicians, poets, and other writers derive assistance from those who have passed on, just the same as those who are manifesting any accepted phase of mediumship. The Bible refers to spiritual gifts in 1 Corinthians 12:4, saying, ''Now there are diversities of gifts but of the same spirit.''

20. *Into what two classifications do we divide mediumship?*

Into mental and physical phases.

21. *What are the mental phases subject to?*

To the mind of the medium; all mental phases must come through the mind of this human instrument.

22. *What are the physical phases subjective to?*

The manifestations of physical mediumship do not come through the mind of the sensitive but are subjective to his or her physical condition. Just as certain chemicals and acids are needed in a battery to generate power, so are they needed in the body of a medium in order to produce the physical phenomena. That is the reason why all cannot be physical mediums; they do not have these necessary chemicals nor can the spirit forces succeed in building them up.

23. *What are the principal phases of mental mediumship?*

Clairvoyance, clairaudience, clairsentience, inspirational writing and speaking, psychometry, and mental healing.

24. *What are the principal phases of physical mediumship?*

Trumpet, levitation of objects and persons, materialization, dematerialization of matter, slate writing, automatic writing, magnetic and spiritual healing, and spirit photography.

25. *Does the success of a circle depend entirely upon the medium?*

Indeed not! No matter how good the medium, the circle cannot be successful unless the mental attitude of those sitting in that circle is right.

26. *Do you believe a medium can contact any spirit whom she or he might desire to?*

No. Any medium who claims that she or he can is making a misstatement. All spirits have not learned the laws of communication, some do not even know that they can communicate, and again all spirit entities are not able to manifest through the same vibration. You have met people here upon the earth plane to whom you have instantly taken a dislike; you were not in harmony with them nor they with you. If you could not come into each other's vibration on earth with any degree of success, it stands to reason that they would not vibrate harmoniously with you when in spirit. The same natural law of attraction controls both the earth and the spirit people. You often hear a spirit say in a trumpet circle, "I could not get through that vibration," or "This is such a splendid vibration in which to manifest,'' proving that all entities cannot manifest in the same vibration.

27. *What is the first step toward developing mediumship?*

To acquire the art of concentration.

28. *What is concentration?*

Concentration is the ability to focus the mind upon a certain thought or object and to hold it there to the exclusion of all else, entirely submerging yourself in this one thought. You will find as you develop that you can become more and more oblivious to everything going on about you and will gradually attain the art of perfect concentration.

29. *How do you attain concentration?*

By going into the silence alone and endeavoring to train the mind along this line. Absolute relaxation of mind and body is the first step; then try to shut out all sight and sound of the material world and visualize that upon which you would concentrate, trying to tune in with that spark of the infinite within yourself, to the great divine mind or infinite intelligence which controls all things.

30. *Can all people attain this ability in the same way?*

No, indeed! Some can concentrate while writing, others on music, some upon objects they are able to visualize, while others are able to gaze directly at a person and immediately lose themselves in concentration as they are reading this person.

31. *What do we gain by concentration?*

The ability to concentrate is a great asset to business and professional people as well as the medium, for it teaches them not to scatter their forces but to successfully direct them toward the accomplishment of one effort at a time. When they have once attained the ability to concentrate, they are able at will to tune in with the divine forces, obtaining guidance in solving life's problems for themselves and others.

32. *What is a clairvoyant?*

Properly speaking, a clairvoyant can see, hear, and sense the spirit people and their messages, but that it may be more clearly understood, we subdivide it into three phases: clairvoyance, clairaudience, and clairsentience.

33. *Can all three of the phases be developed by one medium?*

Yes, but this is not common. Some can only see while others can neither see nor hear, merely sensing all their messages. A medium that can see, hear, and sense them is indeed fortunate for he or she has every opportunity of receiving these marvelous and convincing proofs from these beloved ones in the higher world.

34. *Can you give a Bible reference which proves clairvoyance?*

Yes, indeed! In John 4:16–19, Jesus reads clairvoyantly for Mary at the well; 2 Kings 6:17; Chronicles 26:16; Daniel 8:3, in which Daniel has a clairvoyant vision; and many others.

35. *What is clairvoyance?*

It is the ability to see with the spiritual eye those who have made their change called death and to see their names, symbols, and messages many times written out in the air; sometimes called soul-seeing or lucidity.

36. *What do you mean when you speak of symbols?*

Nearly all clairvoyants receive symbols from their guides which mean certain things. There is no set way of interpreting these as each medium and guide seem to have their own code. The medium must learn to understand their meaning and to weave it all together in an intelligent message.

37. *Do you believe a clairvoyant can foretell future happenings as well as read the past?*

Yes, to a certain extent. The past has already happened, of course, and is naturally easier to read. The spirit friends have a better understanding of the law of cause and effect than we do and can see the direct results of our actions. Again they may have something in mind in which they intend to assist us, and if nothing happens to interrupt it comes to pass as they have foretold.

38. *Do you believe they can foretell death?*

In some rare cases, yes, but the majority of spirits tell us that they do not know any more about it than we of earth. They can only tell when the administering angels begin to gather by the bedside that death is about to occur.

39. *Do you believe that we can create thought images which are so vivid that we confuse them with things seen clairvoyantly?*

Absolutely, yes. It is possible to build in your own mind a thought image that is so real that unless you are fully developed clairvoyantly it is difficult to discriminate between the two. Constant practice and thorough development enable us to overcome this, however.

40. *How can we best develop clairvoyance?*

By sitting regularly at a stated time and trying to tune in with the spirit forces, trying to see with that spiritual eye those higher vibrations of the spirit people which the physical eye is not capable of receiving. The best time to sit is when you are able to put aside all material cares and absolutely relax, making the mind receptive. Clairvoyance can be developed in the daylight as well as in the dark.

41. *Do you believe that we are ever clairvoyant while sleeping?*

Yes, often. If we place ourselves in an attitude of expectancy just before sleep, we are more apt to see visions while in that state. Many believe that the soul leaves the body during sleep, going out upon the spiritual planes, but when awakened all experiences while there fade into oblivion.

42. *What is clairaudience?*

It is the ability to hear with the spiritual ear the whisperings of those who have made the change called death—soul-hearing.

43. *Do you believe that spirits can become annoying to a person who is clairaudient by constantly trying to talk to them?*

Perhaps they do in some cases, but it is all unnecessary, one does not need to heed that which they hear from spirit friends any more than that which they hear from the earth people. Perfect control of your own thoughts helps you to attune yourself to spirit vibrations only when you so desire.

44. *Can everyone become clairaudient?*

No, we do not believe so. Clairaudience comes to us through the ability of developing the inner spiritual ear to the point where it can catch these higher vibrations of sound which are inaudible to the physical ear. It seems that we cannot all of us develop that ability any more than we can all develop the physical phases. I believe that each human soul has some one phase of mediumship in which she or he excels, and it is that phase that she or he should seek to bring out the strongest.

45. *What conditions are essential for developing clairaudience?*

Freedom from all material thoughts, absolute quiet, and a passive

mind that one may listen with that spiritual ear for the higher vibrations of sound coming from spirit.

46. *What is clairsentience?*

It is the most common of all these phases of a clairvoyant, more
generally known as impressional mediumship. Many mediums get
their messages entirely in this way, neither hearing nor seeing the
spirit people, only sensing them and receiving impressionally their
messages.

47. *How can we differentiate between the real message of spirit
and our own thoughts?*

The first thought that comes to us is usually that of the spirit, the
longer we think about it before giving it out the more it is tinged
with our own personality. Only by practice and development are we
able to tell the spirit impressions from our thought vibrations.

48. *What is psychometry?*

Technically speaking the word means soul-measuring. It is the
mediumistic ability to read from the vibrations emanating from
different articles.

49. *Is psychometry the same as clairvoyance or clairaudience?*

No. As before stated, clairvoyance is the development of the
spiritual eye and clairaudience of the spiritual ear. Psychometry
could more directly be likened to clairsentience, for both are
impressional to a certain extent.

50. *What is the best way to develop psychometry?*

Take a letter or any other object and hold it in your hand. Try to
relax and to tune in to its vibrations, receiving any impressions that

you can regarding it or its owner, or naming spirits that it might attract.

51. *Do you think psychometry can always be depended upon?*

Not at first perhaps. In developing any phase of mental mediumship, the spirit is the sender and the medium the receiver. One must always give out freely that which they believe they are receiving from spirit, for only by constant practice and effort are they able to receive correctly. No medium is infallible, and I have yet to hear a spirit who claims to be. All are prone to error in sending and receiving spiritual telegrams just as we find confusion in our telegrams of earth. So let us use our intelligence in investigating, realizing that in the mass of evidence collected down through the ages, truth stands out predominant above the error.

52. *What is trumpet mediumship?*

It is the ability of the medium to produce, with the assistance of the spirit forces, the phenomena of levitation and voices which are audible to the physical ear. The trumpet, usually of tin or aluminum, is floated about the room by the spirits, not touched by human hand, else it could be termed a fake. The voices of the spirit loved ones are thrown into the trumpet, and we are able to talk to them as of earth.

53. *Why do they use the trumpet?*

Simply to intensify the voices that they may become audible to those in the seance.

54. *What Bible reference can you give to prove that trumpet manifestations were known in those earlier days?*

Exodus 20:18–23. In Exodus 19:16, trumpet voices were received through the mediumship of Moses on Mount Sinai.

55. *Do you hear of instances of levitation very often in the history of spiritualism?*

Yes. D. D. Homes, a noted physical medium, was many times levitated bodily and passed through a window into another building across the street. This was accomplished under strict test conditions. Tables and many other heavy articles of furniture have been known to be levitated by the spirit forces, and the Bible refers to levitation in Ezekiel 3:8, 11, and in Acts 8:39–40 we read of the levitation of Phillip.

56. *How is levitation accomplished?*

The majority of spirit teachers tell us that they draw a substance called ectoplasm (so named by Professor Richet of Paris) from the body of the medium the same as they do in materialization. This is combined with chemicals and strength drawn from the sitters and the atmosphere, and is formed into masses and rods by the spirit chemists and placed under the article they desire to levitate, thus overcoming the law of gravitation. This process is sometimes called *telekinesis*, meaning movement at a distance from the motive cause or agency, without material connection.

57. *How are voices produced?*

The sound vibrations in the air as well as those sent out by the sitters in their conversation are drawn into the trumpet by the spirit forces. These vibrations the loved ones pick up to carry on a conversation through their knowledge of the laws of articulation and by the use of ectoplasmic vocal organs developed in the trumpet.

58. *Why is it that the voices sometimes sound like those of the medium and the sitters?*

The spirit entity has no material vocal organs with which to produce sound and must draw from those of the medium and sitters, picking up the available sound vibrations sent out by the medium and others in the seance; therefore, it is natural that the voices reproduced should sound like those from whom they were drawn. Only by constant manifestation and a thorough knowledge of the laws of communication can the spirit succeed in making the voice sound like the dear familiar tones heard in earth life.

59. *What effect does the skeptic, with many doubts, have upon this manifestation?*

Thoughts are real and active things; a doubt vibration makes conditions that are almost impossible for the spirit forces to puncture. Doubt is a negative force, tearing down rather than building up. No matter how strong the medium may be, the thoughts of the sitters can to a certain extent make or mar a seance. One person can throw out doubt vibrations strong enough to spoil a large circle. One cannot condemn too strongly the investigator refusing to comply with the conditions required for the manifestation. When you visit a foreign country, you must comply with their laws in order to have harmony; so in seeking to contact the spirit world, you must obey the laws in order to get good results. If you do not want to do this, stay out of the seance room, for you are not yet ready to accept spirit phenomena.

60. *What conditions are conducive to good results?*

A passive mind seeking for truth and ready to accept it once found. We do not ask you to be gullible, for that too would be wrong, but do not demand of the spirit. Lead them gently out in your conversation, giving them every opportunity to give you a test without having to puncture a doubt vibration in order to do so. One who talks always receives more than he who sits silent. The very sound of your voice attracts the spirit loved ones, and they are able to gain strength of voice through the vibrations you send out in conversation; if you do not talk, neither can they to any great extent.

61. *What do you mean by a test message?*

A test in the vernacular of spiritualism is a spirit message which reveals facts, names, and dates that prove the personality of the manifesting entity, something that you are positive the medium could not know. It makes it very difficult for the spirit when we demand tests, for there we must contact the doubt vibration again. A name or a date is more difficult for the spirit to give than the message itself, and under some of the conditions brought into the seance room by the investigator, I wonder that they are able to give them at all. The spirit loved ones tell us that they realize the fact that our ever-doubtful minds demand these tests, and they many times come prepared to give them, only to have them torn down by our demands for something entirely different. There is just as much necessity for us to learn the laws of communication from our side of the veil as there is for the spirit to learn it from theirs.

62. *What sort of questions should one ask of their spirit loved ones when attending a seance?*

Questions of a reasonable nature. It is people who do not understand who are prone to demand tests or trivial things. When you demand names or dates as tests, it immediately sets in motion a negative vibration, for you have doubt thoughts in your mind as to their ability to give this information, else you would not have asked for it; these vibrations the spirit forces must puncture ere they can manifest. We sometimes make conditions quite impossible for them by our mental attitude. Be passive and lead the spirit gently out in your conversation, and they can give you tests which will be thoroughly convincing.

63. *What is materialization?*

It is one of the physical phases of mediumship and perhaps the most important; it is at least the rarest and most difficult of all phases. Through the instrumentality of the medium, with the assistance of the spirit guides and chemists, the spirit entity is able to manifest in a body which is a replica of its former physical body and is able to walk and talk as when on earth. This body is built of the same vaporous substance, called ectoplasm, which is utilized in telekinesis. This substance exudes from the body of the medium and is manipulated by the spirit doctors and chemists until it forms a solid substance which can be utilized for the time being as the vehicle through which your beloved who has passed on can manifest to you. This substance is contained within every individual to a certain extent, but the body of a physical medium must contain a superabundance of it in order to produce the phenomena. Those sitting in the seance assist in furnishing the necessary chemicals and strength for the manifestation.

64. *How is the spirit able to manage and manipulate this body?*

Through its own willpower. That is one reason why many spirits find it difficult to talk much in materialization; until they are thoroughly familiar with the laws governing this demonstration, they must constantly concentrate on the body to keep it from dematerializing and to make it look natural.

65. *What is impersonation?*

Impersonation is one of the different stages or degrees of materialization. In this case there is not strength or chemicals enough to produce a full form materialization, and the guides use the body of the entranced medium, draping the ectoplasm over his or her form. This is an authentic phase of mediumship, the same as full form materialization, but of course not as beautiful nor as difficult.

66. *What is etherealization?*

It is materialization to a certain extent, but there are not chemicals enough to form a solid substance of the ectoplasm; it is thin and ethereal, and you can see through it.

67. *Where do the spirits get the clothing worn in materialization?*

By the use of ectoplasm, and they also claim to be able to draw from the material in the room and the clothing worn by sitters enough materials with which to weave their robes. They are also able to draw color pigment from the flowers, rugs, and gowns, and reproduce it in their own garments, weaving in some cases robes and scarfs of beautiful colors.

68. What is transfiguration?

It is similar to impersonation. The body and features of the medium are transfigured to resemble those of the manifesting spirit entity.

69. What reference can you give which proves that materialization was known in biblical days?

Perhaps the outstanding references are found in Matthew 17:1–3, where Moses and Elias materialized through the mediumship of Jesus; in Daniel 5:5, where Belshazzar saw a materialized hand write on the palace wall; in John 20:14, where Mary saw Jesus after his crucifixion; and in Luke 24, where Jesus materializes several times for His disciples and many others.

70. In what way are these phenomena dangerous to the medium?

Each spirit is connected to the medium by an ectoplasmic cord, because the material used to build that body in which they temporarily manifest is drawn from the body of that sensitive; should someone touch a spirit unexpectedly, flash a sudden light, or startle the medium in any way, it might result in serious injury or perhaps death to the instrument, through the nervous shock and the rapid recoil of the ectoplasm back into his or her body. The medium being entranced in the cabinet is powerless to protect her or himself; that is why we should allow in these seances only the most serious of investigators, those who are willing to comply with all required conditions and receive their loved ones in the spirit in which they come—that of love and harmony.

71. *Why is it that some spirits can come farther out from the cabinet and seem to build more lifelike than others?*

There could be several reasons for this: first, perhaps a natural tendency of the spirit to be timid; second, a lack of willpower or of knowledge regarding the laws governing the phenomena; and last but not least, the negative thought vibrations sent out by the sitters and perhaps by the very person to whom this spirit might come. Each time they materialize they become stronger and more natural because they understand the laws better.

72. *Which phase of mediumship does healing come under?*

It really comes under both mental and physical phases of mediumship. The magnetism which is contacted by the laying on of hands is a physical phase, while the mental healing is of the other.

73. *We notice that the two terms* spirit healing *and* spiritual healing *are used. How do you differentiate between the two?*

Spiritual healing is that phase of mediumship in which the spirit doctor works through his human instrument to assist humanity, through the power of divine love, either mentally or through magnetic forces. Magnetic healing is also the same, but spirit healing is that cure that is effected by the spirit entity upon the patient without the aid of a human instrument. This is mental to a great extent, although the teachers tell us they are able to use magnetic forces also. This might also be termed divine healing.

74. *Can everyone become a healer?*

No, indeed, we each have our own phase of mediumship for which we individually are best fitted, and that phase once discovered should be developed to the highest degree.

75. *Who was the greatest spiritual healer the world has ever known?*

Jesus of Nazareth. Without a doubt this was his phase of medi-umship, and many incidents of his marvelous healing powers are given in the Bible. See 1 Kings 17:17–24, where Elijah is the healer; the first four books of the New Testament are full of the healing done by Jesus; also Acts 13–14, which speaks of Peter, John, and Paul carrying on the healing as commanded by Jesus in Matthew 10:8.

76. *What natural law must be understood thoroughly by the spirit who is trying to heal?*

The law of vibration. As before stated, this is effective in all phases of mediumship but especially so in healing. The spirit doc-tors tell us that in mental sickness the vibrations must be lowered while in physical illness they must be raised.

77. *Does distance make any difference in mental healing?*

None at all. The spirit loved ones tell us that they can travel on thought waves at will and so can send out upon the ether thought waves of healing which we know through experience prove very beneficial.

78. *Why should healers always strive to keep every organ of their own bodies clean and healthy?*

Because the spirit operators tell us they are able to draw from the healthy organs of the healer to assist the corresponding diseased organ of the patient. If the healer is not healthy, it is therefore more difficult for the spirit to draw the necessary magnetic forces to accomplish a cure.

79. *Why must we always think right to assist in a healing?*

Our thoughts have a great deal to do with the success of such an operation. Even our medical doctor recognizes the power of auto-suggestion and utilizes it in his profession. Think health constantly, visualize yourself as well and whole, and you are doing your part to assist in bringing about a cure. Use the following healing affirmation frequently: "I am God's perfect child and as such must realize that I have the power within myself to heal myself."

80. *I hear the term inspirational writing used by spiritualists often. Is this a phase of mediumship?*

It is indeed and a most beautiful and constructive one too. Most of our books on spiritualism are inspired writing, and I believe that all poets and authors receive more or less assistance from their spirit helpers. It is a mental phase of mediumship coming through and colored by the mind of the instrument.

81. *How can this phase of mediumship be developed?*

By going into the silence and in a prayerful attitude trying to contact the thought vibrations coming from this higher mind of spirit. That mind is seeking through your instrumentality to assist humanity. Write whatever comes into your mind as you seek to tune in, and gradually as you develop you will be able to receive better, learning to submerge your own personality and receive correctly almost word for word from the spirit.

82. *Do you believe an inspirational writer must be educated in order to write well or can she or he receive wonderful writings regardless of her or his own limitations?*

Inspirational writing comes through the mentality of the medium; therefore he or she limits or assists the communications by his or her own mental status. Sometimes the spirit teachers tell us that they can give us word for word, but many times they give us the thought they intend to convey and we clothe it in our own words; therefore, you see how necessary it is that we have a good vocabulary and use good English. We have a few instances where an illiterate person has been able to write a splendidly constructed article or book, but this is only possible when the instrument is entranced or gets it through automatic writing, and even then the personality of the instrument is bound to creep through more or less.

83. *Do you believe all public speakers to be inspired?*

Yes, to a certain extent. Our best speakers are those who can tune in with the spirit forces and receive inspirationally these beautiful truths from the infinite source of all knowledge. Being perfectly conscious they realize the necessity for a dignified and intelligent presentation at all times.

84. *What is the difference between trance and inspiration?*

In trance the mind and personality of the medium are entirely submerged, the spirit taking full control of the instrument; the medium is unconscious of all she or he says or does. In inspiration the medium is fully conscious and in perfect control of mind and body; she or he simply receives and gives out in her or his own way the words and thoughts dictated by the spirit.

85. *Which do you believe to be the better?*

Many prefer inspiration to trance. In the School of Spiritual Truth trance is not sought except in materialization. There have been too many illiterate and undignified presentations of trance in past years for it to be a very appealing phase to the intelligent investigator.

86. *Do you believe that the great spirit teachers and lecturers of the past ages are apt to manifest through an illiterate, untrained medium?*

Absolutely not. Like attracts like. A master mind of spirit may see great possibilities in an untrained mind of earth and seek to develop it, but the human instrument must do its part to assist in the development by reading and studying and otherwise perfecting him or herself, or else the spirit guides pass on to one whose mentality they can use.

87. *What is automatic writing and what phase of mediumship does it come under?*

In automatic writing the hand of the medium is controlled by the spirit; they write whatever they choose. It is a physical phase of mediumship, for the message written is entirely independent of the mind of the instrument.

88. *We also hear of a phase of mediumship called slate writing. Is this similar to inspirational or automatic writing?*

Neither. The slate writer is a physical medium the same as the automatic writer, but the medium does not do the writing; the spirit does this with its own hand, using the psychic strength of the medium.

89. *What great Bible character can we liken to our slate writer of today?*

Moses, who received the Ten Commandments on tablets of stone. See Exodus 24:12–18.

90. *Must one always place pencils in the slates?*

No, many mediums are able to receive communications in colors as well as in pencil with no crayon or pencil within the slates. The spirit entity is able to draw from the atmosphere and surrounding materials the necessary color pigment with which to write. This does not seem strange when we stop to realize that everything which constitutes matter can be found in the atmosphere.

91. *Is this a very common phase?*

No, it is rather uncommon. While we hear of many slate writers, there are comparatively few who are well known and psychically tested.

92. *Who are the best-known slate writers in America today?*

Pierre L., O. E. Keeler, and Mrs. Laura Pruden, of Cincinnati, Ohio, who received for Horace Leaf, of London, a most convincing message from Sir Arthur Conan Doyle.

93. *What is prophecy and are prophets fortune-tellers?*

Prophecy is that phase of mediumship which enables one to peer into the future and forecast coming events. The spirit who gives these prophecies must have a thorough knowledge of the laws of the universe in order to forecast with any degree of success. A prophet is not a fortune-teller, for there is a wide gulf between the two. A fortune-teller reads by stars, cards, or palms, while a spiritual prophet receives his or her message through spirit communication.

94. *Did we have prophets in biblical times?*

We did, indeed, but none more wonderful than we have now. Although they are not honored today as in biblical times, we still have those who are able to foretell events as did those prophets of past ages. The Bible has many quotations on prophecy; in Psalm 84:9, we read that the people feel that God has cast them off forever because "they see not sign nor is there any amongst us that knoweth how long"; in Samuel 28, which speaks of Saul and the woman of Endor; and in Matthew 26, where Jesus prophecies his own crucifix-ion and his betrayal by Peter. In many other places prophecy is spoken of as both true and false.

95. *How can we best develop that phase of mediumship?*

By giving out freely that which we believe we are receiving from spirit. The prophecies of an undeveloped medium need not neces-sarily be acted upon, but only by constant practice in giving out that which we receive are we able to develop the ability of receiving correctly.

96. *If they can see into the future and foretell coming events, does this not prove predestination?*

Not at all. A prophecy is usually the direct result of the law of cause and effect, the spirit seeing the case being enacted and through its knowledge of natural law knowing its effect.

97. *What is spirit photography?*

This is a physical phase of mediumship and gives to one the power to produce faces and forms of spirit loved ones who have passed on, on a sensitive plate or film, thus producing a spirit picture. It is a very rare phase, Mr. William Hope, of England, having been perhaps the best known.

98. *What do you mean when you speak of the spirit forces passing matter through matter?*

Through the instrumentality of a physical medium, the spirit forces are able to pass solid matter through solid matter without injury to either. This has been accomplished under test conditions, articles from a long distance being transported through the ether and brought into a seance room with closed and locked doors in perfect condition.

99. *What advantage has mediumship been to the world?*

Mediumship has brought comfort to the bereaved of earth and has saved many from taking their lives through grief or temporary depression; it has taught men how to live and understand and follow the laws of God; and last but not least, it has taught man not to fear death but to realize that it is the open portal to eternal life.

100. *What do you believe regarding its progression in the coming years?*

I believe that in the coming years our mediums will be compelled to be fully developed and educated before they are permitted to appear before the public. The illiterate presentations of message work and undignified trance messages and lectures will entirely be done away with, and only the higher and more beautiful presentations of the phenomena of modern spiritualism will be allowed. It will then be on a plane of spirituality and intellectuality which any man can accept regardless of his station in life. I believe that in the years to come you will see a psychic as a part of the efficiency program of our larger business establishments and government offices. The wisdom of this more spiritual plane of life will then be utilized to guide those of earth into higher and better avenues of progression, and man will realize through these teachings a new standard of living and a practical application of religion to his every-day social and economic problems.

A P P E N D I X   I

————○————

The following is reproduced from the Fraudulent Mediums Act, which illustrates how seriously spiritualism is taken in the United Kingdom. In fact, it has been said that next to the Church of England, spiritualism has exercised the greatest influence on British politics and philosophy. In the United States, no equivalent law can be found though separate states and municipalities have passed laws governing "Fortune-Telling" that have been resurrected from time to time in order to prosecute astrologers and so-called gypsies.

The Fraudulent Mediums Act, 1951

Reproduced by permission of H.M. Stationery Office

An Act to repeal the Witchcraft Act, 1735, and to make, in substitution for certain provisions of section four of the Vagrancy Act, 1824, express provision for the punishment of persons who fraudulently purport to act as spiritualistic mediums or to exercise powers of telepathy, clairvoyance or similar powers.

[22nd June 1951.]

Be it enacted by the King's most Excellent Majesty, by and with the advice and consent of the Lords Spiritual and Temporal, and Commons, in this present Parliament assembled, and by the authority of the same, as follows:—

I.—(1) Subject to the provisions of this section, any person who—

    (a) with intent to deceive purports to act as a spiritualistic medium or to exercise any powers of telepathy, clairvoyance or other similar powers, or,

    (b) in purporting to act as spiritualistic medium or to exercise such powers as aforesaid, uses any fraudulent device,

shall be guilty of an offence.

(2) A person shall not be convicted of an offence under the foregoing subsection unless it is proved that he acted for reward; and for the purpose of this section a person shall be deemed to act for reward if any money is paid, or other valuable thing given, in respect of what he does, whether to him or to any other person.

(3) A person guilty of an offence under this section shall be liable on summary conviction to a fine not exceeding fifty pounds or to imprisonment for a term not exceeding four months or to both such fine and such imprisonment, or on conviction on indictment to a fine not exceeding five hundred pounds or to imprisonment for a term not exceeding two years or to both such fine and such imprisonment.

(4) No proceedings for an offence under this section shall be brought in England or Wales except by or with the consent of the Director of Public Prosecutions.

(5) Nothing in subsection (1) of this section shall apply to anything done solely for the purpose of entertainment.

II.—The following enactments are hereby repealed, that is to say—

    (a) the Witchcraft Act, 1735, so far as still in force, and

    (b) section four of the Vagrancy Act, 1824, so far as it extends to persons purporting to act as spiritualistic mediums or to exercise any powers of telepathy, clairvoyance or other similar powers, or to persons who, in purporting so to act or to exercise such powers, use fraudulent devices.

III.—(1) This Act may be cited as the Fraudulent Mediums Act, 1951.

    (2) This Act shall not extend to Northern Ireland.

APPENDIX II

———o———

MR. SLUDGE, "THE MEDIUM"
By Robert Browning

Now, don't sir! Don't expose me! Just this once!
This was the first and only time, I'll swear,—
Look at me,—see, I kneel,—the only time,
I swear, I ever cheated,—yes, by the soul
Of Her who hears—(your sainted mother, sir!)
All, except this last accident, was truth—
This little kind of slip!—and even this,
It was your own wine, sir, the good champagne,
(I took it for Catawba, you're so kind)
Which put the folly in my head!

                                        "Get up?"
You still inflict on me that terrible face?
You show no mercy?—Not for Her dear sake,
The sainted spirit's, whose soft breath even now
Blows on my cheek—(don't you feel something, sir?)
You'll tell?

                    Go tell, then! Who the devil cares
What such a rowdy chooses to . . .

                                Aie—aie—aie!
Please, sir! your thumbs are through my wind pipe,
    sir!
Ch-ch!

                Well, sir, I hope you've done it now!
Oh Lord! I little thought, sir, yesterday,
When your departed mother spoke those words
Of peace through me, and moved you, sir, so much,

You gave me—(very kind it was of you)
These shirt-studs—(better take them back again,
Please, sir)—yes, little did I think so soon
A trifle of trick, all through a glass too much
Of his own champagne, would change my best of
    friends
Into an angry gentleman!

                          Though, 't was wrong.
I don't contest the point; your anger's just:
Whatever put such folly in my head,
I know 't was wicked of me. There's a thick
Dusk undeveloped spirit (I've observed)
Owes me a grudge—a negro's, I should say,
Or else an Irish emigrant's; yourself
Explained the case so well last Sunday, sir,
When we had summoned Franklin to clear up
A point about those shares i' the telegraph:
Ay, and he swore . . . or might it be Tom Paine? . . .
Thumping the table close by where I crouched,
He'd do me soon a mischief: that's come true!
Why, now your face clears! I was sure it would!
Then, this one time . . . don't take your hand away,
Through yours I surely kiss your mother's hand . . .
You'll promise to forgive me?—or, at least,
Tell nobody of this? Consider, sir!
What harm can mercy do? Would but the shade
Of the venerable dead-one just vouchsafe
A rap or tip! What bit of paper's here?
Suppose we take a pencil, let her write,
Make the least sign, she urges on her child
Forgiveness? There now! Eh? Oh! 'T was your foot,
And not a natural creak, sir?

                          Answer, then!
Once, twice, thrice . . . see, I'm waiting to say
    "thrice!"

All to no use? No sort of hope for me?
It's all to post to Greeley's newspaper?

What? If I told you all about the tricks?
Upon my soul!—the whole truth, and nought else,
And how there's been some falsehood—for your part,
Will you engage to pay my passage out,
And hold your tongue until I'm safe on board?
England's the place, not Boston—no offence!
I see what makes you hesitate: don't fear!
I mean to change my trade and cheat no more,
Yes, this time really it's upon my soul!
Be my salvation!—under Heaven, of course,
I'll tell some queer things. Sixty Vs must do.
A trifle, though, to start with! We'll refer
The question to this table?

                                        How you're changed!
Then split the difference; thirty more, we'll say.
Ay, but you leave my presents! Else I'll swear
'T was all through those: you wanted yours again,
So, picked a quarrel with me, to get them back!
Tread on a worm, it turns, sir! If I turn,
Your fault! 'T is you'll have forced me! Who's
     obliged
To give up life yet try no self-defence?
At all events, I'll run the risk. Eh?

                                             Done!
May I sit, sir? This dear old table, now!
Please, sir, a parting egg-nogg and cigar!
I've been so happy with you! Nice stuffed chairs,
And sympathetic sideboards; what an end
To all the instructive evenings! (It's alight.)
Well, nothing lasts, as Bacon came and said.
Here goes,—but keep your temper, or I'll scream!

Fol-lol-the-rido-liddle-iddle-ol!
You see, sir, it's your own fault more than mine;

It's all your fault, you curious gentlefolk!
You're prigs,—excuse me,—like to look so spry,
So clever, while you cling by half a claw
To the perch whereon you puff yourselves at roost,
Such piece of self-conceit as serves for perch
Because you chose it, so it must be safe.
Oh, otherwise you're sharp enough! You spy
Who slips, who slides, who holds by help of wing,
Wanting real foothold,—who can't keep upright
On the other perch, your neighbour chose, not you:
There's no outwitting you respecting him!
For instance, men love money—that, you know
And what men do to gain it: well, suppose
A poor lad, say a help's son in your house,
Listening at keyholes, hears the company
Talk grand of dollars, V-notes, and so forth,
How hard they are to get, how good to hold,
How much they buy,—if, suddenly, in pops he—
"*I*'ve got a V-note!"—what do you say to him?
What's your first word which follows your last kick?
"Where did you steal it, rascal?" That's because
He finds you, fain would fool you, off your perch,
Not on the special piece of nonsense, sir,
Elected your parade-ground: let him try
Lies to the end of the list,—"He picked it up,
"His cousin died and left it him by will,
"The President flung it to him, riding by,
"An actress trucked it for a curl of his hair,
"He dreamed of luck and found his shoe enriched,
"He dug up clay, and out of clay made gold"—
How would you treat such possibilities?
Would not you, prompt, investigate the case
With cow-hide? "Lies, lies, lies," you'd shout: and
    why?
Which of the stories might not prove mere truth?
This last, perhaps, that clay was turned to coin!
Let's see, now, give him me to speak for him!

How many of your rare philosophers,
In plaguy books I've had to dip into,
Believed gold could be made thus, saw it made
And made it? Oh, with such philosophers
You're on your best behaviour! While the lad—
With him, in a trice, you settle likelihoods,
Nor doubt a moment how he got his prize:
In his case, you hear, judge and execute,
All in a breath: so would most men of sense.

But let the same lad hear you talk as grand
At the same keyhole, you and company,
Of signs and wonders, the invisible world;
How wisdom scouts our vulgar unbelief
More than our vulgarest credulity;
How good men have desired to see a ghost,
What Johnson used to say, what Wesley did,
Mother Goose thought, and fiddle-diddle-dee:—
If he break in with, "Sir, *I* saw a ghost!"
Ah, the ways change! He finds you perched and prim;
It's a conceit of yours that ghosts may be:
There's no talk now of cow-hide. "Tell it out!
"Don't fear us! Take your time and recollect!
"Sit down first: try a glass of wine, my boy!
"And, David, (is not that your Christian name?)
"Of all things, should this happen twice—it may—
"Be sure, while fresh in mind, you let us know!"
Does the boy blunder, blurt out this, blab that,
Break down in the other, as beginners will?
All's candour, all's considerateness—"No haste!
"Pause and collect yourself! We understand!
"That's the bad memory, or the natural shock,
"Or the unexplained *phenomena*!"

                                          Egad,
The boy takes heart of grace; finds, never fear,
The readiest way to ope your own heart wide,

Show—what I call your peacock-perch, pet post
To strut, and spread the tail, and squawk upon!
"Just as you thought, much as you might expect!
"There be more things in heaven and earth, Horatio,"
    . . .

And so on. Shall not David take the hint,
Grow bolder, stroke you down at quickened rate?
If he ruffle a feather, it's "Gently, patiently!
"Manifestations are so weak at first!
"Doubting, moreover, kills them, cuts all short,
"Cures with a vengeance!"

                              There, sir, that's your style!
You and your boy—such pains bestowed on him,
Or any headpiece of the average worth,
To teach, say, Greek, would perfect him apace,
Make him a Person ("Porson?" thank you, sir!)
Much more, proficient in the art of lies.
You never leave the lesson! Fire alight,
Catch you permitting it to die! You've friends;
There's no withholding knowledge,—least from those
Apt to look elsewhere for their souls' supply:
Why should not you parade your lawful prize?
Who finds a picture, digs a medal up,
Hits on a first edition,—he henceforth
Gives it his name, grows notable: how much more,
Who ferrets out a "medium"? "David's yours,
"You highly-favoured man? Then, pity souls
"Less privileged! Allow us share your luck!"
So, David holds the circle, rules the roast,
Narrates the vision, peeps in the glass ball,
Sets-to the spirit-writing, hears the raps,
As the case may be.

                              Now mark! To be precise—
Though I say, "lies" all these, at this first stage,
'T is just for science' sake: I call such grubs

By the name of what they'll turn to, dragonflies.
Strictly, it's what good people style untruth;
But yet, so far, not quite the full-grown thing:
It's fancying, fable-making, nonsense-work—
What never meant to be so very bad—
The knack of story-telling, brightening up
Each dull old bit of fact that drops its shine.
One does see somewhat when one shuts one's eyes,
If only spots and streaks; tables do tip
In the oddest way of themselves: and pens, good Lord,
Who knows if you drive them or they drive you?
'T is but a foot in the water and out again;
Not that duck-under which decides your dive.
Note this, for it's important: listen why.
I'll prove, you push on David till he dives
And ends the shivering. Here's your circle, now:
Two-thirds of them, with heads like you their host,
Turn up their eyes, and cry, as you expect,
"Lord, who'd have thought it!" But there's always
        one
Looks wise, compassionately smiles, submits
"Of your veracity no kind of doubt,
"But—do you feel so certain of that boy's?
"Really, I wonder! I confess myself
"More chary of my faith!" That's galling, sir!
What, he the investigator, he the sage,
When all's done? Then, you just have shut your eyes,
Opened your mouth, and gulped down David whole,
You! Terrible were such catastrophe!
So, evidence is redoubled, doubled again,
And doubled besides; once more, "He heard, we
        heard,
"You and they heard, your mother and your wife,
"Your children and the stranger in your gates:
"Did they or did they not?" So much for him,
The black sheep, guest without the wedding-garb,

The doubting Thomas! Now's your turn to crow:
"He's kind to think you such a fool: Sludge cheats?
"Leave you alone to take precautions!"
                                                      Straight
The rest join chorus. Thomas stands abashed,
Sips silent some such beverage as this,
Considers if it be harder, shutting eyes
And gulping David in good fellowship,
Than going elsewhere, getting, in exchange,
With no egg-nogg to lubricate the food,
Some just as tough a morsel. Over the way,
Holds Captain Sparks his court: is it better there?
Have not you hunting-stories, scalping-scenes,
And Mexican War exploits to swallow plump
If you'd be free o' the stove-side, rocking-chair,
And trio of affable daughters?
                                         Doubt succumbs!
Victory! All your circle's yours again!
Out of the clubbing of submissive wits,
David's performance rounds, each chink gets patched,
Every protrusion of a point's filed fine,
All's fit to set a-rolling round the world,
And then return to David finally,
Lies seven-feet thick about his first half-inch.
Here's a choice birth o' the supernatural,
Poor David's pledged to! You've employed no tool
That laws exclaim at, save the devil's own,
Yet screwed him into henceforth gulling you
To the top o' your bent,—all out of one half-lie!

You hold, if there's one half or a hundredth part
Of a lie, that's his fault,—his be the penalty!
I dare say! You'd prove firmer in his place?
You'd find the courage,—that first flurry over,
That mild bit of romancing-work at end,—
To interpose with "It gets serious, this;

"Must stop here. Sir, I saw no ghost at all,
"Inform your friends I made . . . well, fools of them,
"And found you ready-made. I've lived in clover
"These three weeks: take it out in kicks of me!"
I doubt it. Ask your conscience! Let me know,
Twelve months hence, with how few embellishments
You've told almighty Boston of this passage
Of arms between us, your first taste o' the foil
From Sludge who could not fence, sir! Sludge, your
        boy!
I lied, sir,—there! I got up from my gorge
On offal in the gutter, and preferred
Your canvas-backs: I took their carver's size,
Measured his modicum of intelligence,
Tickled him on the cockles of his heart
With a raven feather, and next week found myself
Sweet and clean, dining daintily, dizened smart,
Set on a stool buttressed by ladies' knees,
Every soft smiler calling me her pet,
Encouraging my story to uncoil
And creep out from its hole, inch after inch,
"How last night, I no sooner snug in bed,
"Tucked up, just as they left me,—than came raps!
"While a light whisked" . . . "Shaped somewhat like
        a star?"
"Well, like some sort of stars, ma'am."—"So we
        thought!
"And any voice? Not yet? Try hard, next time,
"If you can't hear a voice; we think you may:
"At least, the Pennsylvanian 'mediums' did."
Oh, next time comes the voice! "Just as we hoped!"
Are not the hopers proud now, pleased, profuse
O' the natural acknowledgment?

                                        Of course!
So, off we push, illy-oh-yo, trim the boat,
On we sweep with a cataract ahead,

We're midway to the Horseshoe: stop, who can,
The dance of bubbles gay about our prow!
Experiences become worth waiting for,
Spirits now speak up, tell their inmost mind,
And compliment the "medium" properly,
Concern themselves about his Sunday coat,
See rings on his hand with pleasure. Ask yourself
How you'd receive a course of treats like these!
Why, take the quietest hack and stall him up,
Cram him with corn a month, then out with him
Among his mates on a bright April morn,
With the turf to tread; see if you find or no
A caper in him, if he bucks or bolts!
Much more a youth whose fancies sprout as rank
As toadstool-clump from melon-bed. 'T is soon,
"Sirrah, you spirit, come, go, fetch and carry,
"Read, write, rap, rub-a-dub, and hang yourself!"
I'm spared all further trouble; all's arranged;
Your circle does my business; I may rave
Like an epileptic dervish in the books,
Foam, fling myself flat, rend my clothes to shreds;
No matter: lovers, friends and countrymen
Will lay down spiritual laws, read wrong things right
By the rule o' reverse. If Francis Verulam
Styles himself Bacon, spells the name beside
With a *y* and a *k*, says he drew breath in York,
Gave up the ghost in Wales when Cromwell reigned,
(As, sir, we somewhat fear he was apt to say,
Before I found the useful book that knows)
Why, what harm's done? The circle smiles apace,
"It was not Bacon, after all, you see!
"We understand; the trick's but natural:
"Such spirits' individuality
"Is hard to put in evidence: they incline
"To gibe and jeer, these undeveloped sorts.
"You see, their world's much like a jail broke loose,
"While this of ours remains shut, bolted, barred,

"With a single window to it. Sludge, our friend,
"Serves as this window, whether thin or thick,
"Or stained or stainless; he's the medium-pane
"Through which, to see us and be seen, they peep:
"They crowd each other, hustle for a chance,
"Tread on their neighbour's kibes, play tricks enough!
"Does Bacon, tired of waiting, swerve aside?
"Up in his place jumps Barnum—'I'm your man,
"'I'll answer you for Bacon!' Try once more!"

Or else it's—"What's a 'medium'? He's a means,
"Good, bad, indifferent, still the only means
"Spirits can speak by; he may misconceive,
"Stutter and stammer,—he's their Sludge and drudge,
"Take him or leave him; they must hold their peace,
"Or else, put up with having knowledge strained
"To half-expression through his ignorance.
"Suppose, the spirit Beethoven wants to shed
"New music he's brimful of; why, he turns
"The handle of this organ, grinds with Sludge,
"And what he poured in at the mouth o' the mill
"As a Thirty-third Sonata, (fancy now!)
"Comes from the hopper as bran-new Sludge, nought
            else,
"The Shakers' Hymn in G, with a natural F,
"Or the 'Stars and Stripes' set to consecutive
            fourths."

Sir, where's the scrape you did not help me through,
You that are wise? And for the fools, the folk
Who came to see,—the guests, (observe that word!)
Pray do you find guests criticize your wine,
Your furniture, your grammar, or your nose?
Then, why your "medium"? What's the difference?
Prove your madeira red-ink and gamboge,—
Your Sludge, a cheat—then, somebody's a goose
For vaunting both as genuine. "Guests!" Don't fear!

They'll make a wry face, nor too much of that,
And leave you in your glory.

                            "No, sometimes
"They doubt and say as much!" Ay, doubt they do!
And what's the consequence? "Of course they
    doubt"—
(You triumph) "that explains the hitch at once!
"Doubt posed our 'medium,' puddled his pure mind;
"He gave them back their rubbish: pitch chaff in,
"Could flour come out o' the honest mill?"
                            So, prompt
Applaud the faithful: cases flock in point,
"How, when a mocker willed a 'medium' once
"Should name a spirit James whose name was
    George,
"'James' cried the 'medium,'—'t was the test of
    truth!"
In short, a hit proves much, a miss proves more.
Does this convince? The better: does it fail?
Time for the double-shotted broadside, then—
The grand means, last resource. Look black and big!
"You style us idiots, therefore—why stop short?
"Accomplices in rascality: this we hear
"In our own house, from our invited guest
"Found brave enough to outrage a poor boy
"Exposed by our good faith! Have you been heard?
"Now, then, hear us; one man's not quite worth
    twelve.
"You see a cheat? Here's some twelve see an ass:
"Excuse me if I calculate: good day!"
Out slinks the sceptic, all the laughs explode.
Sludge waves his hat in triumph!

                            Or—he don't.
There's something in real truth (explain who can!)
One casts a wistful eye at, like the horse

Who mopes beneath stuffed hay-racks and won't
    munch
Because he spies a corn-bag: hang that truth,
It spoils all dainties proffered in its place!
I've felt at times when, cockered, cosseted
And coddled by the aforesaid company,
Bidden enjoy their bullying,—never fear,
But o'er their shoulders spit at the flying man,—
I've felt a child; only, a fractious child
That, dandled soft by nurse, aunt, grandmother,
Who keep him from the kennel, sun and wind,
Good fun and wholesome mud,—enjoined be sweet,
And comely and superior,—eyes askance
The ragged sons o' the gutter at their game,
Fain would be down with them i' the think o' the filth,
Making dirt-pies, laughing free, speaking plain,
And calling granny the grey old cat she is.
I've felt a spite, I say, at you, at them,
Huggings and humbug—gnashed my teeth to mark
A decent dog pass! It's too bad, I say,
Ruining a soul so!

                  But what's "so," what's fixed,
Where may one stop? Nowhere! The cheating's nursed
Out of the lying, softly and surely spun
To just your length, sir! I'd stop soon enough:
But you're for progress. "All old, nothing new?
"Only the usual talking through the mouth,
"Or writing by the hand? I own, I thought
"This would develop, grow demonstrable,
"Make doubt absurd, give figures we might see,
"Flowers we might touch. There's no one doubts you,
    Sludge!
"You dream the dreams, you see the spiritual sights,
"The speeches come in your head, beyond dispute.
"Still, for the sceptics' sake, to stop all mouths,
"We want some outward manifestation!—well,

"The Pennsylvanians gained such; why not Sludge?
"He may improve with time!"

                                    Ay, that he may!
He sees his lot: there's no avoiding fate.
'T is a trifle at first. "Eh, David? Did you hear?
"You jogged the table, your foot caused the squeak,
"This time you're . . . joking, are you not, my boy?"
"N-n-no!"—and I'm done for, bought and sold
     henceforth.
The old good easy jog-trot way, the . . . eh?
The . . . not so very false, as falsehood goes,
The spinning out and drawing fine, you know,—
Really mere novel-writing of a sort,
Acting, or improvising, make-believe,
Surely not downright cheatery,—any how,
'T is done with and my lot cast; Cheat's my name:
The fatal dash of brandy in your tea
Has settled what you'll have the souchong's smack:
The caddy gives way to the dram-bottle.

Then, it's so cruel easy! Oh, those tricks
That can't be tricks, those feats by sleight of hand,
Clearly no common conjuror's!—no indeed!
A conjuror? Choose me any craft i' the world
A man puts hand to; and with six months' pains
I'll play you twenty tricks miraculous
To people untaught the trade: have you seen glass
     blown,
Pipes pierced? Why, just this biscuit that I chip,
Did you ever watch a baker toss one flat
To the oven? Try and do it! Take my word,
Practise but half as much, while limbs are lithe,
To turn, shove, tilt a table, crack your joints,
Manage your feet, dispose your hands aright,
Work wires that twitch the curtains, play the glove
At end o' your slipper,—then put out the lights

And . . . there, there, all you want you'll get, I hope!
I found it slip, easy as an old shoe.

Now, lights on table again! I've done my part,
You take my place while I give thanks and rest.
"Well, Judge Humgruffin, what's your verdict, sir?
"You, hardest head in the United States,—
"Did you detect a cheat here? Wait! Let's see!
"Just an experiment first, for candour's sake!
"I'll try and cheat you, Judge! The table tilts:
"Is it I that move it? Write! I'll press your hand:
"Cry when I push, or guide your pencil, Judge!"
Sludge still triumphant! "That a rap, indeed?
"That, the real writing? Very like a whale!
"Then, if, sir, you—a most distinguished man,
"And, were the Judge not here, I'd say, . . . no
      matter!
"Well, sir, if you fail, you can't take us in,—
"There's little fear that Sludge will!"

                        Won't he, ma'am?
But what if our distinguished host, like Sludge,
Bade God bear witness that he played no trick,
While you believed that what produced the raps
Was just a certain child who died, you know,
And whose last breath you thought your lips had felt?
Eh? That's capital point, ma'am: Sludge begins
At your entreaty with your dearest dead,
The little voice set lisping once again,
The tiny hand made feel for yours once more,
The poor lost image brought back, plain as dreams,
Which image, if a word had chanced recall,
The customary cloud would cross your eyes,
Your heart return the old tick, pay its pang!
A right mood for investigation, this!
One's at one's ease with Saul and Jonathan,
Pompey and Caesar: but one's own lost child . . .

I wonder, when you heard the first clod drop
From the spadeful at the grave-side, felt you free
To investigate who twitched your funeral scarf
Or brushed your flounces? Then, it came of course
You should be stunned and stupid; then, (how else?)
Your breath stopped with your blood, your brain
      struck work.
But now, such causes fail of such effects,
All's changed,—the little voice begins afresh,
Yet you, calm, consequent, can test and try
And touch the truth. "Tests? Didn't the creature tell
"Its nurse's name, and say it lived six years,
"And rode a rocking-horse? Enough of tests!
"Sludge never could learn that!"

                            He could not, eh?
You compliment him. "Could not?" Speak for
      yourself!
"Sir, did that youth confess he had cheated me,
"I'd disbelieve him. He may cheat at times;
"That's in the 'medium'-nature, thus they're made,
"Vain and vindictive, cowards, prone to scratch.
"And so all cats are; still, a cat's the beast
"You coax the strange electric sparks from out,
"By rubbing back its fur; not so a dog,
"Nor lion, nor lamb: 't is the cat's nature, sir!
"Why not the dog's? Ask God, who made them
      beasts!
"D' ye think the sound, the nicely-balanced man
"(Like me"—aside)—"like you yourself,"—(aloud)
"—He's stuff to make a 'medium'? Bless your soul,
"'T is these hysteric, hybrid half-and-halfs,
"Equivocal, worthless vermin yield the fire!
"We take such as we find them, 'ware their tricks,
"Wanting their service. Sir, Sludge took in you—
"How, I can't say, not being there to watch:

"He was tried, was tempted by your easiness,—
"He did not take in me!"

                              Thank you for Sludge!
I'm to be grateful to such patrons, eh,
When what you hear's my best word? 'T is a
        challenge
"Snap at all strangers, half-tamed prairie-dog,
"So you cower duly at your keeper's beck!
"Cat, show what claws were made for, muffling them
"Only to me! Cheat others if you can,
"Me, if you dare!" And, my wise sir, I dared—
Did cheat you first, made you cheat others next,
And had the help o' your vaunted manliness
To bully the incredulous. You used me?
Have not I used you, taken full revenge,
Persuaded folk they knew not their own name,
And straight they'd own the error! Who was the fool
When, to an awe-struck wide-eyed open-mouthed
Circle of sages, Sludge would introduce
Milton composing baby-rhymes, and Locke
Reasoning in gibberish, Homer writing Greek
In noughts and crosses, Asaph setting psalms
To crotchet and quaver? I've made a spirit squeak
In sham voice for a minute, then outbroke
Bold in my own, defying the imbeciles—
Have copied some ghost's pothooks, half a page,
Then ended with my own scrawl undisguised.
"All right! The ghost was merely using Sludge,
"Suiting itself from his imperfect stock!"
Don't talk of gratitude to me! For what?
For being treated as a showman's ape,
Encouraged to be wicked and make sport,
Fret or sulk, grin or whimper, any mood
So long as the ape be in it and no man—
Because a nut pays every mood alike.
Curse your superior, superintending sort,

Who, since you hate smoke, send up boys that climb
To cure your chimney, bid a "medium" lie
To sweep you truth down! Curse your women too,
Your insolent wives and daughters, that fire up
Or faint away if a male hand squeeze theirs,
Yet, to encourage Sludge, may play with Sludge
As only a "medium," only the kind of thing
They must humour, fondle . . . oh, to misconceive
Were too preposterous! But I've paid them out!
They've had their wish—called for the naked truth,
And in she tripped, sat down and bade them stare:
They had to blush a little and forgive!
"The fact is, children talk so; in next world
"All our conventions are reversed,—perhaps
"Made light of: something like old prints, my dear!
"The Judge has one, he brought from Italy,
"A metropolis in the background,—o'er a bridge,
"A team of trotting roadsters,—cheerful groups
"Of wayside travellers, peasants at their work,
"And, full in front, quite unconcerned, why not?
"Three nymphs conversing with a cavalier,
"And never a rag among them: 'fine,' folk cry—
"And heavenly manners seem not much unlike!
"Let Sludge go on; we'll fancy it's in print!"
If such as came for wool, sir, went home shorn,
Where is the wrong I did them? 'T was their choice;
They tried the adventure, ran the risk, tossed up
And lost, as some one's sure to do in games;
They fancied I was made to lose,—smoked glass
Useful to spy the sun through, spare their eyes:
And had I proved a red-hot iron plate
They thought to pierce, and, for their pains, grew
        blind,
Whose were the fault but theirs? While, as things go,
Their loss amounts to gain, the more's the shame!
They've had their peep into the spirit-world,
And all this world may know it! They've fed fat

Their self-conceit which else had starved: what chance
Save this, of cackling o'er a golden egg
And compassing distinction from the flock,
Friends of a feather? Well, they paid for it,
And not prodigiously; the price o' the play,
Not counting certain pleasant interludes,
Was scarce a vulgar play's worth. When you buy
The actor's talent, do you dare propose
For his soul beside? Whereas my soul you buy!
Sludge acts Macbeth, obliged to be Macbeth,
Or you'll not hear his first word! Just go through
That slight formality, swear himself's the Thane,
And thenceforth he may strut and fret his hour,
Spout, spawl, or spin his target, no one cares!
Why hadn't I leave to play tricks, Sludge as Sludge?
Enough of it all! I've wiped out scores with you—
Vented your fustian, let myself be streaked
Like tom-fool with your ochre and carmine,
Worn patchwork your respectable fingers sewed
To metamorphose somebody,—yes, I've earned
My wages, swallowed down my bread of shame,
And shake the crumbs off—where but in your face?

As for religion—why, I served it, sir!
I'll stick to that! With my *phenomena*
I laid the atheist sprawling on his back,
Propped up Saint Paul, or, at least, Swedenborg!
In fact, it's just the proper way to baulk
These troublesome fellows—liars, one and all,
Are not these sceptics? Well, to baffle them,
No use in being squeamish: lie yourself!
Erect your buttress just as wide o' the line,
Your side, as they build up the wall on theirs;
Where both meet, midway in a point, is truth
High overhead: so, take your room, pile bricks,
Lie! Oh, there's titillation in all shame!
What snow may lose in white, snow gains in rose!
Miss Stokes turns—Rahab,—nor a bad exchange!

Glory be on her, for the good she wrought,
Breeding belief anew 'neath ribs of death,
Browbeating now the unabashed before,
Ridding us of their whole life's gathered straws
By a live coal from the altar! Why, of old,
Great men spent years and years in writing books
To prove we've souls, and hardly proved it then:
Miss Stokes with her live coal, for you and me!
Surely, to this good issue, all was fair—
Not only fondling Sludge, but, even suppose
He let escape some spice of knavery,—well,
In wisely being blind to it! Don't you praise
Nelson for setting spy-glass to blind eye
And saying . . . what was it—that he could not see
The signal he was bothered with? Ay, indeed!

I'll go beyond: there's a real love of a lie,
Liars find ready-made for lies they make,
As hand for glove, or tongue for sugar-plum.
At best, 't is never pure and full belief;
Those furthest in the quagmire,—don't suppose
They strayed there with no warning, got no chance
Of a filth-speck in their face, which they clenched
        teeth,
Bent brow against! Be sure they had their doubts,
And fears, and fairest challenges to try
The floor o' the seeming solid sand! But no!
Their faith was pledged, acquaintance too apprised,
All but the last step ventured, kerchiefs waved,
And Sludge called "pet": 't was easier marching on
To the promised land join those who, Thursday next,
Meant to meet Shakespeare; better follow Sludge—
Prudent, oh sure!—on the alert, how else?—
But making for the mid-bog, all the same!
To hear your outcries, one would think I caught
Miss Stokes by the scruff o' the neck, and pitched her
        flat,
Foolish-face-foremost! Hear these simpletons,

That's all I beg, before my work's begun,
Before I've touched them with my finger-tip!
Thus they await me (do but listen, now!
It's reasoning, this is,—I can't imitate
The baby voice, though) "In so many tales
"Must be some truth, truth though a pin-point big,
"Yet, some: a single man's deceived, perhaps—
"Hardly, a thousand: to suppose one cheat
"Can gull all these, were more miraculous far
"Than aught we should confess a miracle,"—
And so on. Then the Judge sums up—(it's rare)
Bids you respect the authorities that leap
To the judgment-seat at once,—why don't you note
The limpid nature, the unblemished life,
The spotless honour, indisputable sense
Of the first upstart with his story? What—
Outrage a boy on whom you ne'er till now
Set eyes, because he finds raps trouble him?
Fools, these are: ay, and how of their opposites
Who never did, at bottom of their hearts,
Believe for a moment?—Men emasculate,
Blank of belief, who played, as eunuchs use,
With superstition safely,—cold of blood,
Who saw what made for them i' the mystery,
Took their occasion, and supported Sludge
—As proselytes? No, thank you, far too shrewd!
—But promisers of fair play, encouragers
O' the claimant; who in candour needs must hoist
Sludge up on Mars' Hill, get speech out of Sludge
To carry off, criticize, and cant about!
Didn't Athens treat Saint Paul so?—at any rate,
It's "a new thing" philosophy fumbles at.
Then there's the other picker-out of pearl
From dung-heaps,—ay, your literary man,
Who draws on his kid gloves to deal with Sludge
Daintily and discreetly,—shakes a dust

O' the doctrine, flavours thence, he well knows how,
The narrative or the novel,—half-believes,
All for the book's sake, and the public's stare,
And the cash that's God's sole solid in this world!
Look at him! Try to be too bold, too gross
For the master! Not you! He's the man for muck;
Shovel it forth, full-splash, he'll smooth your brown
Into artistic richness, never fear!
Find him the crude stuff; when you recognize
Your lie again, you'll doff your hat to it,
Dressed out for company! "For company,"
I say, since there's the relish of success:
Let all pay due respect, call the lie truth,
Save the soft silent smirking gentleman
Who ushered in the stranger: you must sigh
"How melancholy, he, the only one
"Fails to perceive the bearing of the truth
"Himself gave birth to!"—There's the triumph's
        smack!
That man would choose to see the whole world roll
I' the slime o' the slough, so he might touch the tip
Of his brush with what I call the best of browns—
Tint ghost-tales, spirit-stories, past the power
Of the outworn umber and bistre!

                                        Yet I think

There's a more hateful form of foolery—
The social sage's, Solomon of saloons
And philosophic diner-out, the fribble
Who wants a doctrine for a chopping-block
To try the edge of his faculty upon,
Prove how much common sense he'll hack and hew
I' the critical minute 'twixt the soup and fish!
These were my patrons: these, and the like of them
Who, rising in my soul now, sicken it,—
These I have injured! Gratitude to these?

The gratitude, forsooth, of a prostitute
To the greenhorn and the bully—friends of hers,
From the wag that wants the queer jokes for his club,
To the snuff-box-decorator, honest man,
Who just was at his wits' end where to find
So genial a Pasiphae! All and each
Pay, compliment, protect from the police:
And how she hates them for their pains, like me!
So much for my remorse at thanklessness
Toward a deserving public!

                                But, for God?
Ay, that's a question! Well, sir, since you press—
(How you do tease the whole thing out of me!
I don't mean you, you know, when I say "them":
Hate you, indeed! But that Miss Stokes, that Judge!
Enough, enough—with sugar: thank you, sir!)
Now for it, then! Will you believe me, though?
You've heard what I confess; I don't unsay
A single word: I cheated when I could,
Rapped with my toe-joints, set sham hands at work,
Wrote down names weak in sympathetic ink,
Rubbed odic lights with ends of phosphor-match,
And all the rest; believe that: believe this,
By the same token, though it seem to set
The crooked straight again, unsay the said,
Stick up what I've knocked down; I can't help that
It's truth! I somehow vomit truth to-day.
This trade of mine— I don't know, can't be sure
But there was something in it, tricks and all!
Really, I want to light up my own mind.
They were tricks,—true, but what I mean to add
Is also true. First,—don't it strike you, sir?
Go back to the beginning,—the first fact
We're taught is, there's a world beside this world,
With spirits, not mankind, for tenantry;
That much within that world once sojourned here,

That all upon this world will visit there,
And therefore that we, bodily here below,
Must have exactly such an interest
In learning what may be the ways o' the world
Above us, as the disembodied folk
Have (by all analogic likelihood)
In watching how things go in the old home
With us, their sons, successors, and what not.
Oh yes, with added powers probably,
Fit for the novel state,—old loves grown pure,
Old interests understood aright,—they watch!
Eyes to see, ears to hear, and hands to help,
Proportionate to advancement: they're ahead,
That's all—do what we do, but noblier done—
Use plate, whereas we eat our meals off delf,
(To use a figure).

                              Concede that, and I ask
Next what may be the mode of intercourse
Between us men here, and those once-men there?
First comes the Bible's speech; then, history
With the supernatural element,— you know—
All that we sucked in with our mothers' milk,
Grew up with, got inside of us at last,
Till it's found bone of bone and flesh of flesh.
See now, we start with miraculous,
And know it used to be, at all events:
What's the first step we take, and can't but take,
In arguing from the known to the obscure?
Why this: "What was before, may be to-day.
"Since Samuel's ghost appeared to Saul, of course
"My brother's spirit may appear to me."
Go tell your teacher that! What's his reply?
What brings a shade of doubt for the first time
O'er his brow late so luminous with faith?
"Such things have been," says he, "and there's no
    doubt

"Such things may be: but I advise mistrust
"Of eyes, ears, stomach, and, more than all, your
      brain,
"Unless it be of your great-grandmother,
"Whenever they propose a ghost to you!"
The end is, there's a composition struck;
'T is settled, we've some way of intercourse
Just as in Saul's time; only, different:
How, when and where, precisely,—find it out!
I want to know, then, what's so natural
As that a person born into this world
And seized on by such teaching, should begin
With firm expectancy and a frank look-out
For his own allotment, his especial share
I' the secret—his particular ghost, in fine?
I mean, a person born to look that way,
Since natures differ: take the painter-sort.
One man lives fifty years in ignorance
Whether grass be green or red,—"No kind of eye
"For colour," say you; while another picks
And puts away even pebbles, when a child,
Because of bluish spots and pinky veins—
"Give him forthwith a paint-box!" Just the same
Was I born . . . "medium," you won't let me say,—
Well, seer of the supernatural
Everywhen, everyhow and everywhere,—
Will that do?

                              I and all such boys of course
Started with the same stock of Bible-truth;
Only,—what in the rest you style their sense,
Instinct, blind reasoning but imperative,
This, betimes, taught them the old world had one law
And ours another: "New world, new laws," cried
      they:
"None but old laws, seen everywhere at work,"
Cried I, and by their help explained my life

The Jews' way, still a working way to me.
Ghosts made the noises, fairies waved the lights,
Or Santa Claus slid down on New Year's Eve
And stuffed with cakes the stocking at my bed,
Changed the worn shoes, rubbed clean the figured slate
O' the sum that came to grief the day before.

This could not last long: soon enough I found
Who had worked wonders thus, and to what end:
But did I find all easy, like my mates?
Henceforth no supernatural any more?
Not a whit: what projects the billiard-balls?
"A cue," you answer: "Yes, a cue," said I;
"But what hand, off the cushion, moved the cue?
"What unseen agency, outside the world,
"Prompted its puppets to do this and that,
"Put cakes and shoes and slates into their mind,
"These mothers and aunts, nay even schoolmasters?"
Thus high I sprang, and there have settled since.
Just so I reason, in sober earnest still,
About the greater godsends, what you call
The serious gains and losses of my life.
What do I know or care about your world
Which either is or seems to be? This snap
O' my fingers, sir! My care is for myself;
Myself am whole and sole reality
Inside a raree-show and a market-mob
Gathered about it: that's the use of things.
'T is easy saying they serve vast purposes,
Advantage their grand selves: be it true or false,
Each thing may have two uses. What's a star?
A world, or a world's sun: doesn't it serve
As taper also, time-piece, weather-glass,
And almanac? Are stars not set for signs
When we should shear our sheep, sow corn, prune
        trees?
The Bible says so.

                              Well, I add one use
To all the acknowledged uses, and declare
If I spy Charles's Wain at twelve to-night,
It warns me, "Go, nor lose another day,
"And have your hair cut, Sludge!" You laugh: and
    why?
Were such a sign too hard for God to give?
No: but Sludge seems too little for such grace:
Thank you, sir! So you think, so does not Sludge!
When you and good men gape at Providence,
Go into history and bid us mark
Not merely powder-plots prevented, crowns
Kept on kings' heads by miracle enough,
But private mercies—oh, you've told me, sir,
Of such interpositions! How yourself
Once, missing on a memorable day
Your handkerchief—just setting out, you know,—
You must return to fetch it, lost the train,
And saved your precious self from what befell
The thirty-three whom Providence forgot.
You tell, and ask me what I think of this?
Well, sir, I think then, since you needs must know,
What matter had you and Boston city to boot
Sailed skyward, like burnt onion-peelings? Much
To you, no doubt: for me—undoubtedly
The cutting of my hair concerns me more,
Because, however sad the truth may seem,
Sludge is of all-importance to himself.
You set apart that day in every year
For special thanksgiving, were a heathen else:
Well, I who cannot boast the like escape,
Suppose I said "I don't thank Providence
"For my part, owing it no gratitude"?
"Nay, but you owe as much"—you'd tutor me,
"You, every man alive, for blessings gained
"In every hour o' the day, could you but know!

"I saw my crowning mercy: all have such,
"Could they but see!" Well, sir, why don't they see?
"Because they won't look,—or perhaps, they can't."
Then, sir, suppose I can, and will, and do
Look, microscopically as is right,
Into each hour with its infinitude
Of influences at work to profit Sludge?
For that's the case: I've sharpened up my sight
To spy a providence in the fire's going out,
The kettle's boiling, the dime's sticking fast
Despite the hole i' the pocket. Call such facts
Fancies, too petty a work for Providence,
And those same thanks which you exact from me
Prove too prodigious payment: thanks for what,
If nothing guards and guides us little men?
No, no, sir! You must put away your pride,
Resolve to let Sludge into partnership!
I live by signs and omens: looked at the roof
Where the pigeons settle—"If the further bird,
"The white, takes wing first, I'll confess when
     thrashed;
"Not, if the blue does"—so I said to myself
Last week, lest you should take me by surprise:
Off flapped the white,—and I'm confessing, sir!
Perhaps 't is Providence's whim and way
With only me, i' the world: how can you tell?
"Because unlikely!" Was it likelier, now,
That this our one out of all worlds beside,
The what-d'you-call-'em millions, should be just
Precisely chosen to make Adam for,
And the rest o' the tale? Yet the tale's true, you know:
Such undeserving clod was graced so once;
Why not graced likewise undeserving Sludge?
Are we merit-mongers, flaunt we filthy rags?
All you can bring against my privilege
Is, that another way was taken with you,—

Which I don't question. It's pure grace, my luck:
I'm broken to the way of nods and winks,
And need no formal summoning. You've a help;
Holloa his name or whistle, clap your hands,
Stamp with your foot or pull the bell: all's one,
He understands you want him, here he comes.
Just so, I come at the knocking: you, sir, wait
The tongue o' the bell, nor stir before you catch
Reason's clear tingle, nature's clapper brisk,
Or that traditional peal was wont to cheer
Your mother's face turned heavenward: short of these
There's no authentic intimation, eh?
Well, when you hear, you'll answer them, start up
And stride into the presence, top of toe,
And there find Sludge beforehand, Sludge that sprang
At noise o' the knuckle on the partition-wall!
I think myself the more religious man.
Religion's all or nothing; it's no mere smile
O' contentment, sigh of aspiration, sir—
No quality o' the finelier-tempered clay
Like its whiteness or its lightness; rahter, stuff
O' the very stuff, life of life, and self of self.
I tell you, men won't notice; when they do,
They'll understand. I notice nothing else:
I'm eyes, ears, mouth of me, one gaze and gape,
Nothing eludes me, everything's a hint,
Handle and help. It's all absurd, and yet
There's something in it all, I know: how much?
No answer! What does that prove? Man's still man,
Still meant for a poor blundering piece of work
When all's done; but, if somewhat's done, like this,
Or not done, is the case the same? Suppose
I blunder in my guess at the true sense
O' the knuckle-summons, nine times out of ten,—
What if the tenth guess happen to be right?
If the tenth shovel-load of powdered quartz

Yield me the nugget? I gather, crush, sift all,
Pass o'er the failure, pounce on the success.
To give you a notion, now—(let who wins, laugh!)
When first I see a man, what do I first?
Why, count the letters which make up his name,
And as their number chances, even or odd,
Arrive at my conclusion, trim my course:
Hiram H. Horsefall is your honoured name,
And haven't I found a patron, sir, in you?
"Shall I cheat this stranger?" I take apple-pips,
Stick one in either canthus of my eye,
And if the left drops first—(your left, sir, stuck)
I'm warned, I let the trick alone this time.
You, sir, who smile, superior to such trash,
You judge of character by other rules:
Don't your rules sometimes fail you? Pray, what rule
Have you judged Sludge by hitherto?

                                        Oh, be sure

You, everybody blunders, just as I,
In simpler things than these by far! For see:
I knew two farmers,—one, a wiseacre
Who studied seasons, rummaged almanacs,
Quoted the dew-point, registered the frost,
And then declared, for outcome of his pains,
Next summer must be dampish: 't was a drought.
His neighbour prophesied such drought would fall,
Saved hay and corn, made cent. per cent. thereby,
And proved a sage indeed: how came his lore?
Because one brindled heifer, late in March,
Stiffened her tail of evenings, and somehow
He got into his head that drought was meant!
I don't expect all men can do as much:
Such kissing goes by favour. You must take
A certain turn of mind for this,—a twist
I' the flesh, as well. Be lazily alive,

Open-mouthed, like my friend the ant-eater,
Letting all nature's loosely-guarded motes
Settle and, slick, be swallowed! Think yourself
The one i' the world, the one for whom the world
Was made, expect it tickling at your mouth!
Then will the swarm of busy buzzing flies,
Clouds of coincidence, break egg-shell, thrive,
Breed, multiply, and bring you food enough.

I can't pretend to mind your smiling, sir!
Oh, what you mean is this! Such intimate way,
Close converse, frank exchange of offices,
Strict sympathy of the immeasurably great
With the infinitely small, betokened here
By a course of signs and omens, raps and sparks,—
How does it suit the dread traditional text
O' the "Great and Terrible Name"? Shall the Heaven
        of Heavens
Stoop to such child's play?

                            Please, sir, go with me
A moment, and I'll try to answer you.
The "*Magnum et terribile*" (is that right?)
Well, folk began with this in the early day;
And all the acts they recognized in proof
Were thunders, lightnings, earthquakes, whirlwinds,
        dealt
Indisputably on men whose death they caused.
There, and there only, folk saw Providence
At work,—and seeing it, 't was right enough
All heads should tremble, hands wring hands amain,
And knees knock hard together at the breath
O' the Name's first letter; why, the Jews, I'm told,
Won't write it down, no, to this very hour,
Nor speak aloud: you know best if 't be so.
Each ague-fit of fear at end, they crept
(Because somehow people once born must live)

Out of the sound, sight, swing and sway o' the Name,
Into a corner, the dark rest of the world,
And safe space where as yet no fear had reached;
'T was there they looked about them, breathed again,
And felt indeed at home, as we might say.
The current o' common things, the daily life,
This had their due contempt; no Name pursued
Man from the mountain-top where fires abide,
To his particular mouse-hole at its foot
Where he ate, drank, digested, lived in short:
Such was a man's vulgar business, far too small
To be worth thunder: "small," folk kept on, "small,"
With much complacency in those great days!
A mote of sand, you know, a blade of grass—
What was so despicable as mere grass,
Except perhaps the life o' the worm or fly
Which fed there? These were "small" and men were
     great.
Well, sir, the old way's altered somewhat since,
And the world wears another aspect now:
Somebody turns our spyglass round, or else
Puts a new lens in it: grass, worm, fly grow big:
We find great things are made of little things,
And little things go lessening till at last
Comes God behind them. Talk of mountains now?
We talk of mould that heaps the mountain, mites
That throng the mould, and God that makes the mites.
The Name comes close behind a stomach-cyst,
The simplest of creations, just a sac
That's mouth, heart, legs and belly at once, yet lives
And feels, and could do neither, we conclude,
If simplified still further one degree:
The small becomes the dreadful and immense!
Lightning, forsooth? No word more upon that!
A tin-foil bottle, a strip of greasy silk,
With a bit of wire and knob of brass, and there's
Your dollar's worth of lightning! But the cyst—

The life of the least of the little things?

                                        No, no!
Preachers and teachers try another tack,
Come near the truth this time: they put aside
Thunder and lightning: "That's mistake," they cry,
"Thunderbolts fall for neither fright nor sport,
"But do appreciable good, like tides,
"Changes o' the wind, and other natural facts—
" "Good' meaning good to man, his body or soul.
"Mediate, immediate, all things minister
"To man,—that's settled: be our future text
" 'We are His children!' " So, they now harangue
About the intention, the contrivance, all
That keeps up an incessant play of love,—
See the Bridgewater book.

                                        Amen to it!
Well, sir, I put this question: I'm a child?
I lose no time, but take you at your word:
How shall I act a child's part properly?
Your sainted mother, sir,—used you to live
With such a thought as this a-worrying you?
"She has it in her power to throttle me,
"Or stab or poison: she may turn me out,
"Or lock me in,—nor stop at this to-day,
"But cut me off to-morrow from the estate
"I look for"—(long may you enjoy it, sir!)
"In brief, she may unchild the child I am."
You never had such crotchets? Nor have I!
Who, frank confessing childship from the first,
Cannot both fear and take my ease at once,
So, don't fear,—know what might be, well enough,
But know too, child-like, that it will not be,
At least in my case, mine, the son and heir
O' the kingdom, as yourself proclaim my style.
But do you fancy I stop short at this?

Wonder if suit and service, son and heir
Needs must expect, I dare pretend to find?
If, looking for signs proper to such an one,
I straight perceive them irresistible?
Concede that homage is a son's plain right,
And, never mind the nods and raps and winks,
'T is the pure obvious supernatural
Steps forward, does its duty: why, of course!
I have presentiments; my dreams come true:
I fancy a friend stands whistling all in white
Blithe as a boblink, and he's dead I learn.
I take dislike to a dog my favourite long,
And sell him; he goes mad next week and snaps.
I guess that stranger will turn up to-day
I have not seen these three years; there's his knock
I wager "sixty peaches on that tree!"—
That I pick up a dollar in my walk,
That your wife's brother's cousin's name was
        George—
And win on all points. Oh, you wince at this?
You'd fain distinguish between gift and gift,
Washington's oracle and Sludge's itch
O' the elbow when at whist he ought to trump?
With Sludge it's too absurd? *Fine, draw the line
Somewhere, but, sir, your somewhere is not mine!*

Bless us, I'm turning poet! It's time to end.
How you have drawn me out, sir! All I ask
Is—am I heir or not heir? If I'm he,
Then, sir, remember, that same personage
(To judge by what we read i' the newspaper)
Requires, beside one nobleman in gold
To carry up and down his coronet,
Another servant, probably a duke,
To hold egg-nogg in readiness: why want
Attendance, sir, when helps in his father's house
Abound, I'd like to know?

                                                    Enough of talk
My fault is that I tell too plain a truth.
Why, which of those who say they disbelieve,
Your clever people, but has dreamed his dream,
Caught his coincidence, stumbled on his fact
He can't explain, (he'll tell you smilingly)
Which he's too much of a philosopher
To count as supernatural, indeed,
So calls a puzzle and problem, proud of it:
Bidding you still be on your guard, you know,
Because one fact don't make a system stand,
Nor prove this an occasional escape
Of spirit beneath the matter: that's the way!
Just so wild Indians picked up, piece by piece,
The fact in California, the fine gold
That underlay the gravel—hoarded these,
But never made a system stand, nor dug!
So wise men hold out in each hollowed palm
A handful of experience, sparkling fact
They can't explain; and since their rest of life
Is all explainable, what proof in this?
Whereas I take the fact, the grain of gold,
And fling away the dirty rest of life,
And add this grain to the grain each fool has found
O' the million other such philosophers,—
Till I see gold, all gold and only gold,
Truth questionless though unexplainable,
And the miraculous proved the commonplace!
The other fools believed in mud, no doubt—
Failed to know gold they saw: was that so strange?
Are all men born to play Bach's fiddle-fugues,
"Time" with the foil in carte, jump their own height,
Cut the mutton with the broadsword, skate a five,
Make the red hazard with the cue, clip nails
While swimming, in five minutes row a mile,
Pull themselves three feet up with the left arm,

Do sums of fifty figures in their head,
And so on, by the scores of instances?
The Sludge with luck, who sees the spiritual facts
His fellows strive and fail to see, may rank
With these, and share the advantage.

                                    Ay, but share
The drawback! Think it over by yourself;
I have not heart, sir, and the fire's gone grey.
Defect somewhere compensates for success,
Everyone knows that. Oh, we're equals, sir!
The big-legged fellow has a little arm
And a less brain, though big legs win the race:
Do you suppose I 'scape the common lot?
Say, I was born with flesh so sensitive,
Soul so alert, that, practice helping both,
I guess what's going on outside the veil,
Just as a prisoned crane feels pairing-time
In the islands where his kind are, so must fall
To capering by himself some shiny night,
As if your back-yard were a plot of spice—
Thus am I 'ware o' the spirit-world: while you,
Blind as a beetle that way,—for amends,
Why, you can double fist and floor me, sir!
Ride that hot hardmouthed horrid horse of yours,
Laugh while it lightens, play with the great dog,
Speak your mind though it vex some friend to hear,
Never brag, never bluster, never blush,—
In short, you've pluck, when I'm a coward—there!
I know it, I can't help it,—folly or no,
I'm paralyzed, my hand's no more a hand,
Nor my head a head, in danger: you can smile
And change the pipe in your cheek. Your gift's not
    mine.
Would you swap for mine? No! but you'd add my gift
To yours: I dare say! I too sigh at times,

Wish I were stouter, could tell truth nor flinch,
Kept cool when threatened, did not mind so much
Being dressed gaily, making strangers stare,
Eating nice things; when I'd amuse myself,
I shut my eyes and fancy in my brain
I'm—now the President, now Jenny Lind,
Now Emerson, now the Benicia Boy—
With all the civilized world a-wondering
And worshipping. I know it's folly and worse;
I feel such tricks sap, honeycomb the soul,
But I can't cure myself: despond, despair,
And then, hey, presto, there's a turn o' the wheel,
Under comes uppermost, fate makes full amends;
Sludge knows and sees and hears a hundred things
You all are blind to,—I've my taste of truth,
Likewise my touch of falsehood,—vice no doubt,
But you've your vices also: I'm content.

What, sir? You won't shake hands? "Because I
        cheat!"
"You've found me out in cheating!" That's enough
To make an apostle swear! Why, when I cheat,
Mean to cheat, do cheat, and am caught in the act,
Are you, or, rather, am I sure o' the fact?
(There's verse again, but I'm inspired somehow.)
Well then I'm not sure! I may be, perhaps,
Free as a babe from cheating: how it began,
My gift,—no matter; what 't is got to be
In the end now, that's the question; answer that!
Had I seen, perhaps, what hand was holding mine,
Leading me whither, I had died of fright:
So, I was made believe I led myself.
If I should lay a six-inch plank from roof
To roof, you would not cross the street, one step,
Even at your mother's summons: but, being shrewd,
If I paste paper on each side the plank
And swear 't is solid pavement, why, you'll cross

——— O ———

Humming a tune the while, in ignorance
Beacon Street stretches a hundred feet below:
I walked thus, took the paper-cheat for stone.
Some impulse made me set a thing o' the move
Which, started once, ran really by itself;
Beer flows thus, suck the siphon; toss the kite,
It takes the wind and floats of its own force.
Don't let truth's lump rot stagnant for the lack
Of a timely helpful lie to leaven it!
Put a chalk-egg beneath the clucking hen,
She'll lay a real one, laudably deceived,
Daily for weeks to come. I've told my lie,
And seen truth follow, marvels none of mine;
All was not cheating, sir, I'm positive!
I don't know if I move your hand sometimes
When the spontaneous writing spreads so far,
If my knee lifts the table all that height,
Why the inkstand don't fall off the desk a-tilt,
Why the accordion plays a prettier waltz
Than I can pick out on the piano-forte,
Why I speak so much more than I intend,
Describe so many things I never saw.
I tell you, sir, in one sense, I believe
Nothing at all,—that everybody can,
Will, and does cheat: but in another sense
I'm ready to believe my very self—
That every cheat's inspired, and every lie
Quick with a germ of truth.

                                    You ask perhaps
Why I should condescend to trick at all
If I know a way without it? This is why!
There's a strange secret sweet self-sacrifice
In any desecration of one's soul
To a worthy end,—isn't it Herodotus
(I wish I could read Latin!) who describes
The single gift o' the land's virginity,

Demanded in those old Egyptian rites,
(I've but a hazy notion—help me, sir!)
For one purpose in the world, one day in a life,
One hour in a day—thereafter, purity,
And a veil thrown o'er the past for evermore!
Well, now, they understood a many things
Down by Nile city, or wherever it was!
I've always vowed, after the minute's lie,
And the end's gain,—truth should be mine henceforth.
This goes to the root o' the matter, sir,—this plain
Plump fact: accept it and unlock with it
The wards of many a puzzle!

                       Or, finally,
Why should I set so fine a gloss on things?
What need I care? I cheat in self-defence,
And there's my answer to a world of cheats!
Cheat? To be sure, sir! What's the world worth else?
Who takes it as he finds, and thanks his stars?
Don't it want trimming, turning, furbishing up
And polishing over? Your so-styled great men,
Do they accept one truth as truth is found,
Or try their skill at tinkering? What's your world?
Here are you born, who are, I'll say at once,
Of the luckiest kind, whether in head and heart,
Body and soul, or all that helps them both.
Well, now, look back: what faculty of yours
Came to its full, had ample justice done
By growing when rain fell, biding its time,
Solidifying growth when earth was dead,
Spiring up, broadening wide, in seasons due?
Never! You shot up and frost nipped you off,
Settled to sleep when sunshine bade you sprout;
One faculty thwarted its fellow: at the end,
All you boast is "I had proved a topping tree
"In other climes"—yet this was the right clime
Had you foreknown the seasons. Young, you've force

Wasted like well-streams: old—oh, then indeed,
Behold a labyrinth of hydraulic pipes
Through which you'd play off wondrous waterwork;
Only, no water's left to feed their play.
Young,—you've a hope, an aim, a love: it's tossed
And crossed and lost: you struggle on, some spark
Shut in your heart against the puffs around,
Through cold and pain; these in due time subside,
Now then for age's triumph, the hoarded light
You mean to loose on the altered face of things,—
Up with it on the tripod! It's extinct.
Spend your life's remnant asking, which was best,
Light smothered up that never peeped forth once,
Or the cold cresset with full leave to shine?
Well, accept this too,—seek the fruit of it
Not in enjoyment, proved a dream on earth,
But knowledge, useful for a second chance,
Another life,—you've lost this world—you've gained
Its knowledge for the next. What knowledge, sir,
Except that you know nothing? Nay, you doubt
Whether 't were better have made you man or brute,
If aught be true, if good and evil clash.
No foul, no fair, no inside, no outside,
There's your world!

                           Give it me! I slap it brisk
With harlequin's pasteboard sceptre: what's it now?
Changed like a rock-flat, rough with rusty weed,
At first wash-over o' the returning wave!
All the dry dead impracticable stuff
Starts into life and light again; this world
Pervaded by the influx from the next.
I cheat, and what's the happy consequence?
You find full justice straightway dealt you out,
Each want supplied, each ignorance set at ease,
Each folly fooled. No life-long labour now
As the price of worse than nothing! No mere film

Holding you chained in iron, as it seems,
Against the outstretch of your very arms
And legs i' the sunshine moralists forbid!
What would you have? Just speak and, there, you see!
You're supplemented, made a whole at last,
Bacon advises, Shakespeare writes you songs,
And Mary Queen of Scots embraces you.
Thus it goes on, not quite like life perhaps,
But so near, that the very difference piques,
Shows that e'en better than this best will be—
This passing entertainment in a hut
Whose bare walls take your taste since, one stage
    more,
And you arrive at the palace: all half real,
And you, to suit it, less than real beside,
In a dream, lethargic kind of death in life,
That helps the interchange of natures, flesh
Transfused by souls, and such souls! Oh, 't is choice!
And if at whiles the bubble, blown too thin,
Seem nigh on bursting,—if you nearly see
The real world through the false,—what *do* you see?
Is the old so ruined? You find you're in a flock
O' the youthful, earnest, passionate—genius, beauty,
Rank and wealth also, if you care for these:
And all depose their natural rights, hail you,
(That's me, sir) as their mate and yoke-fellow,
Participate in Sludgehood—nay, grow mine,
I veritably possess them—banish doubt,
And reticence and modesty alike!
Why, here's the Golden Age, old Paradise
Or new Eutopia! Here's true life indeed,
And the world well won now, mine for the first time!

And all this might be, may be, and with good help
Of a little lying shall be: so, Sludge lies!
Why, he's at worst your poet who sings how Greeks
That never were, in Troy which never was,

Did this or the other impossible great thing!
He's Lowell—it's a world (you smile applause),
Of his own invention—wondrous Longfellow,
Surprising Hawthorne! Sludge does more than they,
And acts the books they write: the more his praise!

But why do I mount to poets? Take plain prose—
Dealers in common sense, set these at work,
What can they do without their helpful lies?
Each states the law and fact and face o' the thing
Just as he'd have them, finds what he thinks fit,
Is blind to what missuits him, just records
What makes his case out, quite ignores the rest.
It's a History of the World, the Lizard Age,
The Early Indians, the Old Country War,
Jerome Napoleon, whatsoever you please,
All as the author wants it. Such a scribe
You pay and praise for putting life in stones,
Fire into fog, making the past your world.
There's plenty of "How did you contrive to grasp
"The thread which led you through this labyrinth?
"How build such solid fabric out of air?
"How on so slight foundation found this tale,
"Biography, narrative?" or, in other words,
"How many lies did it require to make
"The portly truth you here present us with?"
"Oh," quoth the penman, purring at your praise,
"'T is fancy all; no particle of fact:
"I was poor and threadbare when I wrote that book
"'Bliss in the Golden City.' I, at Thebes?
"We writers paint out of our heads, you see!"
"—Ah, the more wonderful the gift in you,
"The more creativeness and godlike craft!"
But I, do I present you with my piece,
It's "What, Sludge? When my sainted mother spoke
"The verses Lady Jane Grey last composed
"About the rosy bower in the seventh heaven

"Where she and Queen Elizabeth keep house,—
"You made the raps? 'T was your invention that?
"Cur, slave and devil!''—eight fingers and two
    thumbs
Stuck in my throat!

                Well, if the marks seem gone,
'T is because stiffish cock-tail, taken in time,
Is better for a bruise than arnica.
There, sir! I bear no malice: 't isn't in me.
I know I acted wrongly: still, I've tried
What I could say in my excuse,—to show
The devil's not all devil . . . I don't pretend,
He's angel, much less such a gentleman
As you, sir! And I've lost you, lost myself,
Lost all-l-l-l- . . .

              No—are you in earnest, sir?
O yours, sir, is an angel's part! I know
What prejudice prompts, and what's the common
    course
Men take to soothe their ruffled self-conceit:
Only you rise superior to it all!
No, sir, it don't hurt much; it's speaking long
That makes me choke a little: the marks will go!
What? Twenty V-notes more, and outfit too,
And not a word to Greeley? One—one kiss
O' the hand that saves me! You'll not let me speak,
I well know, and I've lost the right, too true!
But I must say, sir, if She hears (she does)
Your sainted . . . Well, sir,—be it so! That's, I think,
My bed-room candle. Good-night! Bl-l-less you, sir!

————————

R-r-r, you brute-beast and blackguard! Cowardly
    scamp!
I only wish I dared burn down the house
And spoil your sniggering! Oh what, you're the man?

You're satisfied at last? You've found out Sludge?
We'll see that presently: my turn, sir, next!
I too can tell my story: brute,—do you hear?—
You throttled your sainted mother, that old hag,
In just such a fit of passion: no, it was . . .
To get this house of hers, and many a note
Like these . . . I'll pocket them, however . . . five,
Ten, fifteen . . . ay, you gave her throat the twist,
Or else you poisoned her! Confound the cuss!
Where was my head? I ought to have prophesied
He'll die in a year and join her: that's the way.
I don't know where my head is: what had I done?
How did it all go? I said he poisoned her,
And hoped he'd have grace given him to repent,
Whereon he picked this quarrel, bullied me
And called me cheat: I thrashed him,—who could
    help?
He howled for mercy, prayed me on his knees
To cut and run and save him from disgrace:
I do so, and once off, he slanders me.
An end of him! Begin elsewhere anew!
Boston's a hole, the herring-pond is wide,
V-notes are something, liberty still more.
Beside, is he the only fool in the world?

APPENDIX III

——○——

Directory

Following is a list of persons and organizations mentioned in this work that welcome contact from readers. Please mention Zolar when you write or call, and be sure to enclose a self-addressed, stamped envelope for easy reply.

Mediums/Channels

Dr. Estyne Del Rio
30 East End Avenue
New York, NY 10028
212–794–9417

Rev. B. Anne Gehman*
7630 Little River Turnpike #801
Annandale, VA 32301
703–941–4334
Summers:
15 Cleveland Street
Lily Dale, NY 14752
716–595–2620

Patricia Hayes
Post Office Box 767121
Roswell, GA 30076
404–887–5824

Rev. Robert W. Johnson
Post Office Box 1011
Highland, NY 12528
914–691–7014
212–288–1249

Gretchen C. Lazarony*
Post Office Box 797
Crystal Beach, FL 34256
813–785–9571
Summers:
11 Marion Street
Lily Dale, NY 14752
716–595–3380

Margaret M. Macauley
c/o Janet Kasper
212–873–3758

Pat Rodegast
c/o Valerie Mylonas
48 Reicherts Circle
Westport, CT 06880

Rev. Shirley C. Smith*
14 Cottage Row
Lily Dale, NY 14752
716–595–3452
716–442–3752

*These persons may also be contacted through the Lily Dale Assembly Office.

Rev. John C. White*
Post Office Box 455
Station H
Montreal, Quebec 43G 2L5
Canada
514–765–0867

Summers:
3 Cleveland Avenue
Lily Dale, NY 14752
716–595–3752

Pamela White/Cheryl Williams*
1145 Stephens Street, #3
Brigham Hall
Cassadaga, FL 32706
904–228–3638

Summers:
3 Melrose Park
Lily Dale, NY 14752
716–595–3927

Linda Willows
Wyndhom Foundation
Post Office Box 126
Irvington, NY 10533

Julie Rosa Winter
35 West 15 Street
New York, NY 10011
212–807–7352

Schools/Educational Programs

Patricia Hayes School of Inner Sense
Development/Arthur Ford Academy/
Ro-Hun Therapy
Post Office Box 767121
Roswell, GA 30076
404–887–5824

Offers residential courses at all levels of development, as well as periodic
seminars throughout the United States.

Rev. Joseph Sax, Secretary
Morris Pratt Institute
11811 Watertown Plank Road
Milwaukee, WI 53226
414–774–2994

Offers correspondence studies in the history, science, philosophy, and religion
of spiritualism, as well as residential classes each summer at Lily Dale
Assembly. All courses are approved by the N.S.A.C.

Spiritual Frontiers Fellowship (SFF)
10819 Winner Road
Independence, MO 64052
816–254–8585

Offers year-round programs and lectures throughout the United States. To obtain
information on the location of chapters, call or write to this address.

Pauline Swann, Secretary
Universal Spiritualist Association
Maple Grove
5848 Pendleton Avenue
Anderson, IN 46011
317–644–0371

Offers year-round residential week and weekend seminars in all aspects of
metaphysics, spiritualism, and esoteric studies. Features prominent guest
mediums and teachers from all parts of the world.

Spiritualist Camps

Robert J. Pries, President
Sherry L. Calkins, Secretary
Lily Dale Assembly
5 Melrose Park
Lily Dale, NY 14752
716–595–8721; 8722

Has offered residential courses in spiritualism and allied subjects since 1879,
from June 27 to September 1. Summer home for the famed Morris Pratt
Institute. Complete program available for each year's activities in May of each
year. Send $2.00 to cover program costs.

Warren Smith, President
Pauline Swann, Secretary
Universal Spiritualist Association
Maple Grove
5848 Pendleton Avenue
Anderson, IN 46011
317–644–0371

Offers summer institute programs in spiritualism, metaphysics, and esotericism.
Free detailed brochure upon request.

Cassadaga Spiritualist Camp
Post Office Box 152
Cassadaga, FL 32706
904–228–2525

Offers varied winter programs in spiritualism from September 22 to May 25.

Sun Spiritualist Camp Association
#2 Star Route
Box 596
Tonopah, AZ 85354

Offers varied winter programs in spiritualism from November to May.

Spiritualist Organizations

Rev. Joseph H. Merrill, President
Rev. Elizabeth R. Edgar, Secretary
National Spiritualist Association of
Churches (N.S.A.C.)
Post Office Box 128
Cassadaga, FL 32706

Warren Smith, President
Rev. Pauline Swann, Secretary
Universal Spiritualist Association
Maple Grove
5848 Pendleton Avenue
Anderson, IN 46011

Publication

The National Spiritualist
Summit Publications by Stow
Post Office Box 30172
Indianapolis, IN 46230

Published monthly at $7.00 per year. Official organ for N.S.A.C.

Books and Supplies

National Spiritualist Association
of Churches
Post Office Box 128
Cassadaga, FL 32706

Free list of spiritualist books. Send self-addressed, stamped envelope.

Venture Bookshop
Post Office Box 249
Highland Park, IL 60035

Planchettes, Ouija Boards, books, and other supplies. Request catalog.

APPENDIX IV

──────○──────

Additional Readings

Blunsdon, Norman. *A Popular Dictionary of Spiritualism.* New York: The Citadel Press, 1962.

Boddington, Harry. *The University of Spiritualism.* London: Spiritualist Press, 1947.

Brown, Slater. *The Heyday of Spiritualism.* New York: Hawthorn Books, 1970.

Cook, Mrs. Cecil M. *How I Discovered My Mediumship.* Chicago: Lormar Press, 1919.

Douce, P. M. *Incredible Alliance.* Philadelphia: Dorrance and Co., 1975.

Doyle, Sir Arthur Conan. *The History of Spiritualism.* New York: Arno Press, 1975.

Edmunds, Simeon. *Spiritualism: A Critical Survey.* Hertfordshire, England: Aquarian Press, 1966.

Ford, Arthur. *Nothing So Strange.* London: Psychic Press, Ltd., 1966.

Ford, Arthur. *Unknown But Known.* New York: Harper & Row, 1968.

Garrett, Eileen J. *The Sense and Nonsense of Prophecy.* New York: Creative Age Press, 1950.

Grimshaw, Thomas. *Our Declaration of Principles.* Milwaukee: Morris Pratt Institute.

Hardinge, Emma. *Modern American Spiritualism.* New Hyde Park, NY: University Books, 1970.

Hayes, Patricia. *The Gatekeeper.* Durham, NC: Dimensional Brotherhood, 1981.

Hayes, Patricia, and Marshall Smith. *Extension of Life: Arthur Ford Speaks.* Roswell, GA: Dimensional Brotherhood Publishing House, 1986.

Hudson, Thomas Jay. *The Law of Psychic Phenomena.* Chicago: A. C. McClurg & Co., 1916.

Johnson, Robert W. *Mystical Thoughts for Meditation: He Sends You Knowledge.* Highland, NY: Alpha Centauri Publishers, 1980.

Jones, Lloyd Kenyon. *Development of Mediumship.* Chicago: Lormar Press, 1919.

Kardec, Allan. *The Book of Mediums.* New York: Samuel Weiser, 1978.

Kardec, Allan. *The Spirits' Book.* Mexico: Amapse Society Mexico, 1857.

Khei, F.R.C. *A Brief Course in Mediumship.* Mokelumne Hill, CA: Health Research, 1965.

Leonard, John C. *The Higher Spiritualism.* Washington, DC: The Philosophic Book Co., 1927.

The Lyceum Officer's Manual. Manchester, England: The Spiritualists Lyceum Union, 1952.

Myers, F. W. H. *Human Personality and Its Survival of Bodily Death*. New York: University Books, 1961.

Owen, Robert Dale. *The Debatable Land Between This World and the Next*. New York: G. W. Carleton & Co., 1871.

Pebbles, J. M. *The General Principles and the Standard Teachings of Spiritualism*. Mokelumne Hill, CA: Health Research, reprint 1969.

Podmore, Frank. *Mediums of the Nineteenth Century*. New Hyde Park, NY: University Books, 1963.

Prince, Walter Franklin. *The Psychic in the House*. Boston: Boston Society for Psychical Research, 1926.

Ramacharaka, Yogi. *The Hindu-Yogi Science of Breath*. Chicago: Yogi Publication Society, 1904.

Rodegast, Pat. *Emmanuel's Book*. New York: Some Friends of Emmanuel, 1985.

Samadhi, Delta. *The Master Key to Psychic Unfoldment*. Los Angeles, CA: Crossley Pub. Co., 1931; reprinted Mokelumne Hill, CA: Health Research, 1968.

Spiritualist Manual. Cassadaga, FL: Spiritualist Association of Churches, 1911.

Spraggett, Allen with William V. Rauscher. *Arthur Ford: The Man Who Talked With the Dead*. New York: New American Library, 1973.

Stead, W. T. *The Blue Island*. London: Hutchinson & Co., 1922.

Theobald, Morell. *Spirit Workers in the Home Circle*. London: T. Fisher Unwin, 1888.

Tuttle, Hudson. *The Arcana of Spiritualism*. Manchester, England: The Two Worlds Publishing Co., 1921.

Vishita, Swami Bhakta. *Genuine Mediumship: The Invisible Powers*. Chicago: The Occult Publishing Co., 1919.

Wallis, E. W., and M. H. Wallis. *A Guide to Mediumship and Psychic Development*. Chicago: The Progressive Thinker.

Walmsley, D. M. *Anton Mesmer*. London: Robert Hale, 1976.

Weed, Joseph J. *Complete Guide to Oracle and Prophecy Methods*. West Nyack, NY: Parker Publishing Co., 1971.

INDEX

———o———